GUILT

Theory and Therapy

by Edward V. Stein

L

GEORGE ALLE

RUSKIN HOUSE

PRINTED IN GREAT BRITAIN
by Photolithography
JOHN DICKENS & CO LTD
NORTHAMPTON

FOREWORD

I suppose the writing of most books affects the author's life more than the reader's. Almost half my life has been spent, with varying degrees of intensity, researching the problem with which this book wrestles. When I first began to study guilt, early in my graduate studies, very few people knew much about the subject, and few seemed interested. Since that time, numerous writers have begun to address its importance.

It is disconcerting, when a person thinks he is building the only bridge across a formidable chasm, to look up and see a driver zipping by on one that seems to have been thrown up overnight. Many books on guilt have appeared while this one has been germinating in my mind during years of counseling and seminars with students. It is a conceit to think others were not wrestling equally hard with the subject. (Their contributions will be alluded to in the pages that follow.)

I have tried to be faithful to the spirit of Camus's advice in the second volume of his notebooks: "It is in order to shine sooner that authors refuse to re-write. Despicable. Begin again." There have been many beginnings, but pregnancies, even for books, must eventually terminate.

What has been personally most revelatory about this pursuit has been the discovery that *the greatest anguish and the greatest benediction in human life are rooted in an almost identical dynamic, with very subtle early nuances making massive ultimate differences.*

If there is any way out of man's inhumanity toward man, it

will be through our understanding of, and ability to influence favorably, his guilt-self-esteem system. In this system lie the roots of his self-love and self-hate. These are what he projects in his human relationships, the cisterns from which he draws the refreshing or the bitter resources for his way through life. War, race hatred, the exploitation and carnage of evil social systems, will bend ultimately only to the spiritual-psychological force of men and women who love themselves enough to extend this same attitude toward others.

The notion of inevitable progress seems to have much historically against it. Yet mankind, like the lower life forms, has continually transgressed boundaries his "wisdom" deems unbreachable. There is a spirit in the life process that tends to transcend, to stand out from, its present incompleted realizations. When we participate in this transcendence we know what it is to experience what theologians call "ecstasy." Thus it is that I see in the understanding of the guilt process insights into both the *source* and the *goal* of religious experience.

Jesus once remarked that "except ye . . . become as little children, ye shall not enter into the kingdom of heaven." The behavioral sciences, acting from other presuppositions, have long since clarified the importance of the first few years of human life in terms of the "set" of those molar systems which become interpretive of future experience. Yet research and theory regarding this most critical study for mankind are still sparse.

It will eventually be seen that the future of the world revolves around the nuclear family unit. The understanding of its influence alone will deliver us from another kind of nuclear power.

Theology is largely the abstracted mythical projection and extrapolation of parent-child dynamics. This is not to deride it, but to express my conviction about how God got himself into man's thought. Moreover, I think his participation in history will best be understood *in conjunction with* the understanding of the biosocial dynamics of familial process as it registers in the fundaments of the individual psyche.

Freud's anxiety thesis about the origin of religion has not

Don Gresswell Ltd., London, N.21 Cat No. 1208   DG 02242/71

GUILT: THEORY AND THERAPY

BY EDWARD V. STEIN

The Stranger Inside You

been fully absorbed even yet. The metaphysical riders attached to his metapsychology are too disturbing. Now that theology has endured the "God is dead" experience, it may also be prepared to absorb and fully utilize in its conceptions the exposure of the dynamics that project (and the dynamics that would kill) the father, human or symbolic extrahuman.

Only at this point in time are science and faith becoming aware that they have in the human being a truly common phenomenological focus and in his origins as a person a key to their hoary pasts and mutual future: The only key that can keep that future open and possible.

Acknowledgments are due here to a patient and supportive wife and family who have long "endured" this manuscript's voracious demands, to friends and students whose stimulating questions and insights have kept this venture alive, and to Mrs. Maggie Arms and Mrs. Ruby Egnew whose faithful midwifery at the typewriters through a hot July have finally brought this manuscript to birth.

E. V. S.

San Anselmo, California

CONTENTS

Nothing is more seductive for man than his freedom of conscience, but nothing is a greater cause of suffering.

—*Fyodor Dostoevsky*

Nikos Kazantzakis, in his autobiography, Report to Greco, *wrote:*

Blowing through heaven and earth, and in our hearts and the heart of every living thing, is a gigantic breath—a great Cry—which we call God. Plant life wished to continue its motionless sleep next to stagnant waters, but the Cry leaped up within it and violently shook its roots: "Away, let go of the earth, walk!" Had the tree been able to think and judge, it would have cried, "I don't want to. What are you urging me to do! You are demanding the impossible!" But the Cry, without pity, kept shaking its roots and shouting, "Away, let go of the earth, walk!"

It shouted in this way for thousands of eons; and lo! as a result of desire and struggle, life escaped the motionless tree and was liberated.

Animals appeared—worms—making themselves at home in water and mud. "We're just fine here," they said. "We have peace and security; we're not budging!"

But the terrible Cry hammered itself pitilessly into their loins. "Leave the mud, stand up, give birth to your betters!"

"We don't want to. We can't!"

"You can't, but I can. Stand up!"

And lo! after thousands of eons, man emerged, trembling on his still unsolid legs.

The human being is a centaur; his equine hoofs are planted in the ground, but his body from breast to head is worked on and tormented by the merciless Cry. He has been fighting, again for thousands of eons, to draw himself, like a sword, out of his animalistic scabbard. He is also fighting—this is his new struggle—to draw himself out of his human scabbard. Man calls in despair, "Where can I go? I have reached the pinnacle, beyond is the abyss." And the Cry answers, "I am beyond. Stand up!"

This book is about the Cry . . .

Chapter I

GUILT: WHY SO IMPORTANT?

If we are going towards a human era of science, it will be eminently an era of human science. Man, the knowing subject, will perceive at last that man, *"the object of knowledge,"* is the key to the whole science of nature.[1]
—*Pierre Teilhard de Chardin*

Guilt is the peg on which the meaning of "man" hangs. It is also the peg on which man too often hangs himself.

An adequate understanding of the nature and function of guilt could contribute much to civilization and the solution of man's perennial plight. Sigmund Freud spoke of the sense of guilt as *"the most important problem in the evolution of culture."*[2]

So also the British psychoanalyst Ernest Jones: "The troubles from which the world suffers at present can, in my opinion, very largely be traced to the manifold attempts to deal with the inner sense of guiltiness, and therefore any contribution that will illuminate this particular problem will be of the greatest value."[3]

These men call attention to both the positive and negative implications of this inner dynamic which is so central to the human being. Freud realized that culture is impossible *without it,* and Jones implies that culture is well-nigh impossible *with* it. It is exactly this intransigence which makes the subject so difficult of resolution and so impervious to easy answers. It is not hard to see why, as *question* and *quest,* man has sought an answer to and a release from this which, perhaps more than any other single factor, makes him *man*. When it is absent entirely, he is less than man. Present too constantly or too oppressively, it may lead to illness and insanity. Only in delicate balance is man, through his guilt dynamism, capable of the highest reaches of human community.

Helen Lynd writes that the fact that guilt as *concept* and *word* is often avoided in modern speech and writing and has been retranslated does *not* mean that it is not a part of the reality with which man must contend. As she puts it:

> Terms associated with guilt have tended to be dropped as inciters to desirable action. Sophisticated parents, teachers, or therapists no longer say that a child is good or bad. But the words good and bad have been replaced by mature and immature, productive and unproductive, socially adjusted and maladjusted. And when these words are used by the teacher, the counselor, or the therapist they carry the same weight of approbation and disapprobation as the earlier good and bad . . . (together they constitute as rigid a code as that of any church or creed). An individual feels the appropriate guilt if he does not attain maturity in the prescribed manner.[4]

Guilt, by *any* name, resembles a "law of gravity" of human existence. It is the dynamic principle operative in man which verifies the fictitiousness of his total autonomy and the validity of his dependence upon all the rest of life, essentially the human community, and supremely, the source and principle of all life, God—the ground of our being.

Guilt begins in love, is impossible without love, and paradoxically is only cured by love. It is the most horrible and one of the most hopeful facts for man. It is the *experience* of antilife, anticommunity, antilove which, as limit, as void of being, turns man to seek its opposite. It is "hell." It is life that is anxious for love. It is loveless life fixed with "no exit." It is life experiencing hatred, and the worst of all hatreds, hatred of self.

Just as life is the mysterious complexity of *organization* that spells interdependence of cell upon cell, so is guilt the psycho-biological-spiritual phenomenon which maintains when that interdependence is violated.

Withdrawal, tension, startle-pattern—these are fundamental reflexes for biological survival. Anxiety is the phenomenological awareness of, and participation in, these threat experiences for conscious life. *Guilt is the special form of anxiety experienced by humans-in-society, the warning tension of life principles violated, of conditions of human social existence transgressed, of sociospiritual reality ignored or affronted, of God alienated, of self being destroyed.*

Guilt is man risking life as not-man, evolution in reverse, man regressing to the inhuman, the meaningless, the chaotic. Freud and the Bible are consistent regarding this subject's importance as the birth pain of civilization, the beginning of theology, the new dimension in evolution that separates the beast from the human. To understand it in its complexities is a first step in understanding who we are as humans and the unilinear direction of our existence.

Erich Fromm writes in his book *The Art of Loving:*

> What is essential in the existence of man is the fact that he has emerged from the animal kingdom, from instinctive adaptation, that he has transcended nature—although he never leaves it; he is a part of it—and yet once torn away from nature, he cannot return to it; once thrown out of paradise—a state of original oneness with nature—cherubim with flaming swords block his way, if he should try to return. Man can only go forward by developing his reason, by finding a new harmony, a human one, instead of the prehuman harmony which is irretrievably lost.[5]

Modern man is caught in a morass of intellectual and spiritual confusion. His identity is in question; the meaning and goals of his existence are problematic. The theologian and the psychiatrist are equally hard put for answers concerning the direction of wholeness. Both are realizing that mutual understanding is important if man is to be rescued from himself and the self-destructive levels of his guilt. Current exploration is doing much to clarify this area as the common ground upon which the scientific and the aspirational in human life can meet.

The truth-value dichotomy is the lumpy bit in philosophy's

diet and one that emerges most clearly in the problem of guilt, where the descriptive and the valuational meet.

Paul Tournier, a Swiss psychotherapist, captures the scope of the issue in these words:

> Guilt is . . . a religious problem which interests theologians, a social problem which interests sociologists, and and a psychological problem which interests psychologists. But it does not let itself be dissected. It is a human problem, a form of suffering peculiar to man, and of concern to the doctor because his vocation is the relief of all suffering.[6]

So would we like to emphasize three general catagories of importance in current thought which may be served by a deeper understanding of guilt. They may occupy varying degrees of relevance in the mind of the reader. These are *psychological, sociological,* and *theological.* As one whose vocation is in psychology and theology, I am aware of the frequent reticence, if not antipathy, with which representatives of these disciplines often regard each other. I am counting on a certain large-mindedness in these groups in the remainder of this book and will proceed without apology to reflect on the subject from both perspectives. It is to be hoped that what may be gained from either side will not be unduly marred by natural reluctance to identify entirely with the author's personal syntheses and prejudices. It may be that just as the science of medicine has had to reexplore primitive potions to find in them the essences of the most sophisticated modern drugs—e.g., rauwolfia for chlorpromazine—so may the science of psychology be led to reexplore religious concepts for their hidden, life-sustaining verities. Only the bold researcher, more interested in truth than in his pride, will tramp the ineluctable jungles of ancient ideas for the stuff which sustains life, however entangled in archaic verbiage or hidden by dogmatic undergrowth.

PSYCHOLOGICAL ASPECTS

Psychologists, of all persuasions, are concerned with those factors which account for and control human behavior. Since few, if any, hold out for a purely instinctual theory of behavior, the problem of how inner biological urgings become modified and adapted to the outer physical, social, or psychological environment is of major interest. Much of Freud's life was concerned with the solution of this problem. The growth of ego psychology as a special emphasis within psychoanalysis has been around this focal point of the meeting, fusion, and/or confusion of inner and outer reality.

The problem as it lies before psychology seems to be binary: (a) What internal forces or principles are normally at work to inhibit, express, and control instinctive or "primary drive" behavior? and (b) To what extent are these forces or principles influenced by, or capable of being influenced by, the social environment of the person and under what conditions?

The inferential conceptualizations of psychoanalysis and the existentialist psychologists have gone farthest in wrestling with these issues. The analytic ego psychologists, especially Erikson and Hartmann, have brought the problems to most intense focus in theoretical terms, as they relate to the subjective sense of identity and to the psychotherapeutic process in its involvement with prevailing value systems. The existentialist psychologists wrestle with the same problems, not so much from a structured theoretical-scientific perspective as from a phenomenological and internal stance, interpretive of the private meaning states of the subject. It is conceivable that the latter may turn out to be the *only* possible position for the clinician, but, if so, it would seem to preclude any scientific generalizations concerning internal psychological processes and to convert psychology into a humanistic philosophy rather than a science. This is a conclusion held by many positivistic psychologists.

If one looks at the broad sweep of the psychoanalytic preoccupation with guilt, he sees the reflections of Freud on its dynamics moving through various evolutionary stages (as traced, for example, by Clara Thompson[7] and Patrick Mullahy[8]). Freud's insights are picked up and elaborated by interested students such as Oscar Pfister,[9] Theodor Reik,[10] and John C. Flugel[11] in ways that emphasize their religious connections and references. Then, in the works of Fromm, Horney,

Hartmann, Erikson, C. Buhler, Odier, Wheelis, and many others, the unique implications of guilt and the value problem for the self-in-society as normally and pathologically understood become amplified. It is not our task here to elaborate this development in its details, nor to try to comprehend all these, but simply to call attention to the proliferation of concern for the issues involved and to try to rough out the horizon against which some of them may be profitably discussed.

It is possible to project a schema that groups some of the *psychological* factors that we shall concern ourselves with: (*a*) *the origin and development of guilt*, (*b*) *the nature of the guilt dynamic within the individual*, (*c*) *how external social environment and internal guilt process influence and reflect each other*, (*d*) *the question of healthy and unhealthy dimensions of guilt for the individual and for society as a whole, and* (*e*) *the involvement of psychology in the value systems and normative structures of society as it seeks a science of individual behavior and as it participates in the therapeutic task of helping maladjusted or conflict-ridden persons.*

It will be apparent that (*a*) through (*c*) in the foregoing are largely summarizing historical and descriptive concerns, whereas (*d*) and (*e*) move into areas of normative and conjectural significance fraught with much meaning for the future of humanity, most especially in an age moving rapidly into dimensions of great manipulative significance in eugenics, mass communication, subliminal suggestion, "scientific" thought control, and social planning.

That the latter issues bid well to become momentous (assuming, hopefully, that we surmount the present political-military obstacles of nuclear power) seems an understatement. If man continues his accelerated comprehension of the processes of growth, education, and direction of human life, then *which* specific planned goals for his future shall be chosen and idealized as normative become apocalyptically important. Time is running out.

The well-known Skinner-Rogers dialogue has heightened awareness of the Promethean options now being explored by behavioral scientists.[12] It is no longer a question of *whether* man can control other men through subtle conditioning processes. This is already happening. As Skinner shows, it always has been happening. We have long used censure and punishment as forms of "aversive conditioning" and praise and reward as reinforcement of approved behavior.[13] What he advocates is a wholesale espousal of the process, the utilization of conditioning techniques to produce a good and happy society. "Sooner or later the law must be prepared to deal with all possible techniques of government control."[14] Skinner's *Walden Two* is his projection of his modern utopia "a proposal to apply a behavioral technology to the construction of a workable, effective, and productive pattern of government."[15]

Carl Rogers, responding as a psychologist of a different persuasion, writes:

> Skinner and I are in agreement that the whole question of the scientific control of human behavior is a matter with which psychologists and the general public should concern themselves. As Robert Oppenheimer told the America Psychological Association . . . the problems that psychologists will pose for society by their growing ability to control behavior will be much more grave than the problems posed by the ability of physicists to control the reactions of matter. I am not sure whether psychologists generally recognize this. . . .
>
> With these . . . points of basic and important agreement, are there then any issues that remain on which there are differences? I believe there are. They can be stated very briefly: *Who will be controlled? Who will exercise control? What type of control will be exercised? Most important of all, toward what end or what purpose, or in pursuit of what value, will control be exercised?*[16]

It is interesting that Rogers, a notedly optimistic humanist, criticizes as one weak point in Skinner's utopian objectives his "serious underestimation of the problem of power."[17] And "the major flaw" in Skinner's review of what is involved in the scientific control of human behavior Rogers sees to be "*the denial, misunderstanding, or gross underestimation of the place of ends, goals or values in their relationship to science.*"[18]

It is plain to see that broadly dispersed knowledge of the

human being and how he becomes what he is, as well as how
he influences successors in relationships, is imperative. A clear
insight into the guilt process as the fulcrum of civilization,
specially in reference to normative value systems, becomes
elementary to any intelligent wrestling with the human problem.

SOCIOLOGICAL ASPECTS

However concerned sociologists may be with mass reactions, humans-in-groups, and situational gestalten, they are
constantly forced to consider the colorations and vectors produced within these by the inner histories of the individual
personal units. Especially significant are the inner shared
value systems by which group cohesiveness becomes a reality
as well as the way a group introduces or induces these in its
members.

Freud, in his little book *Group Psychology and the Analysis
of the Ego*,[19] began early to point up the significance of shared
orientations in group responses to a leader.

Riesman's *The Lonely Crowd* was one of the more ambitious efforts (since Max Weber) to interpret the interaction of
the individual's guilt system and mass values.[20] Fromm's *Escape from Freedom* analyzed similar dynamics in a totali-
tarian European setting.[21] Whyte's study *The Organization
Man*[22] explores value conformity as a condition of business
advancement, and Erikson's *Childhood and Society*,[23] the interaction of personal identity and values. All these works
dramatize the relevance of the individual's inner ego-superego
relationships to his behavior in groups.

A study entitled *Variations in Value Orientations*[24] is a sophisticated approach to the interrelationships existing between
a culture and its members respecting the *required* and *permit-
ted* variations of behavior and the values which motivate and
circumscribe it. It seeks to elaborate and specify these variations and model contiguities not only within one culture but
among five different cultures within the American Southwest.
The authors raise again the question of cultural relativity and

universals within human value orientations which promise to provide a theoretical framework against which the problem of guilt may be more profitably discussed and into which, at some point, it must eventually be meshed. They write: "The view advanced here is that variation in value orientations is the most important type of cultural variation and is, therefore, the central feature of the structure of culture."[25]

At practical, casework levels, the sociologist is pressed to deal with guilt and superego meanings in the field of social pathology. What makes a delinquent, criminal, or "psychopathic" personality? What *is* each of these, if they are distinct entities? By what criteria does one or *can* one determine norms? Where lies the dividing line between "healthy" social adjustment and chameleonlike immersion in conformity or rebellious digression?

These are questions that cannot even be intelligently asked, much less answered, apart from intimate acquaintance with the guilt process and its norm-sustaining, group-cohesive relevance. This book cannot pretend to deal in even a limited way with many of these questions. It does hope to focus briefly on superego factors in some delinquency and suggest the relevance of the whole study for the increasing clarification of social pathology.

RELIGIOUS ASPECTS

The understanding of the guilt process is most pertinent to any healthy theological perspective that would relate to an anthropology integral with contemporary science. A portion of the book will devote itself to the interdisciplinary significance of guilt in the effort to solve the human equation as it reaches across the boundaries of psychology, medicine, and theology.

The Judeo-Christian tradition has long wrestled with guilt and forgiveness, not only in an abstract conceptual form but in a concrete, historical, and existential way as one of man's central problems.

Oscar Pfister, an early student of Freud, practicing psychoanalyst as well as a Reformed Protestant pastor in Zurich, explored, from an analytic perspective, the vagaries of this development as various theological and ritualistic codes have been interpreted through institutional rites.[26] He was one of the first to see the sweeping implications of psychoanalysis for theology and to suggest directions for study.

R. S. Lee,[27] an English writer, elaborates a view of Christianity which seeks to clarify the fact that it is meant to be a religion of relationship rather than exclusively a religion of conscience more (or basically) affirming what he calls an "ego religion" rather than a "superego religion."

Both Pfister and Lee, having been immersed in psychoanalytic thought, show the possibilities for the reviewing of religious meaning from this stance, especially respecting guilt. Their work involves not only a clarifying of the old distinction between theological conceptions of legalism and grace, but they also bring into the discussion the deepening implications of these concepts that accrue when they are refracted into some of their subtler psychological components through the lens of depth psychology, much as radiations from distant nebulae, though long with us, give up new meanings when perceived through a radio-telescope.

The work of both Pfister and Lee touches on the confusion entailed for religion and psychiatry in the distinction between neurotic and normal guilt. It is perhaps the failure to draw this distinction clearly that, more than any other single factor, caused (and causes) religious counselors to compound pathology as often as being agents of its cure. It is probably also for this reason that religious leaders have earned the frequent antipathy of psychiatrists.

The confusion is not all one-sided, however. Psychiatry has found itself forced to deal with normal levels of guilt and unable to dismiss all guilt as pathology. Further, it is now engaging itself in the question of authentic values. Heinz Hartmann's work in *Psychoanalysis and Moral Values*[28] is a case in point. A. H. Maslow goes so far as to say:

> The state of being without a system of values is psychopathogenic, we are learning. The human being needs a framework of values, a philosophy of life, a religion or

religion-surrogate to live by and understand by, in about the same sense that he needs sunlight, calcium or love.[29]

The issues are far from settled, in fact, scarcely raised. One well-known figure in psychological circles, O. H. Mowrer, has opened up the discussion in a way that makes radical claims to reorient the problems around conscious confessional levels. He seeks to reinvoke theological-moral expectations and to repudiate many existing psychiatric assertions vis-à-vis pathological guilt.[30]

Mowrer's emphasis on real guilt, "sin," and values has been a much needed corrective in traditional academic psychological circles. It has sparked a great deal of action and study of a subject which has long been sitting in the center of the therapeutic parlor but which, like the proverbial family black sheep, has only been alluded to in guarded, embarrassed terms and hushed voices. One could wish that the reemphasis might be less oriented around extremes of analytic iconoclasm and theological moralism. The latter are leading to partisan enthusiasms which the author believes may have a long-range destructive potential.

"Reality" and "Integrity" therapists are focusing on the *responsibility* of the human being and finding that treating people like adults often taps deep inner resources.[31] The extent to which the success of these approaches lies in their novelty, in the sociopathic drift of our culture, in the decline of neurotic guilt-inducing parents, the general impact of psychoanalytic theory, and/or the absence of similar opportunities in many of our churches is conjectural. Berne has found similar responses on our different theoretical grounds.[32]

Obviously many people do have genuine guilt problems and need to deal with them directly, confessionally, and in reparative ways. This includes neurotics and psychotics whose troubles may be deeply enmeshed in their inauthentic, existentially guilty behavior. Anton Boisen's early insights here are being borne out.[33] It remains to be seen, however, to what extent confessed, relieved, and accepted neurotics are still neurotics who need further therapy. It is also a question whether other acceptance that relieves guilt is achieved at the price of genuine inner freedom—the price of moralistic conformity.

All the foregoing takes on a proportion of major significance, not only for the psychiatric and religious community but also for the average man who too often must live out his days on the meaning crumbs that fall to him from the theoretical table. For, after all, if he *is* guilty and needs a conscious confessional experience, that is one thing. If he just *feels* guilty and needs psychiatric deliverance from a "false" feeling, that is another. But if the professionals argue unendingly that he is neither this nor that, or that he is both, they become party to his illness or confusion. This book will seek to explore some of these issues.

Chapter II

THE GUILT PROCESS:
SOME QUESTIONS AND ASSUMPTIONS

Being human means . . . man has become aware that he himself is the door to the deeper levels of reality.

—Paul Tillich[1]

Guilt, like light, is one of those phenomena everybody knows about from direct experience yet few can explain in theoretical ways. It enters significantly into several important disciplines: law, medicine, religion, psychology, anthropology, and sociology, to name but the most obvious. Much harm has ensued from confusion about the referential meanings of the term "guilt" as it overlaps multiple areas of life.

For example, for want of precision in the use of the concept, people have been punished legally who undoubtedly should have been dealt with psychiatrically, and probably in some instances vice versa. Great chunks of history are marked by human agony directly related to the misunderstanding of guilt—the Inquisition, witch-hunting, punitive treatment of psychotics, "holy" wars (!), race hatred, etc. The current unsettled problem of the homosexual, as well as many efforts to legislate sexual behavior, constitute areas where medical-legal-psychological-religious ideas often interact as much confused with guilt as informed by factual data.

We will not concern ourselves with legal or sociological but essentially with psychological and religious dimensions of the topic. We wish to examine the psychological rootage out of which the guilt process emerges. Though this is still a highly speculative venture, it is abetted by the fact that empirical observations of children and of conditions relevant to pathology and normalcy have been going on for some decades now and lend new strength and precision to inferential projections concerning the origins of guilt.

GUILT DEFINED

Guilt will be defined here as a state of tension or anxiety over internalized aggression (self-hatred) or loss of self-love. These are reflections of early experiences with significant emotional figures in the environment, usually the parents. Internally and phenomenologically guilt is anxiety, pain, displeasure, depression, remorse, because of the violation of some internalized values rooted in an emotional relationship. The threat of anticipated guilt anxiety *normally* cues off the control system, inhibiting impulse expression. The failure of this conscience warning, in the case of impulses which break through into action, results in *normal guilt* (remorse). However, as Freud saw, the *wish* itself may activate the guilt system, resulting in neurotic self-condemnation and self-punishment at unconscious levels of function.

There is thus a warning system (feelings of conscience) and an after-the-fact punitive system. In the neurotic, the "fact" will be an unconscious impulse and the punishment will be unconscious, both expressing themselves simultaneously in a symptom. Neurotic guilt may also be, and eventually *will* be, complicated by factual behavior which violates his value system and adds real guilt. It is probably Freud's underestimation of the latter which greatly complicated treatment and has continued to complicate treatment theory. As will be brought out later, several current therapeutic emphases attempt to deal with this lacuna.

Medard Boss, the Daseinsanalyst, makes it clear that this school of thought considers man "primarily guilty." Man's guilt begins with his birth, at which time his debt to life, as it unfolds itself to him and challenges the potentials of his being, begins. This is a creditable philosophical-religious stance with which we do not basically contend; however, it in some senses bypasses the psychological goal of trying to understand the way in which this primary guilt becomes evident, variegated, and/or muted in various personalities.[2]

Guilt having been defined in the above manner, various problems immediately emerge.

1. *What are the dynamics of the impulse system to be controlled?* Any discussion of psychodynamics immediately involves one in an implicit theoretical stance. We wish to make that explicit (though it must already be apparent) and to say that we draw heavily upon the psychoanalytic and depth psychological background current in much clinical thought respecting guilt. Later in this chapter we will clarify some of the reasons for retaining this position and in the next chapter will consider some options and modifications of the position as it is articulated in various writers such as Fromm, Klein, and Ausubel. The burden of this book, however, will reflect a psychoanalytic inclination. An eclectic has been defined as "a person who has read two books on a subject." In the present state of confusion concerning guilt it is very difficult to maintain a rigid theoretical stance, however much one reads. We affirm here, though, the significant value of the love-hate polarities of Freudian theory since these dynamics seem to be central to the infant-parent relation, the internalization of which has so much to do with the guilt process. At the same time, this does not obligate us to espouse the extremities of Freud's thought regarding "death instinct, *fundamental* dualism, etc."

2. *Is the guilt system organic, inherited, automatic, and constitutional or is it learned, environmentally induced, something that comes from the outside?* Or, is it a combination of these two? Before the advent of Freud's psychological scalpels for the dissection of the human psyche, it was held by many thinkers that guilt was essentially something *given* in the organism. The term "constitutional psychopath" was often applied to persons who seemed from an early age to be lacking a guilt control system for impulse. It was felt that these persons were born into the world with some constitutional inadequacy which made it impossible for them to function morally.

3. Obvious questions followed: *If it is* given, *why is there*

so much variety in moral opinion and behavior? Why does it not run a more consistent pattern throughout the whole of humanity? Why, for example, is aggression approved in some cultures and frowned upon in others? Why was a Hebrew stoned to death for the kind of sexual involvement with another man's wife which would be normative in an Eskimo culture—indeed, for the very behavior that an Eskimo would be ostracized for *failing* to participate in?

4. *If guilt is* learned—*an environmental conditioning process—why is there such a widespread similarity of moral and ethical opinion in widely separated cultures,* and how is there so much conformity within a given culture or subculture, sometimes apparently in spite of opposite home backgrounds?

Further, if it is *learned* and something that involves the processes of consciousness, how is it that some people tend to have a very sensitive awareness of the contents of a particular cultural value system without these contents affecting their practical behavior?

5. *If guilt is a combination of constitutional givens and also conditioning experiences, what are the factors interacting to produce the particular varieties of guilt experience which do occur?* Such a complex question seems impossible to answer. It probably *is,* in a definitive sense, but we will try to organize such fruitful theoretical suggestions as have been contributed by those who have wrestled most with this problem.

6. *A central problem for medicine: How to influence the* organism organically through electric and chemotherapies to maximize the capacity for dealing with psychological stress and the possibility of reversing processes (psychological or somatic) which become so extreme in the pathological forms of guilt? Sometimes somatic therapy is the only form of therapy used. At other times, it is a temporizing which permits a less contaminated theater for psychotherapeutic reconstruction.

7. *A central problem for psychology:* What *exactly* happens in the training and growing-up process to develop guilt or its absence and what combination of events seems reliably to

work toward health or pathology? How can these be prevented or modulated in the case of pathology? How can they be reinforced and stimulated in healthier situations?

THEORETICAL CONSIDERATIONS

We shall adopt for this book, not uncritically, Freud's concept of the superego. Our reasons are as follows:

1. Guilt is a *conflict phenomenon* involving dynamic polarities, and the ego-superego poles provide a meaningful dynamic framework for this discussion.

2. It offers continua for the varying *intensities* (positive and negative) evident in the guilt spectrum.

3. It affords, in a meaningful conceptual way, *a symbolic shorthand* for the vagaries of the guilt function in respect to the personalized and anthropomorphic *otherness* of conscience. (Some would disavow it as a purely fictitious construct. They don't deal with memory this way; yet, in some real sense, the superego is part of the memory system—the part with the warning finger which taps the dallying ego on the shoulder in warning or applies the whole hand in punishment if unheeded.)

Various *critical questions regarding the superego concept* suggest themselves to be explored:

1. The importance of the *sexual* element in its genesis vs. the *authority-power* element in the initiation and perpetuation of the superego in the personality.

2. The *temporal* factor. What is the timing of the emergence of the superego? Is it as abrupt in its emergence as Freud seems to imply or not? Does it begin in earliest affective experiences of infancy and precede ego development as Klein elaborates? What is the relation of the superego to the total aging process, that is, how is it modified throughout the early and childhood developmental period by varied social experiences?

3. *The topographical factor.* Is the superego actually a specialized psychic system which contains separate contents (over against an ego with different contents) or is the

superego really a shorthand term for a combination of
feelings surrounding the ego contents? Moreover, in what
way are contents and feelings connected in either case?

4. *The factor of permanence.* What accounts for change
in the value system of a person? Why is it that some highly
intelligent people seem to be so inflexible regarding value
changes? Is morality always a *reflected* morality of an authoritarian parent? When and how, if ever (totally), does
it become *mine?* The ego seems always to be involved in
some way in the guilt process. In what way is it involved?

The foregoing assumptions and questions are posed as a
background against which the discussion of guilt can take
place. Our concern in the next chapter will be to trace the
development of the superego in the child and to see the way
in which variations in this development impinge upon variations in the total character and behavior.

Chapter III

SUPEREGO FORMATION

What we idealize determines what we believe controls
the universe and what we strive to emulate.

—*A. D. Weisman*[1]

Guilt is experienced as conflict, tension, anxiety, depression,
remorse. Any discussion of guilt will therefore be arid unless
what is in conflict can be differentiated and understood. Because Freud gave us the tools for such discussion, it is not
surprising that clinicians and theorists return to his concepts
and dynamic orientation, sometimes reluctantly.

Freud's term *superego* retains its value as *symbol for a
psychic function* even where one may differ with his particular formulations of the details of its origins and nature. If we
would eliminate the term "superego" for any number of suggested reasons (anthropomorphic, superfluous, unobservable,
etc.), then we must posit something (some function or dynamic element) in its place to account for the *conflict* of
guilt—essentially a feeling conflict rather than a conceptual
disparity, though the latter may be involved.

We shall adopt Freud's term "superego" for the discussion
of guilt, showing later some modifications that have been
suggested. It will be our objective to sketch briefly the broad
outlines of his theory concerning the superego and then to
relate other writers to his thought, drawing upon all of them
for subsequent treatment of the problem.

It will be well in all of the following to keep three basic
questions in mind:

1. What are the *content* and *function* of the superego?
2. *When* is it established in the personality?
3. *How* is it established?

Freud projected his view of personality as a trifunctional unity of id-ego-superego. These terms represent essentially the *passionate,* the *rational,* and the *moral* in man.

Freud envisioned the newborn infant as a psychobiological organism, dominated by "the pleasure principle" (seeking pleasure in the form of the reduction of anxiety-tension and the return to a state of bearable organismic tonicity, which for the infant is, at first, largely euphoric sleep). Psychologically, the newborn infant is essentially id (although many analysts believe the rudiments of all three psychic systems are present). By the term "id" Freud meant "everything that is inherited, that is present at birth, that is fixed in the constitution—above all, therefore, the instincts, which originate in the somatic organization and which find their first mental expression in the id in forms unknown to us."[2]

He also characterized the id as "a chaos, a cauldron of seething excitement." It is that part of the psyche which connects directly with somatic processes and "takes over from them instinctual needs and gives them mental expression." The id is entirely unconscious and it is only through an extension of the id, the ego, that instinctual needs reach consciousness and are related to the external world.[3]

The ego thus is the organizing, ordering center of personality, the rational, logical focus of the self which largely controls the discharge of id impulses and passions. It is for the most part conscious, although it extends into the unconscious and involves unconscious mechanisms of defense.

Freud saw the development of the superego to be a result of man's long infantile dependency and his constitutional bisexuality. The child is under the sway of powerful parents whom he comes to love and hate in special ways because of his and their sexual natures. This love and hate reach such intensity as to force a largely permanent psychological precipitate, the superego.

The infant (we will follow Freud in using the male as a paradigm) is, in the earliest stages of his development, attached to the mother as a sexual object and identifies in some measure with both parents but basically with the father.[4] As his sexual attachment to the mother increases in intensity (some time between the ages of three and six), he experiences the father as an obstacle to his full possession of the mother and has intensely hostile feelings toward him as a result. This is the classical Oedipus complex.

His desire both to be like the father and to be rid of him is an ambivalence that underlies the incest-murder taboos of many cultures and, for Freud, explains the universal relevance of the Oedipus myth. The anxiety that underlies the boy's instinctual ambitions and the anticipated punishment Freud termed "castration anxiety," the appropriate talion reaction to his wish. Freud summarizes:

> An ambivalent attitude to the father and an object rela-
> tion cf a purely affectionate kind to the mother make up
> the content of the simple positive Oedipus complex in
> the boy.[5]

The Oedipus complex is the critical turning point in the child's character. Whether and how it is resolved has much to do with his psychic future. In the normal progression, the boy must give up his sexual love of the mother. This, Freud felt, demanded some psychological substitute. There will follow "either an identification with the mother or an intensified identification with the father."[6]

Both the boy and the girl may resolve the Oedipus conflict in either direction, that is, through major identification with either father or mother. Which direction they move is determined by the relative strength of their masculine and feminine dispositions. Freud explains the feminine Oedipus attitude ("Electra complex") as originating in envy for the male organ, with rejection of the mother as the primary love object "for having sent her into the world so insufficiently equipped." In her resentment she gives up her mother and puts someone else in place of her as the object of her love— her father.[7]

Freud amplified this further, indicating that the simple Oedipal resolution probably was rare. That, more often, most people are involved in double identifications, that is, with father and mother and that the sexual disposition will determine the balance.[8]

Freud writes:

> *The broad general outcome of the sexual phase governed by the Oedipus complex may, therefore, be taken to be the forming of a precipitate in the ego, consisting of these two identifications in some way combined together. This modification of the ego retains its special position; it stands in contrast to the other constituents of the ego in the form of an ego-ideal or superego.*[9]

The superego consists of a double dynamic: "you ought" and "you ought not" in its relation to the ego. This is the result of the original parent identifications, namely, that there are some things that should be emulated (the values) and some that must be foregone (sexual privilege).

The achievement of this resolution is brought about by *repression* of the Oedipal incest-murder wishes. The ego achieves this through the reinforcement of its repressive capacities by means of identifying with the prohibiting parent.

Freud adds:

> The more intense the Oedipus complex was and the more rapidly it succumbed to repression (under the influence of discipline, religious teaching, schooling and reading) the more exacting later on is the domination of the superego over the ego in the form of conscience or perhaps of an unconscious sense of guilt.[10]

The great contribution of Freud to the understanding of the problem of guilt lies exactly here. He has given us an imaginative representation of the way in which the internal, personalized, punitive voice of conscience—acting both consciously and unconsciously—is established. Through identification, the parent image, probably that of both parents, is internalized as prohibiting or approving the wishes and behavior of id-ego.

Freud saw the superego as largely unconscious, by virtue of its origin in the repressed Oedipus complex. For this reason, it may and often does function in relation to the impulses of the id independently of conscious awareness. The conflicts going on are often only "felt" by the person as depression, anxiety, or other symptoms.

Freud made no major distinction between the ego ideal and the superego.[11] Subsequent writers have seen this as a weakness and have built elaborate extrapolations from the distinction.[12]

It seems to this author that *Freud was correct in rejecting a sharp distinction.* In that he saw the superego as a dynamic internalization of the parent figure or figures, it follows that the interrelationships of ego and superego will reflect the subtleties of ambivalence and, with accompanying projective distortions, all of the melding of positive and negative feelings that flow between parent and child. *A clean-cut positive/ negative, ego ideal/superego delineation is no more to be expected internally than is such an unambiguous parent-child relationship interpersonally.*

The underlying dynamics of personality, as of all life, Freud attributed to two basic instincts, the erotic and the death instincts. The former is a unifying, positive, and life-furthering force, the latter a destructive, aggressive, life-diminishing force seeking quiescence. He saw these two forces active in the id, and by the displacement, active in the superego's relation to the ego. When living up to the ego ideal a person experiences his internalized parents affirming his actions. He experiences the love impulse internally in a manner reflective of his parents' previous stance toward him. When his impulses or actions violate the values he has taken over from his parents, he experiences *loss of this love* or, more forcefully, *punitive internal aggression* turned against his ego. The anxiety associated with the *expectation* of such loss of love or self-aggression is termed "feelings of conscience" or the "conscience warning signal." The *experiencing* of such internal loss of love or self-punishment is guilt feeling.

Not infrequently, one reads criticisms of the superego concept because of its "anthropomorphic" quality, implying that a more neutral, less personal explanatory principle or dynamic would be more "scientific." Yet *it is exactly this quality which renders it an appropriate symbol psychologically.* In pathological degrees of guilt, not only is anxiety experienced, but definite voices, and not uncommonly, faces are hallucinated.

We know from the phenomena of multiple personality that "molar" repression takes place. Seemingly unitary "personalities" replace each other. Since the mind is capable of functioning in this way, and since such molar clusters of organized intrapersonal dynamics do occur around certain meaning loci such as a name or an image, it seems inordinate to criticize the superego concept on the basis of "anthropomorphism." There is some interesting support for this position in the Berne-(Penfield) conception of *parent* "ego states," although it is clear that Berne rejects a direct equivalence.[13]

Once this possibility is granted, namely, that an "internalized parent" may function in relation to the rest of the self as giving supplies of hatred and love in reaction to the wishes and actions of the id-ego, Freud's hypothesis fits the complexities of guilt dynamics most aptly.

J. C. Flugel elaborates from Freudian theory four main sources of the superego's development. These are (1) secondary narcissism in which the original primary narcissism (love of ego by the id) is directed to the ego ideal, (2) the incorporation or introjection of parental ideals and attitudes, (3) "recoil against the self of aggression aroused by frustrating objects in the outer world," and (4) moral masochism, in which the relation of ego to superego is that of masochist to sadist and in which self-punishment is tinged with satisfaction.[14]

One researcher questioned Freud's notion of "aggression turned against the self," a necessary conceptual correlate of the superego construct. His effort to test this possibility experimentally is instructive and interesting. In a doctoral dissertation, entitled *The Violation of Prohibitions in Solving of Problems,*[15] Donald MacKinnon set up an open-book test situation with 93 college students in which they were able to cheat if they chose to. They were photographed and recorded, so that the violators and nonviolators were known.

The expectation from Freudian theory was that those with a stronger superego would tend to *internalize* more aggression and those with a weaker superego would tend to *externalize* aggression more. As it turned out, both in language and behavior, those who *cheated* tended significantly more to strike out in their frustration against external objects, to walk about, to swear, etc. The *noncheaters* (presumably used to a superego internalization of aggression) tended to express their anger against themselves, biting their skin, fingernails, pulling their hair, etc.

To summarize: For Freud the problem of guilt is to be understood in terms of the personality, driven by instinctual forces of love and hate from the id, seeking to find satisfaction and release of these drives by means of the ego (rational control system and organizing center). The ego must relate the inner needs not only to an external real environment of satisfying resources but also to a complex and vague "social reality," a system of values mediated to him through his parents or other emotionally significant surrogates. This "value environment" becomes *dynamic* for him through the process of identification and introjection by which he internalizes as his superego the parental ideals. Freud made clear his belief that the child adopts the parental *superego* more than parental *behavior* as his superego content. This internal memory constellation, ego ideal, or parent image is the focal medium through which self-evaluation, self-love, self-hatred, and punishment are channeled. Through it the instinctual forces of the id are fed back as feeling states to the ego. Guilt is ego anxiety over punishment or loss of love from the superego.

A somewhat ludicrous analogy I have often resorted to with students may be helpful here. If one were to imagine a young driver learning to drive an automobile equipped with power brakes, with his mother and father sitting anxiously in the back seat, one would have a fair model of the problem. The road, the other cars, etc., constitute the hazards of reality. The power of the engine is the id, the driver is the ego. The parents mediate the traffic rules (values), the meaning of traffic lights, how to avoid other cars, etc. Guilt might be likened to the power brakes, where, at the driver's will, some of the power of the engine is drawn off to slow or stop the car. At first the brakes are applied at the behest of the parents (who know the traffic rules), in concern for their love or fear of their punishment. Gradually the young driver learns the rules for himself. He is now in possession of a superego. Not only in the sense that he has learned the traffic "rules" but in the sense that he continues to hear his parents' voices and to feel their feelings toward himself, long after they are no longer in the back seat. If these feelings were too intense, he may drive with too much guilt, with one foot dragging on the brake, a neurotic condition we will discuss later. Lacking such feelings, he will tend to use the rules expediently in a psychopathic self-interest.

CRITICS OF FREUD

Aside from many current general theoretical critiques of Freudian theory (see Hall and Lindzey, *Theories of Personality*) several specific critiques are leveled in respect to his superego concept by other psychologists concerned with guilt, some of them also psychoanalytically inclined. In the main, these focus on three objections: (1) the *timing* of superego development, (2) the *sexual etiology* of its appearance, and (3) the *superfluity* of the concept. A fourth objection, leveled by Mowrer, in respect to its role in pathological repression, we will deal with in another chapter.

Melanie Klein

This prominent woman psychoanalyst, herself a student of Ferenczi and Abraham and a pioneer in child psychiatry, has had a major impact on British psychiatry. Her most signal contribution to guilt theory lies in her questioning of both the *timing* and *genesis* of the superego. In essence, she asserts that guilt and superego begin in *the first year of life*, perhaps as early as six months, and, further, that *they arise in the intimate infant-mother dynamics* rather than in the triangular Oedipus conflict.

Flugel states that in this new emphasis she followed the thought of Abraham and Ferenczi.[16] Abraham, in his discussion of pregenital stages had hinted at a possible guilt in connection with the anal stage,[17] and Ferenczi went so far as to speak of a "sphincter-morality," where "the anal and urethral identification with the parents . . . appears to build up in the child's mind a sort of physiological forerunner of the ego-ideal or superego."[18]

These suggestions were, Klein noted, reinforced by certain observations of Freud and Fenichel and various members of the British school, as well as her own analyses of children under three years.[19]

Klein's work in this area emphasizes the dynamics of ambivalence in the infant in the "depressive position," as she speaks of it. This occurs probably as early as "four to six months" of age as the infant, in the normal process of feeding, is frustrated. When the mother's breast for any reason is not satisfying, the frustration arouses unpleasant sadistic instincts, and aggressive biting and expulsion (as well as psychological projecting of "bad" feelings onto the now "bad" breast) occur. Anxiety over the impulse and over the loss of the loved object follows. There then ensues an introjection in an attempt to recover the lost object.[20]

This cycle of projection and introjection continues, not only through the oral stage but also through the other pregenital stages of infancy, accompanied by both an increment of sadistic defusion of aggression from libidinous drives, and a gradual refusion (in the normal instance) as the child's perception of the parent becomes more modified by reality. As the movement proceeds, the parent is seen in the infant's sadistic projections as possessing all the biting, defecating, castrating fury that the infant is presumably experiencing instinctually through the several stages of psychosexual development.[21]

For various dynamic reasons, introjection of the fearful parent may occur. Such reasons may be: mimicking to avoid attack (identifying with aggressor) or taking on the power of the aggressor to resist attack, or being good enough not to be attacked. All of this, of course, is complicated by the inclination of the infant mind toward feelings of omnipotence about its thought processes, e.g., the possibility that "wishes may kill," thus amplifying the dangers. We will return later to this problem of omnipotence as an important aspect of superego development. It is sufficient to note here that, in Klein's thought, the normal pattern is for some of the aggression of the parent to be seen as "firm strength" that, as reality becomes clarified, may be relied on by the child to protect him from the anxiety of his own raw instincts.[22]

Another factor of importance is the infant's concern to make restitution when it has attacked the loved-feared object. Klein's contribution of this notion of the infant's reparative gesture comes out of her clinical work and constitutes insight also into the early mechanisms of guilt removal apparent in more developed form in obsessive-compulsive symptomatology as well as normal behavior.[23]

Klein does not see herself in contradiction to Freud's superego theory but as enlarging it and clarifying the precursors of the completed superego. To let her sum up in her own words:

> In my experience, the super-ego, as well as guilt, starts in infancy. The fantastic nature of the early introjected figures corresponds to the immature stage of the ego and to the prevalence of the phantasy life. When in the infant's mind feelings of well-being and love predominate, he feels the mother to be ideally good, but in states of discomfort, frustration and hatred, she turns for him into an extremely bad—a persecuting—object. The father, too, is introjected as a good and as a persecutory object. Such good and bad internalised figures constitute the external ego and exercise a powerful influence over the infant's mind. All these figures are focused as persecutory and depressive anxieties which, in my view, are the elements of early guilt.
>
> Freud's concept of guilt and of the superego as a sequel to the Oedipus complex relates to the climax of the superego development. The figures underlying the early superego gradually change until they assume the form in which the super-ego is active in a child of five years and later.[24]

Klein's work had a definite impact on psychological thought in modifying the previous fixedness of Freud's theory of the *timing* of superego emergence. *Not only does it raise major implicit questions about the* necessity *of the Oedipal triangle as a* precursor *of conscience but it moves the weight of the progression somewhat away from the* libidinous *in the direction of the* power *factor.* Subsequent theorists have followed and reinforced the movement in this direction, as we shall attempt to clarify. Some of their motivation springs from anthropological findings which have raised questions about the universality of the Oedipus complex.[25]

Klein's rooting of guilt in ambivalence allows the retention of the superego concept (as internalized parent) without the absolutizing of the Oedipus complex which Freud's position demands. It must be allowed, however, that it is not seen by her as any questioning of the ultimate arrival of the Oedipus triangle, indeed only making it more inevitable.[26]

Klein's emphasis on the anxiety produced by ambivalence as the basis of guilt is very important. Her remark that "what originates the formation of the super-ego and governs its earliest stages are the destructive impulses and the anxiety they arouse"[27] brings to the fore the fact that guilt hinges on the subtle balances of: power controlling power, power controlling sex, and love controlling both. The latter is implicit, in that if the child did not experience such satisfying care he would not develop the requisite anxiety over his destructive impulses. In fact, there is considerable evidence that death would ensue or at least pathology.[28]

Erich Fromm

Erich Fromm sees the origin of conscience essentially in the child's response to *power*. It is not necessarily focused on the sexual conflict, though this may be a phase of it, or in some instances a central factor, but most often the issue is that of authority. It is therefore true for Fromm as for Klein that the superego need not wait for its emergence upon the sexual-Oedipal conflict. It emerges, rather, out of the resolution of the power-fear struggle of the infant in relation to the parental authority.

Fromm criticizes Freud's concept of the superego as "only

one form of conscience or, possibly, a preliminary stage in the development of conscience."[29] By this he sets it over against the "humanistic" conscience.

According to Fromm, the superego is to be equated with what he calls "the authoritarian conscience." This is the conscience that basically is experienced in the child in a polar way as (from the child's side) fear and (from the parent's side) a powerful authority who must be obeyed. The child sees himself symbiotically related to this authority figure in such a way that his life is by sufferance of the authority and his survival through internalization of the authority and a dutiful patterning of his life after the authority's wishes. Fromm admits that often the authority is idealized and then reintrojected in idealized form.

Behavior in this situation is governed almost entirely by the authority's decision and by dutiful compliance rather than by the individual's evaluation of the issues in a rational way that leads to an ethical decision. Norms are accepted "not because they are good" but "because they are given by the authority."[30] "Good conscience" involves pleasing the authority, and "bad conscience" lies in displeasing the authority. Fromm sees this as not really guilt but fear.

Even though there is an inclination to emulate the authority, there is also a psychological barrier to the limits of this, and the child must be on guard lest his imitation of the authority seem to question the latter's power. Duty and subservience are the prime virtues; the prime offense is disobedience.

The basic dynamic of the relationship lies in the child's feeling of security through his participation in the power of the authority and his feeling of anxiety and emptiness in any tension between himself and the authority. Rejection or isolation is like death, or facing the "horror of nothingness." "Even punishment is better than rejection."[31]

Having established the dynamics of the authoritarian conscience as that of a symbiotic fear-duty relationship, Fromm explores the *contents* of such a conscience. In addition to disobedience being the cardinal sin and obedience the cardinal virtue, he sees the primary effect in a stifling of productiveness: "To the extent to which he feels dependent on powers transcending him, his very productiveness, the assertion of his will, makes him feel guilty."[32]

"Good conscience" in such a system actually comes from the subduing of one's independence, the awareness of inferiority and guilt and even cruelty toward the self. A rationalization occurs in which the weakened self is made to seem "just punishment for sin." "The fact of his loss of freedom is rationalized as proof of guilt, and this conviction increases the guilt feeling induced by the cultural and parental systems of value."[33]

On the roots of neurosis, Fromm disagrees partially with Freud. He believes that it is not the sexual but the *power* rivalry which largely originates both neurosis and the chronic guilt of the authoritarian conscience. The struggle of the child is essentially for freedom from the coercive power of parents. If the child never wins, he will be neurotically bound. Normalcy lies in his winning the struggle, biasing the outcome in the direction of his own self-realization, the fulfillment of his inner potentialities and productiveness. In Fromm's words:

> The most important symptom of the defeat in the fight for oneself is the guilty conscience. If one has not succeeded in breaking out of the authoritarian net, the unsuccessful attempt to escape is proof of guilt, and only by renewed submission can the good conscience be regained.[34]

Over against this authoritarian conscience Fromm sets as an ideal the "humanistic conscience." By this he means, "not the internalized voice of an authority whom we are eager to please and afraid of displeasing; it is our own voice, present in every human being and independent of external sanctions and rewards."[35] It is "knowledge within oneself," with an emotional quality which makes more than an abstract judgment. It is "the reaction of our total personality," a "reaction of ourselves to ourselves," *"the voice of our loving care for ourselves."*[36]

Contrasting them, Fromm writes:

> Humanistic conscience is the expression of man's self-interest and integrity, while authoritarian conscience is

concerned with man's obedience, self-sacrifice, duty, or
his "social adjustment." The goal of humanistic conscience is productiveness and, therefore, happiness, since
happiness is the necessary concomitant of productive
living.[37]

By thus differentiating, Fromm makes a contribution at the
same time that he puts us in a quandary. He helps us to see
the way in which the power aspects of conscience may be
perverted to self-destructive ends in the effort to resolve fear
and anxiety in relation to the symbiotically significant authority. He clarifies the distortions of the "ought" and the paradoxical absurdities of "guilt experienced as virtue" in the authoritarian, dependent, and freedom-threatened person.

On the other hand, he sets up in this way what seems to
be an artificial antinomy. *He seems to put a negative valence
on all the power aspects of superego and to derogate any
dependence or compliance as a crippling abandonment of
freedom. The obverse of this, of course, tends to apotheosize
rebellion as well as freedom and to elevate rejection of any
dependence or veneration to an ultimate.*

It is true that there is a stage in the process of development
in which the courage to defy authority (which probably after
all, in a healthy person, is grounded in the confidence that
the authority will *not* destroy) in order to test values for oneself is a necessary movement in maturation. However, it does
not seem to enter Fromm's system as a possibility that a *good*
authority may will and encourage the freedom and independence of the child. All authority seems to be caricatured as
hostile power. Even when it is benevolent it tends to be seen
as a ruse. Benevolent power of restraint may be a necessary
part of our "loving care for ourselves."

Fromm does assert that his delineation of the authoritarian
conscience as totally over against the humanistic conscience
is an artifice. He admits that "they are, of course, *not separated in reality and not mutually exclusive in any one person. On the contrary, actually everybody has both 'consciences.'
The problem is to distinguish their respective strength and
their inter-relation.*"[38]

It becomes apparent therefore that Fromm may be leading

us into a cul-de-sac by setting up such a sharp distinction, however suggestive and helpful. He seems to equate the self-restrictive, internal-aggressive, or "thou shalt not" aspects of superego with *destructive* values and only the positive, free, ego-ideal aspects of superego with health values. This seems to the author an unwarranted dichotomy. It sets the stage for Fromm's later hedonic calculus: humanistic values = self-realization. It also raises the question, however, of whether the conscience struggle of the mature man is ever free of some elements of self-negation, anxiety, the desire to please the internalized authority.

Fromm, as McKenzie points out,[39] tends to replace the dynamics of the *ought* with a self-interest ethic based on some rational awareness of an objective criterion by which the productive good can be discerned. *It always remains a question whether the affective dynamics of the sense of obligation or oughtness can be reduced to an objective calculus of self-realization.*

Fromm seems rightly to want to move us from an ethic of *fear* to an ethic of intelligent self-conscious and loving co-operativeness with some objective value reality in the universe. It is a question whether this can occur by way of shifting the hate-love attitudes toward the self (which flow from the relation to the parental authority) entirely into an unanxious self-love dimension freed to explore some "inner voice" dispassionately. This appears to be an attempt to shift the *feeling* aspect of conscience or superego onto a cognitive level, where conscience pain can be avoided by purely rational operations.

Putting the problem as simply as possible, superego is internalization of positive and negative *affects* toward the self in response to values espoused or denied by the ego. Granted that the ego functions better if these affects are not crippling, overwhelming, or too grossly negative; the healthy person will be able to test reality for himself and modify these feelings. Yet to assume that the humanistic or healthy conscience can ever be *divested* of negative elements (or ought to be entirely) or that it can simply be reduced to an operation of rational calculation is to want to *eliminate* the superego in its full vitality in favor of an idealized ego which probably does not exist.

What Fromm seems to be saying is that any "oughtness" that rightly governs one's behavior should come from a rational assessment of reality—a kind of Q.E.D. at the end of a syllogism. What is *true* for me as self-realization is what I should feel guilty over if I violate it. Yet if (when!) such rationality is violated, *what* feelings occur and where do they come from? Just the "tut-tut, you made a mistake" level of awareness, or a real sense of anxiety over separation from one's internalized ideal self? Should this kind of guilt anxiety be eliminated? This is a kind of moral "fear" which has its origins in the relation to the original parent image, even though greatly modified. To eliminate it would be comparable to tranquilizing the ego of one's concern about jumping off high buildings or grasping high voltage wires.

We come here to a point where there exists considerable disagreement about the origin of conscience. That is whether an authoritarian conscience is a necessary stage in the evolution of any conscience, prior to the full development of rationality. Julian Huxley suggested this, and Fromm takes issue with him, believing that it would not be necessary in a nonauthoritarian environment, admitting however that "only the future development of mankind can prove or disprove the validity of this assumption."[40]

Fromm rightly recognizes the overlapping and confusion between an authoritarian conscience and his humanistic conscience and that sometimes we feel a sense of obligation to perform even cruel or evil acts. However, it does not seem possible to eliminate the irrational feeling element of "the ought" (which must be the dynamic of even a rational ethic) by tending to equate it all with authoritarianism and irresponsible or vindictive power. Fromm seems to do this. This brings us to a representative of another possibility in the theoretical understanding of superego emergence, David Ausubel.

David Ausubel

One of the more sophisticated theoreticians of recent years in respect to the problems of conscience and guilt is David

Ausubel. In his book *Ego Development and the Personality Disorders*,[41] he traces very carefully the formation of conscience and the development of guilt feeling in connection with ego formation.

His theory is elaborated with the support of research in developmental psychology, reflecting the work of Piaget, Gesell, Havighurst, and others who have made recent contributions in this area, as well as revealing a knowledge of the classical writers. His work is perhaps the most carefully systematized treatment to date.

Although employing many psychoanalytic insights, Ausubel at the outset rejects several basic psychoanalytic assumptions. The most important for our purposes is his rejection of the superego concept as necessary or adequate for the expression of, and understanding of, the theory of guilt.[42]

In place of the superego he uses the term "conscience." He prefers to remain with this term because he sees the whole process of guilt conflict and the role of values in the personality as centered in the *ego* rather than in what he considers a mythical superego. He asks the question: "If the ego tests reality and represses socially unacceptable elements of the id, why then do we need a superego, which is the 'heir' of an instinctual oedipus conflict?"[43]

He also raises questions about the necessity for an unconscious superego apart from the ego and an ego ideal over against the ego.[44] We have questions about his dismissal of the superego concept and its replacement by the term "conscience," but we will discuss this later.

Accepting, for the moment, his notion of conscience as purely an ego function, what does Ausubel say about its development?

Essentially, he understands the child's development, both ego-wise and conscience-wise, as a *power* problem in relation to the parent. Early experiences of powerful adults responding to his cries and giving him attention tend to lead to and amplify the feeling of *omnipotence* in the child. The infant does not understand that the parental response to his needs and cries is an act of parental love and duty, and thus, by the time he reaches ten months of age he begins to feel that "par-

ents are deferential and permissive because of an obligatory
need to submit to his powerful will."[45] He develops a sense of
omnipotence about his will, which, by the tenth month, is
sufficiently grounded that the infant will express real rage if
his will is not satisfied.

*Ausubel places great importance upon this development in
the infant and makes its resolution the central point in his
personality theory.*

If a child continues to grow with an illusion about his omnipotence in relation to reality (and this is possible because
of the way parents may help him to continue the illusion),
then the child is headed for trouble. Especially is this true
in the area of conscience and the formation of a healthy value
system.

Ausubel sees as critical for the development of normal
personality what he calls the process of "devaluation" of omnipotence. This process he terms "satellization" (a function
closely reminiscent of the ego defense mechanism "altruistic
surrender" borrowed by Anna Freud from Edward Bibring[46]).
By this Ausubel means that the infant, facing the crisis of
recognition that he is not omnipotent, but in a real sense dependent upon the love and power of the parents, must go
through a stage in which he surrenders his notion of omnipotence and maintains his self-esteem by a compromise: that of
identification. In other words, he is not omnipotent, but his
parents are, and by identifying with them he basks in the
light of their strength and feels a new security and self-esteem
in this relationship. "Since he cannot manipulate reality successfully enough to gratify omnipotent fancies, the next best
thing, therefore, is to become a satellite of persons who obviously *are* omnipotent."[47]

Ausubel does not see this satellization process occurring
inevitably. There are certain prerequisites for it which he
articulates. These include *sufficient altruistic satisfaction of
the child's needs by the parents to arouse a natural response
of affection for them in the child,* and also a *genuine acceptance of the child by the parents* that is not conditional upon
his fulfilling any special requirements, being a reflection of
their love for him as *their* child. Such intrinsic valuation of

the child by the parents becomes the core of his inner self-acceptance and security.[48]

There are negative implications which Ausubel draws from the above. He points out that narcissistic parents who reject their children or value the child on the basis of his potential for fulfillment of some frustrated ego ambitions of their own are likely to produce a child incapable of satellization and who lacks intrinsic status. Such a child will tend to perpetuate his omnipotent strivings and try to extort from his environment whatever he can get.[49]

The *qualitative* properties of the personality which must be brought under the influence of satellization are: "the extent of hedonistic motivation, the need for immediacy in gratification, the degree of executive dependency, and the concept of moral responsibility."[50]

Ausubel pictures the infant and the mature adult at opposite poles in respect to these qualities.

The following outline will attempt to depict briefly the stages in normal satellization which Ausubel elaborates and, parallel to these, the particular evolutionary phases of conscience as these take place concurrently with and within the ego development:[51]

AGE	EGO	CONSCIENCE
0 to 2½ years	*Presatellization Stage*	
	Gradual distinguishing of self from environment.	"Inhibitory control" based on "learning to anticipate and avoid punishment." Inhibition reduces the pain of deprivation, isolation, or disapproval for unacceptable behavior.
	Development of pre-verbal concept of self and discovery of volitional power of crying and vocalization.	
	Gradual emergence of verbal symbolization with emerging freedom from dependence on objects for expression.	Parental values "not truly" internalized. No internalization of sense of obligation as yet. Conformity still based on fear. *No true guilt yet,* only anxiety.

Sense of volitional om-
nipotence rather than
awareness of parental
altruism.

Dependence upon par-
ent for fulfillment of
his will (executive de-
pendence). After 27
months: possibility of
identification and self-
criticism.

2½ to 4 years   *Early Satellization*
                    Stage

Discovery by infant
that he is not omnipo-
tent and that he is de-
pendent on parents'
goodwill (volitional de-
pendence). Ego-deval-
uation crisis, forcing
ego reorganization:

Emerging "need to as-
similate parental values
and . . . gradual emer-
gence of a feeling of
obligation to conform
to them . . ." (after
early period of nega-
tivism).

Crisis: continue fantasy
       of omnipotence
       (or)
       accept reality of
       dependence.

Period of uncritical sub-
servience reinforced by
parental prestige, re-
ward, threat, and child's
physical dependence.
Movement toward true
conscience.

Early resistance to, then
frequently acquiescence
in,

Compromise: Maintain
self-esteem through
SATELLIZATION:
Achieving indirect sta-
tus by *transfer of omni-
potence fantasy to par-
ents and basking in
their power and good-
ness.*

(At 3 years: decline in
resistive behavior.)

4 years

New surge of negativism, self-assertion based on new (more realistic) executive competence, independence. Increased self-confidence.

Crisis: Whether to attempt complete assertion of exaggerated self-confidence or to recover comfort of dependent status. Growth of self-critical faculty and true guilt.

"Despite the boisterous, aggressive and competitive characteristics of four-year-old negativism, the effects of early satellization are not completely lost. Evidence of guilt feelings is present, and the influence of conscience is discernible if only in the elaborate efforts made to justify violations of the accepted behavior. Neither moral values nor moral obligation are rejected outright." (P. 422.) Imaginative excuses, projections, and rationalizations indicate incomplete acceptance of satellization.

5 to 8 years

Later stages of satellization

5 is a "relatively quiet, well-conforming age."

Decline in self-exuberance.

Heightened self-critical faculty.

Fluctuations of self-assertiveness but movement toward greater satellization up to age of 8, "at which time, identification with the parent is at a maximum."

"Stabilization and internalization of sense of moral obligation as a result of gains in self-critical ability."

Conscience functions to a greater degree "in the absence of external coercive agents."

Reinforcement by guilt feelings.

Conscience still not divorced from external authorities.

Moral absolutism.

8 years and up   *Desatellization in Pre-*
                    adolescent

Movement from this | "Decline in moral ab-
age on tends to be to- | solutism."
ward peer-group iden-
tifications and weaken- | Conscience becomes
ing gradually of depen- | "less   authoritarian,"
dent tie upon parents. | "more reciprocal."
"We-feeling" with peer
group "recapitulates his | Morality acquires more
relation to his parents. | generality, abstractness
. . ." This movement is | less egocentric.
also in direction of | Shift from parents to
teachers and parent-sur- | society as locus of
rogates. Desatellization | moral accountability.
may be resisted or com-
plicated by parental (or
child) reluctance to sur-
render child's depen-
dent status or through
arousal of unusual guilt
feeling over same.

Desatellization in Ado-
lescent

A continuing of previ- | Intensification of pre-
ous stage with a sharp- | vious stage, plus "trend
ening of the depen- | toward expediency and
dence-independence | conformity" (more in-
struggle. A reactivation | terest in extrinsic sta-
of the self-assertion of | tus), "cynicism," also
the 2½-year-old, . . . | toward more "tolerance
"but the battle of voli- | and flexibility." More
tional independence lost | awareness of *context* of
then most be won now" | moral decision.
(p. 83). Movement to-
ward adult ego class
and sex status.

It can be seen that one of Ausubel's major contributions is his clarification and specification, supported in many instances by empirical observation, of the developmental sequences in the relationship between child and parent as these elaborate

both *ego* and *conscience*. He has put into bas-relief the power
factors as they seem to shift loci between child and parent in
the determination and control of impulse expression, and he
has given us what is probably as accurate a description of
the authoritative conscience (Fromm) or superego (though
he will not call it this) as we may expect concerning its outward manifestations and possible internal *meanings*.

It is the opinion of this author, however, that *Ausubel has
much overemphasized the power factor and too much under-
played the love element*. He does mention it in his reference
to the necessity for unconditional acceptance of the child and
an altruistic concern for the child's needs as necessary prerequisites for satellization. Yet he writes as though this were
some kind of constant while the struggle with power was the
only variable of any importance—as though one aspect of
the parent could be introjected dependably once for all while
the power aspect of the parent was related to in some isolated
ambivalent fashion.

As indicated previously, Ausubel rejects the superego concept on various grounds. We would like to present these in
capsule form and react to them in similar fashion.

1. Ausubel rejects the synonymous use of "superego" and
"conscience" as "unprecise" and "misleading," "since superego
does not refer to the developmental conscience described
above as a part of the ego, but to a separate, reified layer of
personality derived from a specific, inevitable, and universal
event in psychosexual development."[52]

Reaction: "Reification" is no more true of Freud's "superego" than it is of Ausubel's "ego." If it is accepted as a shorthand symbol for a special function or series of functions—in
this case *those feelings toward the self surrounding responses
to the internalized values which reflect identifications with,
and introjections of, the parents*—then it has a connotative
value of great importance even for "conscience" in Ausubel's
theory. Freud recognized the preliminary developmental roots
of the superego. It is possible to disagree with Freud as to
the absolute degree or universality of the incestuous sexual
crisis and still retain the superego symbol, just as it is possible

to retain the concept of "evolution" without subscribing to all of Darwin's entailed interpretations.

> 2. Ausubel agrees with Sherif and Cantril's objection that . . . there is for the individual no psychological difference either in the genesis of or the function of "moral" codes (which psychoanalysts separate out as the "superego") and other norms of behavior the individual learns. The emerging developing ego is in large part composed of *all* these interiorized social values.[53]

Then he adds: "The values subsumed under conscience are *merely internalized in an ethical context* and are *more closely related to such factors as self-criticism, obligation, self-control and guilt feelings.*"[54]

Response: We would agree that the codes or contents of morality are essentially ego factors. (The psychopathic personality *learns* them.) But what does Ausubel mean by "*merely* internalized in an ethical context," and "more closely related to . . . [orectic] factors"? This is the whole point! Why is it that contents of morality can be so ineffectively incorporated into the ego? Is it not exactly that the *feelings toward the self of approval and disapproval* that constitute the essence of the superego (the internalized parent) were not introjected, identified with? There are no guilt feelings because the *source* of those feelings has not been introjected. Ausubel would say this is because "satellization" did not occur, but he also admits that when satellization does *not* occur it is because the *love* relation between parent and child was not adequate. Is this not a possible tacit admission that the internalization of those feelings toward the self that the parents held (essentially, superego) is determinative both of positive conscience and of negative conscience (or positive and negative superego feelings)? Is not this what Ausubel means when he refers to the "ethical context" in which values are internalized, i.e., some emotionally significant figure is conveying positive or negative feelings toward the subject about the importance *for the relationship* of adopting the conceptual code or content of the value?

3. Ausubel criticizes the poor conceptualization of the rationale for the superego as something "special and apart from the ego," especially concerning reality testing, ego–superego–ego-ideal distinctions, and the question of superego as *cause* or *product* of repression of the Oedipus complex.[55]

Reaction: What is "reality testing" of values if not a behavioral exploration to discover whether the superego (internalized parental feelings toward the self re these values) warnings and threats will be borne out?

Are polarities between ego and superego any more tenuous than complex polarities between one aspect of an ego and another (unnamed) aspect when one is trying to explain why value contents are not integrated as determinants in guilt-producing fantasy or motor activities sanctioned by the ego?

Further, is it not possible to conceptualize superego as functioning at preliminary levels of significance (such as presatellization levels of obligation) and, later, in more crystallized or set forms of importance, when true existential realization of reality-for-survival is experienced (such as the sense of obligation in the later stages of satellization)?

4. Ausubel rejects the sexual Oedipal conflict as the basis of identification with the parent's values as "impressionistic," based on "retrospective clinical material," and not based on any "unequivocal clinical findings" concerning the derivation of hostility toward same-sex parents based on sexual rivalry.[56]

Reaction: The author would question under what conditions Ausubel would judge sex-rival hostility as "unequivocal" as satellization, while agreeing with Ausubel at the same time that it is a question whether value rivalry with the parent must reach the level of castration anxiety before true identification can become effective and "crystallized" in the personality.

5. Ausubel contends:

The superego concept . . . ignores all of the developmental evidence available on the growth of conscience— from complete infantile amorality to a sense of moral responsibility based first on fear of punishment, later on uncritical satellization, and finally on rational notions of

moral reciprocity and functionalism. It is a static concept
which makes no allowances for the fact that the nature
of conscience keeps on shifting.[57]

Reaction: Exactly the opposite! It is because superego theory
explains the very contradictions of developmental theory
that it is such a viable concept, for example, the way in which
internalized feelings about values (because of the significant
tenacity and importance for self-esteem of keeping the internalized unconscious parent image satisfied) so effectively resist change in spite of ego adoption of varying and sometimes
contrary contents. Again, what explains the continuity of the
"sense of obligation" and the vitality of real guilt even when
formerly important values are replaced? What, in psychopathological phenomena, accounts for the pervasive appearance of parental voices (and faces) in psychotic symptomatology?

SUMMARY

At this point, we would like to give some perspective on
the foregoing and summarize in broad scope what seems to
us implicit in the presentation.

We have reviewed the major emphases of Freud, Klein,
Fromm, and Ausubel respecting the underlying dynamics of
superego-conscience development and guilt structure. If we
chart their thinking in the categories we suggested at the
beginning of the chapter, the result is as shown on the facing
page.

	Superego (Conscience) Content	Function	When Established	How Established
Freud (Superego Ego Ideal)	Essentially parent value content. Only partial ego integration, increasing with maturation and analysis (with pathological exceptions). Central dynamic values: pleasure and avoidance of pain.	To protect from anxiety over castration and/or power of same-sex parent.	*During period (height) of Oedipus conflict (approximate 4 to 6 years)*, with predispositions begun in infancy in love-hate relations with parents, especially involving stages of libido development.	Largely by identification with values of threatening parent (incest-murder taboos) and *repression* of threatening impulses.
Klein (Superego Ego Ideal)	Largely the same as Freud. Central dynamic values: pleasure and avoidance of pain.	To protect from anxiety over negative (hate) aspects of ambivalence, loss of loved object, and depression.	In *first year of life* when infant begins differentiating of self and mother in respect to feeding frustration.	Through *introjection-projection* interplay around sadistic, incorporative, and restitutive impulses.
Fromm (Authoritarian Conscience or Superego and/or Humanistic Conscience)	Depends heavily on parents' ability to respect child's freedom and to minimize authoritarian aspects of relation. Rational integration implicitly possible from earliest stages of symbolization.	*Authoritarian conscience:* To protect from fear of authority. *Humanistic conscience:* To increase happiness through productivity, love, rationality.	As early as self vs. authority conflicts can be experienced. As early as rational functions permit.	By *submission* to authority's power and denigration of one's self and ego functions. Through healthy parent-child relationship *emphasizing rational self-affirmation and minimizing fear of authoritarian power.*
Ausubel (Conscience)	Essentially parental value content, largely uncritically adopted until age of eight. Then movement toward de-satellization begins.	To resolve omnipotence conflict and maintain some reflected self-esteem and status during ego devaluation of satellization.	Begins to "focus" about 2½ to 3 years of age	Through satellization and identification.

Chapter IV

SUPEREGO MATURATION

A morality which plays safe, by subjecting itself to an unconditional authority, is suspect. It has not the courage to take guilt and tragedy upon itself. True morality is a morality of risk.

—Paul Tillich[1]

The last chapter presented a gross picture of superego formation, attempting to provide a broad frame of reference against which both superego precursors and superego *maturation* (Some writers resist the use of this term in relation to superego. We hope the remainder of this chapter will justify its employment.) could be discussed. It will soon be evident that in order to understand what happens in later moral development, it is necessary to have a more precise picture of superego formation in its earlier stages.

Unfortunately, the student of guilt, trying to construct a viable theoretical picture, resembles the scientist given the task of planning a moon landing before precision data are in on the topography and consistency of the lunar surface. He must work from coarse observational data and speculative constructs until such time as better data force logical changes.

Research on the elements involved in superego formation has scarcely begun. What there is holds out some hope of eventual assessment of psychoanalytic theory concerning guilt. The findings tend to lend some strength to Freud's general ideas concerning identification with parents and the importance of this for socialization, while raising some serious questions about the interconnection between sex-typing and moral identification.[2, 3]

The groundwork of Freud's contribution is his exposure of the love-power polarity in guilt dynamics. These are the germinal elements in the vicissitudes of moral development with which all subsequent theorists have had to grapple. These elements are dominant in the molar learning processes underlying identification and constitute the reinforcement factors in more specific aspects of moral conditioning. They predispose the infant at a fairly early age (some of it preverbal) to a readiness or set for openness toward, or blatant rejection of (as in the sociopath), the socialization process. These, the *orectic* or feeling bases of moral development, are the *sine qua non* of its occurrence.

Freud's original contributions to the understanding of the processes by which the child's feelings do or do not become structured in a socializing way have been widely reviewed and criticized. Psychoanalysts such as J. C. Flugel,[4] Heinz Hartmann,[5] and Edith Jacobson[6] have presented sensitive interpretations appreciative of his theory. The intensive studies of children under the direction of Anna Freud in the Hampstead Clinic and the preparation of the Hampstead Index on the superego have produced a rich file of clinical material. Much of this is reported in the *Psychoanalytic Study of the Child* in its annuals.[7]

Before looking at some of the efforts to translate and criticize Freud from the perspective of learning theory and empirical experiment, we shall look briefly at the way in which psychoanalysts have elaborated their theory respecting superego development. It is almost impossible in handling this material to tell where dogmatic theory stops and clinical perception begins.

When Freud spoke of the superego as "the heir of the oedipus complex," he drew attention to the idea that it constitutes a precipitation or aggregate collation of experiences with the parents, and that it turned on the particular compromise a child unconsciously achieved between his incestuous and murderous impulses toward his parents. This is why the analysts speak of the *core* of the superego in terms of the control of these two basic impulses.[8] (People who have difficulty with this as the *core* of the socialization process may be helped by conceiving "incest" in the broader terms of wanting to merge with the security figure who reduces tension, and "murder" as the ultimate rage toward any obstacle —in this case, a parental barrier.)

Many possible unique drive combinations could and do occur; however, Freud is criticized by McCord and McCord for failing to include the significance of extraparental authority figures as critical determinants.[9] All of the drive combinations, however, tend to function with varying degrees of stability, coherence, and intensity that reflect, resemble, or refract treatment (or the child's perceptual distortion of it) which the child received from the parents, represented to the ego in ways that are often strongly personalized—as though one or both parents were internally present.

Most children experience the parents in *two* ways: as *ideal models* to follow and as *love-withdrawing authorities* who punish, inhibit, and restrict. These two aspects are often roughly differentiated as *ego ideal* and *superego* respectively with the former being more conscious and the latter largely unconscious.

Over the last decade, much of the writing by psychoanalysts has turned on the distinctions between these two aspects and their interrelationships as well as the precursors from which they emerge. The value of such a distinction is to be seen (beyond that of heuristic curiosity) in the possibility it affords of assessing various stages of pathological regression as well as suggesting ideal directions for education of the young child and optimal parent-child relationships.

Freud himself showed some discrepancies in his use of terms. In his 1914 essay "On Narcissism,"[10] he used the term "ego ideal" to refer to the mental construct the infant developed as a kind of internal focus of narcissistic love in order to repair the ego trauma resulting from his ineffectiveness in the real world, fantasied or real rejection, etc. (A crude analogy might be a kind of "psychic pacifier" in the absence of the real breast.) It represented the idealized aspects of the

parental objects and the idealized possibilities of the self. It
was here distinguished from "conscience" which represented
the negative, critical aspect.

We find these two (negative and positive) elements merged
in his use of "ego-ideal" in his *Group Psychology and the
Analysis of the Ego*.[11] In his 1923 book, *The Ego and the Id*,[12]
"ego-ideal" and "conscience" are synonomous. Freud refers to
the superego in *The New Introductory Lectures*,[13] as the "vehicle of the ego ideal." Thus, after 1923, *superego* was used
by Freud to represent both the positive and negative aspects
of the moral dynamic.

The spate of articles which has appeared in the effort to
unravel the distinctions and interrelationships of the two concepts has been helpfully assessed by Joseph Sandler.[14] The
writers have tended to focus on the positive, libidinous (and,
usually, earlier and more archaic) significance of the ego
ideal, as well as the later, more punitive, and critical meaning
of superego (although the latter also has archaic precursors).
A summary description of the ego ideal might run as follows:

Ego Ideal

The *ego ideal* may be said to be constituted by images of
the parents which are positively cathected, love-giving, need-
gratifying, goal-setting self-esteem providing, and often un-
clearly differentiated self-parent images that are glorified in
fantasy. This latter magical element comes from primitive and
archaic ego elements that obtained before perception was sufficient to differentiate self and object representations.

Edith Jacobson[15] draws attention to movement from this
core of the ego ideal as the fused self- and love-object through
a gradual differentiation of these as the ego develops and reality begins to impinge. A *movement* occurs from a sense of
magical omnipotence of the self toward displacement of this
to the parent (reminiscent of Ausubel's "satellization") as a
glorified image. There also occurs a reality-ordered discovery
of parental limitations which provides a necessary temporary
"disillusionment." If the previous relationship has been poor,
this may result in a cynical character. If it has been good,

the normal response is for the child reactively to reinvest the parental image with idealized powers, much as he does his own ego ideal. (One hears reflections of this process often in a child's grandiose bragging about his parents.) These aggrandized images continue to function throughout life in some measure as a "carrot in front" sort of goal for the ego. There remains a *longing to be one with the love object,* to merge ideal self and ideal object. (The root-closeness of magic, hope, and morality can be seen in this conception of ego ideal.)

It is important to emphasize the foregoing steps: From (1) *fusion* of self and object with omnipotent fantasies, to (2) *differentiation* that leads to surrender of much of omnipotent fantasy to the parental object, to (3) *reality recognition* of parental limitations, and (4) a compensatory kind of *idealization* of parent and self.

The most important things to remember here are the *positive nature* of the ego ideal, its "double face"[16] (i.e., its blending of ideal self-representation and idealized parental object representations), its *rootage in magic and fantasy* (core of narcissistic omnipotence), its *goal contents* (by which the ego measures the self), its personal quality, and its *relation to reality perception.* Edith Jacobson would add a note about a value shift from *pleasure* to *strength.* This is the process of the intrusion of the reality principle on the pleasure principle consistent with Freud's formulations.[17] (The inherent logic in it is this: if the seeking of pleasure leads to a loss of love objects or a rejection of the self, then more important is the kind of *strength* which protects one from such weakness and helplessness.)

The foregoing summary (The student is referred to Edith Jacobson's *The Self and the Object World* for its much more thorough explication. [Cf. note 5.]) has purposely emphasized *one* side of the picture—the positive ego ideal aspect of the superego. This is done for purposes of clarification. It must be emphasized that it is a partial caricature. A parallel caricature would be a description of a person which only summarized his likeable qualities. In actuality, Freud, probably correctly, refused to distinguish neatly in any rigid way this positive ego ideal aspect of the self from the more negative superego qualities, which he sometimes referred to as "conscience." He saw the interaction of ego and superego reflecting the ambivalence and love-hate polarities that are typical of the parent-child relationship,[18] mirroring the simultaneous impact of negative and positive valences. (Hartmann and Loewenstein tend to support this view and resist too radical a separation of ego ideal from superego.)[19] It is this very sensitivity of Freud to the complex molarity of these relationships which makes his dynamic approach so appropriate in the individual instance and so frustrating to theorists who want "nomothetic" as opposed to idiosyncratic categories.

SUPEREGO

To continue the caricature: We may emphasize now the *negative, prohibitive* side of the superego as it functions in the personality. Many of its functions operate at an unconscious level. It is the "image of the hated and feared objects," experienced as critical, demanding voices (there is frequently an auditory emphasis in the superego) punishing the self or threatening punishment, setting boundaries for the self and limits on instinctual expressions. It has its roots in early, pregenital reaction formations of disgust and loathing and shame, variously related to infant ambivalence (cf. Klein), "sphincter morality," anal-sadistic and exhibitionistic impulses. These archaic elements interact with fantasied projections of aggressive and hostile impulses to come to dynamic fruition in what Freud called the "castration complex." It is this latter in its full terrorizing impact on the ego that arises during the Oedipus conflict. It comes about as a result of the incestuous wish for the opposite-sexed parents which leads either to real or fantasied threats of attack or to mutilation by the same-sexed rival.

Definition of the Term "Superego"

As we continue to use the term "superego," unless we wish to emphasize the positive ego ideal or the negative punitive side (in which case we will write superego [+] or superego

[−]), the term will represent the blended identifications of both parental introjects and whatever positive or negative dynamic implications this may have for the particular individual. We will ordinarily, too, be speaking of the "superego proper," i.e., what the psychoanalysts recognize as the heir of the Oedipus complex. Its establishment means: *Fear of parental punishment (castration) or loss of love has now become internalized into a fear of superego punishment or loss of love.* The parental image has become introjected and identification is under way.

A shift has occurred from "sphincter morality" and shame (though this continues to function) in the direction of castration anxiety and/or superego fear (on the negative side), and from magical archaic ego fantasies about omnipotence in the direction of a more reality-oriented, idealized imagery in the ego ideal (on the positive side).

There has also occurred a shift of desire for love-fusion with the parent (whether conceived as incestuous or otherwise) to a desire for fusion of self and parent *images* in the ego ideal, as well as a shift from aggression against the real parents to aggressive relations between ego and superego, with all the ambivalent and punitive innuendos.

Before establishment of the superego proper, thus defined, two other (probably concomitant) developments must occur. We separate them for purposes of clarity, *not* to imply that they are distinct or easily distinguishable from each other or from interaction with the previously described elements. These are *ego maturation* and *identification.*

Edith Jacobson writes:

> The psychic organization is not ready to build up the superego as a functional system before the maturation of the ego and of object relations has progressed to a certain level. I refer to the development of feeling and thought processes, of perception and reality testing, of logical and abstract thinking, of the sense of time, of critical judgment and discrimination, and finally to the development of self and object representations, of affectionate object relations, of ego identifications, and of the executive functions of the ego.[20]

It is when these ego components are sufficiently developed

that the superego as an organized system is sufficiently functional to present fairly stable expressions of the guilt phenomena. One is tempted to conjecture whether it is not the maturation of these ego factors rather than the Oedipal sexual crises that determine the collation of superego functions and the appearance of Oedipal conflicts at about the same time.

It is on the fulcrum of *identification* that the socialization process most crucially turns. As Bernard Diamond put it, "When there is no identification, we are all sociopathic."[21]

Some psychoanalysts (Klein) speak of the early infant confusion of self and object as identification. Others feel this is a mistake and believe that it should be referred to the processes which occur *after* some kind of self-object distinction has been developed.[22] We will refer to it in the latter sense.

Sandler defines identification as "the changing of the shape of one's self-representation on the basis of another representation as a model."[23] It may be conscious or unconscious, specific or molar. Sandler does not believe it is necessarily dependent upon introjection, though it may often be.[24] He distinguishes introjection as "the investment of object representations with an authority or status which they did not previously possess."[25] Superego formation thus involves the introjection of the parental images with special authority and varying degrees of identification with these.

Freud is sometimes represented as picturing identification with only one of the parents (e.g., the boy with the father) and thus woodenly tying all moral identification to sex-role identification. It is true that he often reads this way and that he did tie together sex role and socialization. However, he must also be credited with awareness of the many subtle combinations possible in superego identification. He did emphasize that repression of the Oedipus conflict was made easier by identification with the same-sexed parent and that this was reinforced or obfuscated by the constitutional, biological bias of the child. *He did on the other hand point out that the simple Oedipal solution was probably rare and that most people are involved in double identifications "in some way combined together" with the sexual disposition determining the balance.*[26]

If too strictly interpreted, Freud's tying of superego to sex type can be an obstacle to theory, but without sensitivity to these connections it becomes difficult to understand many varieties of superego pathology and sex deviations.

Bronfenbrenner[27] and Roger Brown[28] both assess a number of recent theoretical critiques and experimental explorations of Freud's identification theory. Most of the writers they review accept the necessity for some such molar learning process as identification. At the same time, they reflect a general discontent with tying model identification so strictly to sex type as Freud seemed to do. They suggest that envy of the social power and instrumental skills of the parent may be as significant as fear of pain or castration in superego establishment.

The experiments that have been performed to explore identification tend, as Brown points out, to support the notion that it is *"power that attracts imitation."*[29] This certainly seems to be evident in the kind of learning that characterizes the sociopath. On the other hand, in itself, it fails to account for genuine socialization and the total guilt process, because it in no way provides for the love dynamic toward self or others, and leaves out the very thing which distinguishes a healthy superego from the sociopathic one. It is the *positive* affects which are internalized and the positive ego ideals of an affectional sort which lend a true moral quality to the superego. As Fromm so clearly pointed out, this is the basis of a humanistic as opposed to a fear-ridden authoritarian conscience. It is because of this that Freud recognized the significance of the libidinous affects and their vicissitudes in superego establishment and the fact that it is because power provides or limits access to these that it becomes so important to identify with it.

SUPEREGO DIMENSIONS

The superego as a fairly stabilized function in the personality may be viewed from the perspective of four different dimensions. These are *feeling, content, timing,* and *control. It is the way in which these factors are integrated or function reciprocally in a discordant fashion which determines the ultimate outcome for a particular individual's moral behavior and attitudes.*

Feeling

Feeling accounts for the sense of "oughtness" that Kant epitomized as the essence of moral motivation. Irrespective of what *contents* are held to be the norms for the individual or society, if feelings or emotions concerning these are not *supportive* of the contents, the person will not be sufficiently motivated to let the contents direct his behavior or function as personal goals. For example, the sociopath knows what the code *content* is. He can repeat it on tests and he can even play the role of a sophisticated socialized member of society. But the *feelings* that motivate this behavior, in case after case, turn out to be those of expediency. He is not apparently constrained by identification feeling from the most brutal crimes, nor, having committed them, does he experience the feeling of guilt, self-reproach, self-punishment, or the withdrawal of self-love.

The feeling level of superego may vary on a wide continuum from almost *no* feeling of guilt to an intense feeling of self-punishment and self-destructiveness. The latter is prominent in many pathologies, especially the neuroses, and is perhaps most clearly evidenced in depression and in the obsessive-compulsive neuroses. Much of the feeling tone surrounding the self-evaluation is preverbal and thus mysteriously inaccessible to conscious thought or control, as Klein and Sullivan remind us. When the negative feelings are erotically tinged they produce the varieties of sadomasochism which are so numerous. Karl Menninger in his book *Man Against Himself*[30] explores the wide spectrum of possibilities these may assume.

Odier points up the fact that the moral narcissism of the neurotic conscience results in a tendency to put *principles before persons,* an unloving preoccupation with being right in all events irrespective of the effect upon persons, with the conviction that *La vertu excuse tout* ("Virtue excuses everything").[31] A kind of negative, anxious scanning of life and

future puts avoidance of guilt so much in the foreground that
many human situations are not grasped in their humanness.

The capacity to extend feelings of love and identification
of an empathic sort to another human being, which constitute
the root of all moral behavior, depends on the prior feeling of
love for oneself which can be imaginatively projected. This
primary self-love is the core of a healthy personality and the
basis of ego growth, identification, and the formation of the
ego ideal.

Feeling Intensity. Feeling varies in respect to intensity and
flexibility. Freud believed that feeling toward the self was
the internal reflection of the feeling relationship with the parents.[32] Self-love and self-hatred were the result essentially of
the introjected parent images reacting to id-ego wishes and
behavior.[33] Superego approved impulses and behavior evoke
positive, self-loving feelings. Disapproved impulses and behavior evoke negative, aggressive, and self-hating responses.
Such feeling dynamics he postulated were the result of the
libidinous and aggressive drives *turned inward.*[34] (Cf. Mac-
Kinnon's experiment, p. 36 above.)

Freud recognized that the child's feeling represented his
own aggression as much as or more than the actual treatment
he received, although the latter often influences it. He wrote:

> The original severity of the super-ego does not—or not
> so much—represent the severity which has been experi-
> enced or anticipated from the object, but expresses the
> child's own aggressiveness towards the latter. If this is
> correct, one could truly assert that conscience is formed
> in the beginning from the suppression of an aggressive
> impulse and strengthened as time goes on by each fresh
> suppression of the kind.[35]

It is important to call attention to this *acceleration of intensity* of the superego. Freud saw a mechanism at work
which functioned as a kind of self-perpetuating, self-intensi-
fying superego component.

> In the beginning conscience (more correctly, the anxiety
> which later became conscience) was the cause of in-
> stinctual renunciation, but later this relation is reversed.

Every renunciation then becomes a dynamic fount of conscience; *every fresh abandonment of gratification increases its severity* and intolerance. . . . Renunciation (externally imposed) gives rise to conscience, which then demands further renunciations.[36]

There seems to be no necessarily direct relationship between intensity of guilt and effectiveness of conscience. That is, some neurotics may feel very guilty but it comes at the *wrong time* (too late) and in some criminals apparently their very antisocial behavior may be motivated by intense guilt that needs punishment.[37] It is nevertheless true that, even though feeling may become exaggerated or distorted or ill-timed, especially the negative aspects of it, it is an absolute imperative for superego function.

Feeling Flexibility. This term refers to the gamut of feelings that a person may experience. An individual with a healthy superego experiences a level of self-esteem that is concordant with his behavior. As a sensitive warning instrument, his superego usually functions at a level that maintains a high degree of self-esteem. When he does fail to live up to his central values or approximate these at an acceptable level, his guilt tends to be proportionate and appropriate to his violation. However, when he has made what restitution is possible and remedied the situation in whatever ways he can, he will not normally continue to feel guilt but will be able to achieve equilibrium on the basis of his own capacity for self-love. It is here of course where the larger ethical meanings of behavior become crucial and where religious and cosmic solutions become relevant. Some behavior, e.g., murder, is sufficiently gross as to defy internal redress apart from external social and institutional responses and meanings mediated by a priest or a therapist and even then may be precluded. However, apart from such extremes it is only the pathologically guilty person who maintains a continuous self-negating attitude and who is incapable of a variety of flexible self-attitudes varying from healthy self-esteem to self-punishing guilt and back again, although he may express a reactive and defensive manic elation to resist depression, in which his elation or

"pseudo self-esteem" is an artifice. The capacity to accept
oneself, to accept forgiveness, and feel forgiven for guilt-producing behavior usually reflects the kind of parental response
that met childhood infractions or the child's perceptual distortions of this response. Some authors prefer to speak of
"autonomy" rather than maturation or flexibility, referring
to superego "independence" from the object and from the
drives.[38]

Lack of this flexibility is seen in the *rigid* superego which
may be ruthless and sadistic in its demands. Karen Horney
emphasized this element in the neurotic, who, failing to live
up to the ideal image, tends to *intensify* the expectations and
demands against the ego.[39] The compensatory wish follows
the sense of weakness. Failure leads to a sense of inadequacy.
Inadequacy, in turn, leads to a need to feel stronger and to
try harder, so the neurotic intensifies his fantasy image of his
possibilities and makes greater demands, leading to more impossible expectations and repeated frustration and failure.

Horney writes:

> More and more the neurotic subsitutes grandiose ideas
> for attainable goals. The value they have for him is ob-
> vious: they cover up his unendurable feelings of noth-
> ingness; they allow him to feel important without en-
> tering into any competition and thus without incurring
> the risk of failure or success; they allow him to build up
> a fiction of grandeur far beyond any attainable goal. . . .[40]

Erich Fromm pictures this cycle of rigid demandingness
and inflated expectation in his description of the authoritarian
conscience:

> The authoritarian character, being more or less crippled
> in his productiveness, develops a certain amount of sa-
> dism and destructiveness. These destructive energies are
> discharged by taking over the role of the authority and
> dominating oneself as the servant. . . . What matters is
> the fact that the authoritarian conscience is fed by de-
> structiveness against the person's own self so that de-
> structive strivings are thus permitted to operate under
> the disguise of virtue.[41]

The healthy superego seems to reflect an optimum combination of intensity and flexibility. One might say that it is *intense at the core* regarding empathy, the need for identification with any fellow human, and self-punitive when love and the true conditions of community are violated, while being *more flexible* at the periphery regarding the changing conditions and relativism of mores that seek to implement and protect such core values. Moreover, in regard to the failure of the self to achieve its goal or even to challenge value contents, the healthy superego will reflect a certain perspective, room for mistakes and acceptance of finitude and will allow for exploration, growth, and integration with reality, experiences, as the ego explores its world.

In respect to feeling, the extreme poles of this continuum are seen in the *sociopathic personality* on the one side, and the *obsessive-compulsive neurotic* on the other. The former seems to evidence no guilt feeling, irrespective of his behavior, the latter is constantly dominated by the feeling of guilt, often without major reference to his behavior (though his behavior may intensify his neurotic guilt).

The fact that feeling seems to be so independent a variable in some instances makes it seem irrelevant to behavior. If it is present and functioning, an *intensification* of feeling, especially of a negative sort, does not guarantee and may even impede superego function (analogous to brakes dragging in a car).

Many writers have drawn attention to the fact that there are superego feelings other than guilt. Shame and inferiority feelings are intimately involved in superego activity, although both of them seem to be prior to and functioning before true superego guilt. Freud discussed shame in connection with exhibitionism and related it fairly specifically to this mechanism.[42] Edith Jacobson[43] speaks of it as an early, broad response to awareness of something in ourselves that brings or can bring disgrace to ourselves, humiliating disclosure before others, etc. She emphasizes the *visual* elements in shame, as opposed to a more *auditory* emphasis in guilt, and relates shame to specific instinctual strivings as contrasted with more general inadequacies evident in inferiority conflicts. Shame and inferiority reflect "conflicts that regulate self-esteem in terms of pride and superiority rather than moral behavior in relation to others."[44] Guilt is more focused on hostility and harm to others and is frequently more amenable to reparation.

Jacobson elucidates the important interaction of shame and guilt and their occasionally opposed causes: "A person may feel guilty because of his sexual aggression but will be ashamed of his impotence."[45] Or an incompetent person may rather have it appear that he just isn't trying and is guilty of being lazy rather than experience the shame of trying and having it discovered that he is incapable.

Piers and Singer speak of shame arising "out of a tension between the Ego and the Ego-ideal, not between Ego and Super-Ego as in guilt."[46] This is appropriate as a definition prior to superego formation, but, following development of the superego proper, it seems to demand too distinct a differentiation of ego ideal and superego. The close interaction of these latter makes it very difficult to separate them neatly. One might even speak of guilt as a kind of "moral shame" before the parental introjects.

It is of interest to speculate (in a reverse way) whether one of the reasons *confession* is effective as a guilt-reducing mechanism is because the shame involved before the confessional audience is self-punitive and satisfies the talion expectation of justice in some measure.

Confession in the neurotic is often ineffective. It may provide temporary cessation of anxiety, but it is only momentary and does not restore basic self-esteem. Confession may do more harm than good, especially if it is oriented around the simple reduction of anxiety and is inauthentic regarding the concern to remedy the violation.[47]

Content

Feeling, alone, critical as it is, is not enough in itself. Intense feeling may be attached, because of the vicissitudes of training, to very selfish or very destructive objectives. The apparent altruist may be, while *feeling* virtuous, destroying another human being.

Feelings of equal intensity may accompany the most disparate of ideas. For example, Wilfred C. Hulse, a psychiatrist, indicates that during World War II the American soldier felt guilt over killing, whereas this was rarely the focus of guilt in the German soldier. The latter was able to subordinate himself so completely to the all-powerful authority of a superior officer that guilt was felt only where there was failure to carry out an order.[48] Thus the *content* of the superego may in separate individuals vary to the point of complete antithesis, whereas the "oughtness" or degree of intensity seems to be the more widespread common denominator in guilt feeling.

For the above reason, deploying the feelings from parochial, parental norms in the direction of less private, more objective, more universal norms is critical to general human progress. Some writers describe this deployment as a "development [which] points toward the replacement of automatic affective reactions by more controlled, realistic considerations."[49] Others see it as a "depersonification" of the superego.[50] By this term is meant the neutralization of some of the instinctual drives in the superego structure and a distancing from the parents. This is an unfortunate choice of words. "Depersonification" tends to connote a kind of mechanization of the moral process, a juggling of ethical syllogisms. (This is not what is intended by the term apparently, because Jacobson later emphasizes that the "personal relationship" with our conscience usually continues to some extent.)[51] Evidence repeatedly reminds us that it is the *capacity for identification* (or personal feeling-quality) which must underlie the logical process to prevent its being a psychopathic expediency or casuistry.

Arlow and Brenner paraphrase Freud's famous dictum, "Where id was there shall ego be" to read, "Where superego was there shall ego be." This does more justice to what is being clarified: namely, that this is a necessary *integration* of the private with the public, a blending of the feeling that trickles from the parochial backwaters of a private family spring with the ocean of human values. This must in some measure come about by objective reflection on the varying conditions of human community and the relativistic moralities that attempt to protect and convey these conditions, accompanied by the desire to identify with the larger human community. This will involve ego function: intelligent criticism, exploration of feeling and content, comparison of private with public moralities, rational modification, etc.

Content, therefore, must be dealt with in terms of *realism, applicability,* and *internal coherence.* Much of this is obviously the concern of philosophical ethics and theology. It is highly relevant to the psychology of guilt at several points, however.

Realism, for example, refers to the question of whether some contents are inseparable from the possibility of the existence of *any* community. One measure of "realism" would be whether a large consensus of humans from many cultures over a long time span opted for a particular value. Love and identification seem to come close to such a minimum. Hospital statistics on unloved infants[52] and the data on sociopathy would tend to support this. We wish here not to contend for the ultimate realism of any particular contents (in spite of our convictions that there are such) so much as to point to the importance of this category. The possibility of someday realizing a human global community makes imperative the discovery and inculcation of these contents. It is possible and probable that Freud was overly cynical about these being so antithetical to individual self-realization as he seems to be in *Civilization and Its Discontents.*[53] Angyal's explorations in "homonomy" are important here.[54] In the healthy person the concern for universality is oriented around the realism and validity of the contents. In the unhealthy person it tends to be more oriented around narcissistic feelings of infallibility, megalomania, etc.

Applicability of content raises a separate question. It may, for instance, be true that equal consideration for a fellow human is a universal necessity for the conditions of community at the same time that it is true that survival in a particular subculture or nation may make such a conscience content appear inapplicable or self-destructive. For example, the soldier who is forced to measure patriotism against such a standard, or to weigh the enemy's survival over his own. The loyal German caught in the Nazi perversion is a special case of this, so carefully studied by Erich Fromm.[55] Any major shift of values, such as that occurring in the present, forces the sensitive person to a realism-applicability conflict of this sort around content.

Internal coherence is another important aspect of superego content. Redl and Wineman[56] speak of "value islands" in the personality. By this they mean to emphasize that the superego may be made of heterogeneous and discontinuous contents that exist in isolated clusters. Their term "Swiss cheese superego" connotes the obvious lacunae in the contents of some delinquents' value systems.

Such lack of internal coherence or consistency, however, is not restricted to delinquent personalities. As the Hartshorne and May studies showed, the *specifics* of conscience content are often quite disparate within the same individual (one who cheats may be horror-stricken at stealing, and vice versa).[57] This is a matter of historical record at collective levels also. Western communities most verbal about "Christian love" are often those blotched with unpleasant records regarding war, racial prejudice, inquisitions, and witch-hunting. A great deal depends on the health of the ego in its capacity to bind and integrate value contents and its freedom from denial and repressive distortion of these. There is a sense in which one might speak of many "communities" or organizations as *collusions in repression,* with hatred being reserved for anyone who tends to expose the repression. The therapist knows this hatred firsthand when he unmasks the defenses against such inconsistencies in the neurotic patient.

Part of the reason people arrive at adulthood with internally conflicting value contents is the fact of multiple identification. Different models that have been added to the parental models (which themselves carry inconsistency), such as teachers, peers, etc., carry with them diverse contents. Often these inconsistencies don't come into focus until the identity struggles of adolescence and sometimes not even then.

To summarize with respect to content: the healthy and maturing superego should tend to show a *movement toward the resolution of contradictions in content,* hopefully in the direction of larger public norms and ideally toward universal norms. This movement tends to be an *objectivization* (a disengagement from the parental image which Jacobson calls "depersonification") involving critical ego functions. It will be along dimensions of *realism, applicability,* and *consistency* or *coherence.* Roger Brown's discussion and summary of many of these forces is helpful.

> The moral theory an individual forms out of his own idiosyncratic collection of moral data can cause him to reject the larger part of the conventional morality. From a social point of view the ideal outcome of the moralization of the individual is not acceptance of some static set of folkways but participation in the moral argument of his time and civilization. From the individual point of view the ideal outcome is that rare state which has been mistakenly assumed to be usual, some reasonable consistency among judgment, feeling, and action.[58]

Timing

What is meant by timing in respect to superego function? It is well known that reinforcement—whether a punitive or rewarding reinforcement—of a response to a stimulus is most effective for the learning of that response if it is well-timed in relation to the response. For example, if a child is rewarded or punished at the end of the day for a certain type of behavior, rather than immediately afterward, the reinforcement is not likely to be so effectively related to the behavior. It is more likely to build up a hostility or affection for the person who provides the punishment or reward independently of the behavior.

Such timing may well be an important element in superego function. Joseph Finney, in a very stimulating article,[59] suggests a servomechanism model for the understanding of the guilt process. This is to see guilt as a control mechanism much like other control systems that maintain vital balances in the body. For example, when the body temperature gets too high, certain operations go into effect to remedy the condition. Under stress some of these mechanisms are overworked: feedback is too high or too low. "A medical example is that 'breathing becomes panting'! A psychological example is that the normal use of repression becomes extreme naïveté or un-awareness of one's motivations."[60] He defines psychological sickness "in terms of failing servomechanisms," such as "a person who is irritable, anxious, aggressive on slight provocation, fatigued or depressed"[61] to certain clinically defined extremes.

He continues:

> Among the servomechanisms that control our behavior, human beings have developed one that we call "ego-ideal" or conscience. This is a servomechanism learned in early childhood. . . . Since the processes of self-control by ego-ideal are internal ones, this is a feedback mechanism that we always carry with us. If the process is a well-learned one, it can provide rapid control that will prevent certain actions.
>
> Those who have not developed an effective conscience must rely on other controls, mostly on the punitive reactions of other people. This is intrinsically a slower and less predictable reaction; *it cannot act ahead of time to prevent the forbidden act; it can only act afterward.* Even the anticipatory reaction of fear is much less reliable than control by ego-ideal. And, since the misbehavior has gone far, the corrective action also may go far, in a punitive direction. Thus, the person with a weak conscience subjects himself to harsher controls than the person with a strong conscience. In this respect, a weak conscience is more punitive than a strong one.[62]

Without elaborating all the subtleties of Finney's hypothesis, and at the risk of oversimplification, we would like to stress one of his major points. It is that superego punishment acts as a kind of pain feedback to impede the guilt-producing behavior cycle. If it comes *at the wrong time,* even if it is intense, it may actually worsen, rather than help, the situation. He compares it to someone pushing a child in a swing. If he wishes to stop the child's swing, he must apply force against the pendulum action at *just the right part of the cycle,* otherwise he intensifies the swing. Such a model helps to explain how people with very severe superegos have very poor behavioral control, where some in fact are criminal because of extreme guilt.

The author believes that this suggestion regarding timing is much more important than can yet be substantiated and will turn out to be a critical influence in both penology and guilt therapy.

Time-binding, bringing past and future into present reality considerations, is an important ego function. It seems to be one of the most obvious problems for the child, who finds it hard to wait, to inhibit his immediate responses on behalf of some frustratingly vague and poorly symbolized future. It is also one of the apparent lacunae in the repertoire of delinquent and psychopathic persons. There is a tendency toward immediate discharge of tension. Acceptance of control, and of inhibition, for any human seems only possible in the light of some later expected fulfillment or reward, or may be in some instances accepted only so long as fear of pain outweighs the internal tension for need satisfaction. The time-disturbed person often seems unable to profit from the past or to trust in the future. The connections with antisocial behavior and guilt cry out for experimentation.

Effectiveness of Control

We will let this term denote the responsiveness of the *organism* to the superego function—that is to say, the actual reliability of the superego in controlling behavior or influencing it.

As the last section implied, control is more than a matter of the intensity of psychic energies involved. It is at least, as well, the appropriate timing of the energies in respect to other processes in operation. It is difficult to say exactly what should be included under the rubric of control. The word covers a congeries of functions which merge into some ultimately observable compromise. It is more like the residuum of several streams flowing together than the pressing of a button.

The psychoanalytic ego psychologists, elaborating Freud's structural hypothesis, see behavior as the amalgam of all the dynamic forces of id, ego, and superego in interaction:

> Every action, every thought, every mental act is the result of a compromise or interaction among the various functions of the mind, i.e., among id, superego, and ego.

Every action, every fantasy, every dream, every symptom will be a compromise or resultant of instinctual wishes, of moral demands or prohibitions, of defenses of external factors, and so forth. A correct understanding of this principle of multiple functioning is essential to the proper application of the concepts of the structural theory to both clinical and theoretical problems.[63]

Although behavior is always such a compromise, much of the control process seems to lie in ego-superego interaction and to revolve around anxiety formation and prevention. As a response to the unbearable nature of massive anxiety, the ego develops ways of defending itself against at least the internal drives which tend to develop anxiety-producing situations. These defenses are numerous, but apparently most people settle for a limited number that continue to reappear in human behavior. Many of these are cataloged by Anna Freud: reaction formation, repression, regression, denial, isolation, etc.[64] These defenses may result in a permanent blocking of some drives or neurotic symptom formation. Sublimation and identification are also important ego avenues of instinct control and anxiety reduction. The particular combinations, intensities, and qualities of these forces tend to result in normal or pathological degrees and types of control.[65]

The peculiar capacity to inhibit discharge, "to talk the id out of an immediate gratification," is an ego function that seems to depend on both reality experiences and the compelling impact of identification, i.e., the influencing power of the superego introjects.

Redl reports a very important priority factor here. Namely, that in work with severely disturbed behavior disorders, the child must be dealt with on an ego basis alone first, with every effort made to build up ego resources. Superego appeals, or the effort to control behavior through guilt arousal, only lead to blind and rampant acting out, if ego controls are not first implemented.[66] This may be a reverse way of clarifying what is the control function of the superego: that is, the giving of guilt anxiety signals to the ego on the basis of disparity from identification figures. When these identifications are surrounded with many painful memories, new situations that tend to

arouse these (perhaps castration threats), present such overwhelming anxiety as to demand immediate discharge, hence
the "acting out" in response to authorities.

Superego influence in respect to control thus would seem
to lie at the point of reinforcing ego inhibitory control of
motor discharge through participation in the defense mechanisms (e.g., providing paradigms for reaction formation, sublimation, etc.) and specially through the provision of introjects that present models for the selective screening of possible
behaviors, as well as affective implementation of these by
means of self-esteem and self-punishment.

Control functions of the ego may in some cases involve
the turning of defenses *against* the superego rather than the
id, including repression. Freud discussed this in relation to
the contrast between the absence of conscious guilt in hysteria
as compared with its presence in the depressive and obsessive
compulsive neuroses. He credits the ego with a resistance to
superego pain:

> It is the ego . . . that is responsible for the sense of guilt
> remaining unconscious. We know that as a rule the ego
> carries out repressions in the service and the behest of
> its super-ego; *but this is a case in which it has turned
> the same weapon against its harsh taskmaster.*[67]

In this insight Freud obviously antedates Mowrer's concern
about repression of the superego.[68] Nunberg relates the intensity of the guilt conflict to two factors: It depends, he says,
"on one hand, on the sharpness of the criticism of the superego, and on the other hand, on the power of resistance of the
ego."[69]

The superego influences control mechanisms essentially as a
counterforce (to id impulses) which has become effective
through identification and introjection and which draws upon
id (drive) energies for its intensity.

The healthier and more mature the person, the more control
is in the service of the values genuinely held, and the *less* the
ideal is experienced as disadvantageous (except in moments
of extreme temptation). There is an identification with the
good which relates duty to value rather than to the anxious
avoidance of guilt. Duty to the value may even in some in-

stances be prepared to run the risk of guilt or shame on behalf of the value. The more integrated the personality, the less conflict between the desired and the good (valued) occurs, because the good has come to be desired *for itself* rather than as a reluctant concession for the avoidance of guilt anxiety. Morality is consciously in control. Superego matures or is ego-criticized, ego-evaluated, and ego-incorporated (sometimes only *after* sinning and remorse) to the point where it is allied with the control system as "mine" rather than being experienced (to use Odier's term) only in its "primitive heteronomy."[70]

We have up to this point attempted to summarize the important aspects of superego formation and function and to distinguish between the precursors and the constituents of the superego proper. It is hoped that the aspects emphasized will provide a basis for discussion of guilt in its normal and pathological forms, as well as suggest directions for therapy and a more precise discussion of the wider ramifications of guilt.

It is clear that the superego continues to expand and to develop in most persons on into adulthood. It tends to retain of course the structure that emerges out of crucial early identifications of the preschool years as a kind of core which, however much it may be added to, enriched, or altered by later changes, tends to reemerge in its more primitive forms in pathological regression.

The changes that come about tend to proceed in a variety of ways which have been elaborated by a number of authors. Freud, though emphasizing the "special" place of the first identifications, and stressing their central superego role, added that, "during the course of its growth, the super-ego also takes over the influence of those persons who have taken the place of the parents . . . and whom it has regarded as ideal models."[71] He adds, however, that "these only affect the ego, they have no influence on the super-ego, which has been determined by the earliest parental imagos."[72] In the light of this latter statement, it is difficult to understand one a few pages later that reads, "A psychological group is a collection of individuals, who *have introduced the same person into*

their super-ego, and on the basis of this common factor have
identified themselves with one another in their ego."[73] Apparently he is concerned to stress the homogeneous quality of
the superego in its original core identifications while also allowing for expanding ego identifications in the ego ideal
(superego +). Edith Jacobson reacts to this same statement
of Freud's by saying that "such ego identifications with realistic parental images actually begin to develop in interaction
with superego identifications."[74]

It is this kind of obdurate quality of the original superego
proper which partly prompted Flugel's observation:

> The internalized ideals that correspond to different as-
> pects of the same authorities or to the varying aspects of
> different authorities are never fused into a completely
> harmonious and consistent whole.[75]

Moral maturation seems to involve both the continuation of
the feeling core of the superego and the maintenance of self-
esteem that this affords the ego (with modification of over-
harsh punitive feeling) at the same time that it involves an
ego penetration and growing critical evaluation of contents,
comparison of these with reality, the appropriation of new
ideals and the spreading of motivation from personal parochial introjects to the wider, interpersonal community.

Some writers speak of maturation in terms of "coming to
terms with the Superego."[76] McKenzie writes in reaction to
this:

> It is not a coming to terms with the Super-ego but a
> leaving it behind; it is the passing from the "borrowed
> morality" of the super-ego to the free morality of con-
> science where *oughts, commands,* and prohibitions have
> become moral policemen. We accept these not in virtue
> of external authority, but because we *see* they are true.
> Indeed, to say that moral principles, oughts, and com-
> mands have authority is just another way of saying that
> they are *true.*[77]

The emphasis here is on the movement toward a reality
component in response to judgments concerning intellectual
contents and a movement of *feeling* on the basis of positive

conviction that such contents constitute the true basis of community rather than just that they protect one from superego punishment.

It was Piaget's studies of children and their moral judgments which opened the way to a careful study of content changes in superego functions. He set up many situations in which he could elicit responses from children to moral dilemmas or comparative problems concerning punishment for various infractions.

For example, here are two protocols to which children were asked to react:

> There was once a little girl who was called Marie. She wanted to give her mother a nice surprise, and cut out a piece of sewing for her. But she didn't know how to use the scissors properly and cut a big hole in her dress.
>
> A little girl called Margaret went and took her mother's scissors one day that her mother was out. She played with them for a bit. Then as she didn't know how to use them properly she made a little hole in her dress.[78]

Younger children focused on Marie's *greater damage* as a basis for her being naughtier. Older children picked Margaret on the basis of her *intention*.

Piaget noticed a process of change that seemed fairly uniform among children from an attitude which he called *heteronomous* (the child from approximately four to eight sees the adult authority as sacred and judges behavior by that realistic external standard) toward an attitude which he called *autonomous* (where one becomes aware that moral rules have more of a subjective quality that orients them to peer approval, intellectual judgment, and cooperative decision; they are relativistic rather than absolute).

As Roger Brown, in a helpful summary of Piaget's influence, points out, subsequent research does not support "the associations Piaget proposed between heteronomous morality and unilateral respect for authority and that between autonomous morality and mutual respect between peers,"[79] although it does tend to confirm a "shift from objectivity to subjectivity and from absolutism to relativism."[80]

Kohlberg, following Piaget's tradition, examined the reac-

tions of children to similar but more complex stories than
Piaget had used. The stories often set law over against deeper
human sensitivities that underlie conventional morals. His
work, too, reflects the intimate involvement of the child's intellectual abilities with what emerges and presents an even
more complex development than that of Piaget's heteronomous and autonomous stages. Kohlberg sees a continuous
development of conscience right through adolescence, reach-
ing a culmination in what he calls stage VI, where the individual is capable of independent judgment of moral conduct on the basis of internal sanctions rather than on peer
appraisal.[81]

Although Roger Brown criticizes the psychoanalysts for an
almost complete omission of the intellectual element in superego development,[82] the criticism is not without some rejoinder:

Edith Jacobson traces the development of the superego into
adolescence, with some emphasis on the process of "neutralization of drive," "depersonification," "logical and abstract
thinking," "critical judgment and discrimination," etc.[83] Pre-
pubertal children go through a process of reprojection of their
superego (+ and −) to dominant influential and extrafamilial
persons and run head on into contradictions and conflicts
which demand integrative ego struggles and model conflicts.
These latter reach a confusing turbulence and intensity in
adolescence and are reinforced by intensified instinctual
drives. Code changes and identity struggles are often profound and disturbing. These in large measure center around
the choice of sexual object and the revival of the Oedipal
struggle.

Jacobson summarizes:

> Whereas in childhood the voice of the superego stated:
> "If you identify with the parental moral standards, de-
> mands, and prohibitions, you will be granted sexual
> pleasure in the adult future," it must now convey: "You
> are permitted to enjoy adult sexual and emotional free-
> dom of thoughts and actions to the extent to which you
> renounce your infantile instinctual desires, loosen your
> childhood attachments, and accept adult ethical stan-
> dards and responsibilities."[84]

Chapter V

GUILT IN THE SOCIOPATHIC
PERSONALITY

> There is much that is strange, but nothing that surpasses
> man in strangeness.
>
> —*Sophocles* (Antigone)

The most destructive, costly, and pernicious human beings
in any society are often the sociopathic personalities. Whether
they exercise monolithic power, like a Göring, or function in
relative anonymity, they leave a trail of misery behind them.
History is strewn with their depredations and with malignant
monuments to these men in whom guilt does not function or
is absent. In that they constitute an extreme form, or caricature, they are of special interest in the understanding of
the guilt process.

The "psychopath," as he is often loosely denoted, is variously defined. The American Psychiatric Association refers to
him as "a person whose behavior is predominantly amoral or
anti-social and characterized by impulsive, irresponsible actions satisfying only immediate and narcissistic interests, without concern for obvious and implicit social consequences, accompanied with minimal outward evidence of anxiety or
guilt."

The term "sociopathic personality" is a more precise term
which is broken down into four subheadings: (1) "Antisocial
reactions," (2) "Dyssocial reactions," (3) "Sexual deviation,"
and (4) "Alcohol and drug addiction." We will be most interested in the first and, to some degree, the second. Typology is

always disappointing, in that one label rarely fits a person, and most problems tend to be contaminated by elements that blend into other categories. We wish, however, to concentrate on the more extreme forms of sociopathy as *paradigms of the person in whom the guilt dynamic is absent or so distorted as to be largely ineffective. By guilt dynamic we mean not only the negative and self-punitive elements to which "superego" is too commonly restricted (thus generating theoretical cul-de-sacs) but also the positive ego-ideal aspects of superego which favorably impel decision-making in a prosocial direction as a stable modeling influence. These constitute the internal imagery and role patterns which "are cathected" (or sufficiently reinforcing) to provide valence and evoke identification.*

Frankenstein[1] distinguishes minute differences within the psychopathic category and classifies eleven subtypes emerging from various combinations of maternal-infant relationships in conjunction with an introvert-extrovert typology, with varying degrees (or total lack) of constitutional disposition for anxiety. He draws careful distinctions between pure psychopathy, Aichorn's "Wayward Youth," Bowlby's "Affectionless Thief," Redl's "Children Who Hate," Ophuijsen's "Primary Behavior Disorder," Friedlander's "antisocial character," and sundry psychoanalytic character disorders. It seems to this author that he casts a humorous light on this precision when he adds, later, "No diagnosis of psychopathy can be made with any degree of certainty before the child has reached adolescence," adding the footnote, "With the exception of the very few cases of congenital psychopathy."[2]

The McCords, on the other hand, in their book *Psychopathy and Delinquency*, without deprecating the value of precision in diagnosis or its obvious clinical value, focus on "aggressiveness, guiltlessness, affectional shallowness, and extreme impulsivity" as a central core of the psychopath's syndrome.[3] They emphasize *guiltlessness* and *lovelessness* as the two traits which "conspicuously mark the psychopath as different from other men."[4]

These two factors are recognized by almost all writers as discriminative differentials. Love and guilt (upon its violation) are the minimal conditions for genuine community of any sort and even in their most attenuated, distorted forms of anxious fealty to a criminal subgroup, they are still relevant in distinguishing the antisocial from the dyssocial sociopath. The latter is recognized as capable of at least some group loyalty and value identification, even though it may be very distorted in terms of the larger community or culture. Anxiety is closely interwoven with both the origin and elaboration of love and guilt, and its conspicuous diminution or absence is evident in the antisocial sociopath, with concurrent ego defects.

There is sometimes confusion about a diagnosis of psychopathy when there are admixtures of typical traits with symptoms of other disorders of a neurotic nature. Antisocial sociopathy is usually resorted to only *after* other symptom categories are exhausted. Karpman, for example, goes so far as to say that the true primary psychopath *cannot* develop a psychosis because he lacks guilt and the capacity for regression. He distinguishes the primary type ("anethopath") from the secondary or "symptomatic" type of psychopathy which involves admixtures of classic symptoms of neurosis or psychosis. The anethopath he also subclassifies as either "aggressive-predatory" or "passive-parasitic."[5]

Cleckley[6] attributes the following characteristics to the primary psychopathic personality:

1. Unexplained Failure
2. Undisturbed Technical Intelligence
3. Absence of Neurotic Anxiety
4. Persistent and Inadequately Motivated Antisocial Behavior
5. Irresponsibility
6. Peculiar Inability to Distinguish Between Truth and Falsehood
7. Inability to Accept Blame
8. Failure to Learn by Experience
9. Incapacity for Love
10. Inappropriate or Fantastic Reactions to Alcohol
11. Lack of Insight
12. Shallow and Impersonal Responses to Sexual Life
13. Suicide Rarely Carried Out
14. Persistent Pattern of Self-defeat

SUPEREGO DIMENSIONS

An examination of some of these typical characteristics with reference to our superego dimensions in the last chapter may help to elaborate the bleak but unique picture of the personality in which guilt is not operative.

Feeling

Mankind has long held that the capacity to feel along with one's kind, to put oneself in the other person's shoes, is of the essence in being human. This core of the Christian and Kantian ethic is caught up in the remark by Diamond that "where there is no identification, we are all sociopathic."[7]

The unusual thing about the sociopath is that at a superficial level his feelings seem appropriate. He is often charming, makes a good court appearance, and wins his way enough into the affections of others, to be able to manipulate and exploit them as well as to find sexual experience. He may seem outgoing and spontaneous. He is often sophisticated and alert to prestige modes.

On the other hand, any choice between his egocentric gain and the necessity to set it aside in consideration of another, if it is a real choice, quickly exposes his expediency and the shallowness of his feeling. He is incapable of deep and lasting love relationships. He consistently manipulates and exploits others. His sexual relations are predatory and fickle. He may be aware of the social feelings of others, but he is indifferent to them except as they serve his private ends. A little alcohol or slight frustration may serve to release unlimited but impulsive (rarely planned out) cruelty and destructiveness. He can kill with no qualms of guilt feeling.

Lindner, describing the disparity between the *knowing* and the *feeling* of the psychopath, writes: "He verbalizes about right and he knows what is proper; but he is in the position of those of us who stand in puzzled bewilderment before an abstract work of art. It is there, and we accept it; but we do not feel and, hence, cannot understand it."[8]

Predation, aggressive or passive, seems to be the dominant

feeling orientation: "The world is my oyster." Frankenstein relates this to two major factors in infancy: a predominance of ego expansiveness (ego inflation) with a consequent failure of the "feeling of otherness" to emerge:

> Ego inflation means that the ego, instead of fulfilling its task as the mediator between inner and outer realities and as the organ and agent of conceptual, functional and structural coordination, becomes an "end in itself." Whereas normally the ego fulfills its function by facing and recognizing the non-ego (e.g., other people) as its counterpole, that is, as an independent reality, the psychopath conceives of the non-ego as of an actual or potential part of itself, to be "incorporated" at will. The relationship between the ego and the non-ego, it is true, is disturbed also in the neurotic or psychotic diseases, in waywardness or in primary behavior disorders, in brain injuries, or in feeblemindedness. But in all these pathologies, the feeling of otherness is not only not eliminated but on the contrary is accentuated, and the specific forms in which it *is* accentuated constitute the essential characteristics of the various clinical units. The perception of the non-ego may be distorted by projections (in neuroses), or the non-ego may engulf the ego (in psychoses); the non-ego may be the area of chance occurrences (in waywardness) or the absolute enemy (in primary behavior disorders); it may become almost identical with neural irritation (in brain injuries) or with the "omnipotent," the absolutely separated (in feeblemindedness). It is only in the different forms of psychopathy that otherness is no longer experienced as such, although *intellectually most psychopaths are well able to understand not only the fact but also the individual quality of this otherness.* The boundaries between the ego and the non-ego remain more or less distinct, and it is usually not at all difficult for the psychopath correctly to evaluate differences; often he even excels in it. But this ability, which normally helps to establish and develop the experience of "distance" and thus intensifies polarization, tension, and relatedness, serves the opposite purpose in the life and development of the psychopath, the purpose of "egotropic incorporation."[9]

It will be recalled that this process is very close to what Ausubel means by the "omnipotent fantasy" of the infant

which needs to be limited by the opposing strength of the
parent and undergo "satellization."[10] It is also closely related
to magical, archaic grandiosity which the psychoanalysts see
converted into the ego ideal (normally) by way of a growing
realistic imagery, which acts to limit the fantasies and relate
them to the parental introjects.[11]

It is the failure either of the development of the ego-pro-
cess which leads to satellization or of the normal ego-nonego
reality differentiation which the psychoanalysts refer to that
is so important here. Jacobson writes: "The child will be protected from relapses into the world of magic fantasies of fu-
sions and early infantile types of identifications *to the extent
to which he succeeds in building up true object relations*
which no longer display the narcissistic qualities described
above. This again presupposes the constitution of well-defined self-representations separated by distinct, firm boundaries from the likewise realistic representations of his love
objects."[12]

Frankenstein does not deny that "incorporation" occurs, or
that internal images exist which permit reality responses, but
that instead of carrying the *feeling* of "otherness," "not-mine-
ness," for the psychopath, all ego images carry the feeling of
"my property," property which has lost its independent in-
dividuality, "to be used and disposed of at will," whether an
object belonging to another person, or another person himself.
Put this way, one senses the ease with which the psychopath
can dispose of human life as he would an unwanted insect.
One can also sense the pointedness of Buber's "I-Thou" polarity and Schweitzer's nuclear "reverence for life" as central
ethical insights.

There is evidence that the basic feeling problem that shows
up in the failure of identification and lack of guilt is at root
a low level of anxiety. Lykken's study of anxiety in the sociopathic personality led him to believe that the psychopath has
too low a level of anxiety for efficient conditioning or avoidance learning. In comparison with nonsociopathic controls, the
psychopaths showed little anxiety on a questionnaire measure,
had a lower level of galvanic skin reactivity to a conditioned

stimulus associated with electric shock, and were relatively unable to learn to avoid punished responses in a laboratory learning experiment.[13]

A study investigating the interrelationship of guilt and anxiety was performed by Lowe. He utilized self-report measures, having clinical judges choose MMPI items reflecting guilt and comparing these with results on the Taylor Manifest Anxiety Scale. Seventy psychiatric patients, seventy male psychiatric nurse's aide applicants, and seventy female aide applicants were tested. "The results were interpreted as showing that as far as self-report measures are concerned, scales involving clinical constructs of guilt and anxiety measure the same psychological entity."

Hodges[14] challenges the notion that there is no anxiety in the sociopath and believes that he has a character armor (Reich) and utilizes instinct rather than reaction formations. He agrees with Karpman that the problem is related to a dissociation of feeling and intellect.

A few writers feel that the sociopath suffers from an *oversevere* superego rather than *lack* of a superego.[15] Donnelly, for example, hypothesizes that a large number of them have identified with one parent on a dependent and hostile basis in such a way that gratification is apparently only obtainable by repeatedly violating his own and his parents' value system.[16] If this were so, one would expect signs of guilt to emerge in symptom formation or to show up in test protocols. Lack of such in the psychopath is what leads most writers to trace the difficulty to a more primitive origin than repression.

Redl is quite adamant that he has never met a child, out of hundreds with whom he has worked, who can be spoken of as a pure psychopath or totally conscienceless. He writes: "The concept of a 'child without a conscience'—the so-called 'psychopath' is supposed to belong to this category—can be maintained only in the artificial seclusion of individual interview practice."[17] Redl does see superego deficiencies in respect to value content, signal inadequacy, identification deficiency, guilt displacement, model rigidity, etc.[18]

It is possible that the antisocial sociopath as a pure form does not exist and that it is only lack of patience or perception in the observer that enables him to classify a person as totally devoid of superego or guilt feeling. Clinical consensus and experimental evidence do not seem ready to settle this question. The direction toward which the type points, however, should be clear: the *feeling* of guilt anxiety as it occurs in most people is nearly absent or distorted so much that it seems absent to the observer. If it is present, it is ineffectively present. The result is "hollowness of affect," "incapacity for love," and a poor understanding of the emotional attachments of others which restrain them from alienating behavior.

Rosen and Gregory, assessing the experimental studies on psychopathy and delinquency, cite material which supports the notion that this distortion of feeling roots in a failure of parent-child relationships in infancy. Independent studies by Bandura and Walters, by Merskovitz, Levine, and Spivak, and another by Silverman all tend to support connections between aggressive antisocial behavior and parental rejection or failure to meet the dependency needs of children.[19]

Bandura and Walters, in great detail, summon experimental evidence that throws light on the probably direct relationship between the sociopath's parental modeling (when he has any) and his predatory behavior. Even allowing for the possibility that minimal dependency ties or positive modeling occur, negative modeling goes on.[20] It is oriented around the one who controls resources;[21] aggression may be imitated if it is seen that the aggressor is rewarded,[22] and the parents who utilize only fear to evoke even minimal conformity as often as not evoke imitation of their aggression rather than of the code item,[23] and aggression tends to increase in frequency and generalize.[24]

Robert Lindner, a lifetime student of the psychopathic personality and one of the few psychoanalysts to claim some success in treating such, sees in the psychopath a rejection of the father image and a corresponding fear of castration and aggressive reaction toward authorities who subsequently correspond to the father figure. "In addition, the psychopath is burdened with guilt for the parricidal and incestuous fantasies that plague him unremittingly. Because of this he seeks punishment, goes out of his way to meet it, and does so with a spirit of daring and challenge."[25]

Stabenau, *et al.*, made a comparative study of families of schizophrenics, delinquents and normals (using such devices as The Revealed Differences Test and the Thematic Apperception Test) which reinforces the importance of the presence of warmth and empathy and the promotion of authority in the lives of normals. It also refers to delinquent family environments in such terms as the following: "loose, unstable family organization, shifting of the family roles, undercontrol of affect, and or open conflict among family members. . . . It was uncertain who would be the father, who would be the mother, who would dominate or be the leader."[26]

A study by Sharp, *et al.*, comparing the family interaction of twenty schizophrenic with twenty sociopathic patients, presents some illuminating and supportive protocols: "The mothers of sociopaths did not appear to have been deeply involved with or accepting of their sons at any time. . . . Parents of sociopaths seldom expressed guilt. Parents of schizophrenics frequently expressed guilt feelings. . . . The six sociopaths who received parents' visits were among the least antisocial in the study group."[27]

Such evidence moves in the direction of supporting those theorists who feel the psychopathic distortion is heavily influenced by parent-child relations, and stands over against Cleckley's rather surprising remark that he has not "regularly encountered any specific type of error in parent-child relations in the early history of my cases."[28]

If Frankenstein is correct, it may be that a congenital low level of anxiety or an extremely early distortion of it by parental indolence or rejection is so much the primary dispositional factor that later variations in the relational patterns with parents need follow no set form to account for the disposition.

The feeling distortions that Cleckley mentions certainly congeal around the failure of anxiety to develop over dependency-relatedness, the need for and sensitivity to other-involvement, internal or external (except in the aforementioned

predatory sense): "Persistent and *inadequately motivated*
antisocial behavior," "Irresponsibility," "Incapacity for love,"
"Lack of insight," "Shallow and impersonal response to sexual
life." The failure of identification and introjection precludes
neurotic anxiety and any capacity to accept blame.

Maslow writes of the feeling situation of the psychopathic
personality as follows:

> These are people who, according to the best data avail-
> able, have been starved for love in the earliest months of
> their lives and have simply lost *forever* the desire and
> the ability to give and to receive affection (as animals
> lose sucking or pecking reflexes that are not exercised
> soon enough after birth).[29]

Coming from such a normally optimistic writer, these are
bleak words. Set over against Redl's viewpoint and that of
those who feel that the sociopath operates dissociated from
his feelings, rather than in total absence of them, one is allowed to question whether an ego therapy might not overcome
some of the incapacity for relatedness. Redl believes it does.
It remains to be seen whether further evidence will bear him
out.

The report of the McCords cn the Wyltwick studies would
seem to support Redl's expectations. They speak of both "an
internalization of guilt" and an increase of love and respect
for attending adults even on the part of boys recognized as
"psychopathic," in addition to an increment of "positive ego-
ideals."[30]

Karpman studied the dreams of the psychopath and found
them reflecting the emotional shallowness typical of his waking life. Moreover, the dream responses revealed immediate
discharge of motor impulses and a predominance of actual
fear responses over anxiety responses. With very little symbolism or poetic imagery, the dreams also showed a minimum
of guilt and even of forthright sexual behavior.[31]

Content

The fact that the sociopath's problem lies focally in the
orectic area is evidenced by his ability to articulate the very

code he violates. Intellectually, he often knows what society expects of him and can even feign guilt over its violation. He passes paper and pencil tests concerning the mores with efficiency and can quote the law to the policeman.

The McCords' report of this aspect of the Wyltwick studies again bears out the fact that even the psychopaths agreed with as high as 85 percent of the statements in the code presented to them, representing the expectations of both society in general and the Wyltwick School in particular.[32]

It was for some time held that sociopaths were unusually gifted intellectually. Some indeed have very high intelligence; however, recent research tends to support the position that they represent the expected normal curve of intelligence when studied in sufficiently large numbers.

Craddick reports a study of male prisons, comparing twenty-seven psychopaths with twenty-seven nonpsychopaths, in the hope of testing the theory that psychopaths are differentiated from other prisoners, by a performance score that is higher than a verbal score on I.Q. tests. No difference was found between the two groups, but for *both* groups, performance scores were higher than their verbal I.Q.'s. A possible conjecture is that verbal inadequacy on the part of all these men resulted in a frustration which maximized their tendencies to act out in antisocial ways.[33] Frequently the psychopath is extremely capable of verbal facility. It is still possible, however, that the *differential* is such as to evoke acting out behavior.

Kozol goes so far as to see a kind of identity between psychopathy and genius at the level of their nonconformity, adding: "It is probable that the basic dynamics is the same, but the apparent difference between psychopaths and geniuses is in their goals rather than in their substance."[34]

He sees in both of them a frequent indifference to some of the realities that motivate other men by way of rewards and consequences and implies that the genius may be essentially different only in the fact that his social assaults are more refined. It reminds one of the saying, "Civilization is the product of its outlaws."

Even the study of the moral standards of normals makes it apparent that there is no necessary connection between *content* of the superego and *effectiveness* of moral behavior. Recent studies of student attitudes toward cheating show direct relationships between stress and violation of the code.[35] The fact that the sociopath seems unable to endure stress without acting out, amplifies the fact that this is where his trouble lies—in his impulsivity rather than his intellectual knowledge of the ethical code.

One might think that the sociopathic knowledge of both code and punishments ensuing upon its violation would be sufficient to constrain a highly intelligent person. This in fact is one of the assumptions that observers are continually amazed to find transgressed. There seems to be almost an indifference to the deleterious and self-destructive results of behavior. Hare found in electric-shock experiments that the psychopathic personality is relatively unaffected by the threat of punishment.[36]

A number of experiments have been performed that indicate that a subject's capacity to acquire fear responses may depend on either previous social learning or on constitutional differences. Individuals may learn more or less rapidly or adequately relative to generalized drive or anxiety level. Noxious stimuli and the symbols that reflect them in the subject's memory system simply may not cue off appropriate responses, nor be learned as rapidly by low-anxiety persons.[37]

Aronfreed resists the notion of a unitary source of moral behavior such as the superego and feels that the specific vagaries of socialization are best accounted for by assuming an array of specific anxiety-reducing responses cued off by the subject's cognitive repertoire:

> The anxiety is reducible by a number of different responses which acquire instrumental value because they reproduce certain significant cues which are often associated in the original socializing situation, either with the avoidance or termination of punishment or with the attenuation of the anticipatory anxiety that precedes punishment. The child may then make the relevant cue

producing responses to reduce the anxiety aroused by subsequent transgressions, even in the absence of external punishment. *The use of the term guilt, in this framework, would be appropriate only when the moral responses have a self-evaluative, cognitive component.*[38]

This relating of guilt to specific cognitive cues and special socialization precedents for their occurrence helps to account for the kind of "value islands" and "Swiss-cheese superegos" of which Redl speaks. It also helps us understand dyssocial sociopathy. However, when it is applied to antisocial sociopathy, it raises various problems. Such a person seems capable of reproducing appropriate *cues* but *not* the appropriate responses. It could be, of course, that in the primary socializing experience, conditions reinforced the learning of *cues*, but they were not attached to anxiety-reducing responses (anxiety being apparently absent); rather, they may have been reinforcing in a positive manner (as viewed by the subject) in the sense that they opened up exploitative opportunities independent of self-punitive or reparative feelings.

It has been suggested that the reason why sociopaths do not learn from painful experience is not their incapacity to learn that certain behavior leads to punishment, but that given the failure of one response, the only other dominant responses available are antisocial rather than prosocial options.[39] It is difficult to accept this as an adequate basis for the continuing resistance of the sociopath to change even in the presence of prosocial models.

Bandura and Walters suggest that one reason for the perseveration of deviant behavior in the face of punishment and apparent nonreinforcement may be that unobserved intermittent positive reinforcement may be sufficiently intense. They also suggest that vicarious reinforcement (by observing successful deviants) may act to offset punishment.[40]

Whatever the reasons, the technical intelligence in the sociopath is not disorganized or distorted as it is in psychosis, nor is it delusional or hallucinatory. There *seems* to be no obvious connection between his theoretical thinking and his irrational behavior.[41]

George Kelly's conception of guilt as "perception of one's apparent dislodgment from his core role structure" allows us, however, to see a content problem in the antisocial sociopath.[42] His models having been undependable, or seen as "animals which are concerned primarily with giving milk and making money," he feels no violation of his identity in playing such a conceptual role. Kelly writes:

> He grows up with his core role structured in relationship to such presumed people. When people try to make him feel guilty by pointing out that he is selfish, cruel, or immoral, he may readily agree that he is and concede that it would be nice if he were different. However, he does not experience guilt, for these interpretations are not incompatible with his core role structure.[43]

Such cognitive support of his predatory feelings is one of the likely bases for the intransigence of the psychopath in the face of therapeutic efforts.

Timing

Uniformly the psychopath is reportedly disturbed in his sense of time. This is not a cognitive disorganization regarding a clock or calendar time, but the subjective experience of *enduring*, the necessity for waiting for unseen possible rewards, for restraining impulses toward immediate realization. This is often traced to the experience of the infant, in which "the returning other," the mother who can be trusted eventually to satisfy unfulfilled needs does *not* appear for the infant who becomes psychopathic. This may be due to maternal indolence or rejection or both. It thus becomes difficult for him to justify waiting for rewards. He becomes predacious about exploiting what is at hand and avoiding the risk of never getting it by waiting. Time consideration becomes a painful game he does not wish to play. He lives in the *now*. What suited yesterday's moment does not suit today's, hence he is inconsistent in behavior and in his loyalties. It would be interesting to experiment with psychodrama for psychopaths around *time* issues and themes.

The capacity to endure privation of a minimal sort demands either the imaginative envisioning of specific eventual rewards, reinforcement, satisfaction, *or* the envisioned return of one who can provide *some* justification for waiting.

Frankl has emphasized this dynamic of meaningful goal-hope as the most critical factor for survival under the deleterious conditions of the death camp.[44]

Miller relates a vivid example of this distortion of time in a character disorder's counseling protocol:

> You ask me what I'm going to do when I leave here, Doctor? Well, first I'm going back and talk things over with my wife. I'm going to see if maybe we can get started again. I'm ready to settle down now, and she said that if I could promise to settle down, she'd be ready to talk it over. How long since I saw her, you ask? Six *years,* I guess.[45]

Redl similarly reports this difficulty in realism about time in his "Children Who Hate," especially where the postponement of a desired activity was involved. He notes that when a request was referred to some future, even the following day, it was often experienced as a complete refusal. Similarly, threatened consequences, since they necessitated some image of a self-in-a-future, no matter how dire the possibilities, failed to restrain immediate pleasure possibilities. The following is an excerpt from his records of such a problem:

> We have finally worked a haircut schedule. It was Joe's turn to go with me today to get his haircut. This produced quite a reaction in Larry, who burst into my quarters today after learning from Joe that he was going with me to the barber. He demanded that he be taken today and that's all there was to it. I reminded him that we had all sat down and worked out the schedule and that he had agreed to come after Joe because his shopping trip came before Joe's. He was blind to this reasoning, however, completely swept away by his involvement in this particular need of the moment. "Yeah," he whined and screamed at the same time. "Now I'll never get one. I'll never have one, never, never."[46]

Effectiveness of Control

The social defectiveness of the psychopath is most evident in his impulsiveness, his lack of control. This is not a total

incapacity for inhibition, since, if the situation serves his expediency, he may *seem* socialized. However, the triggering
mechanism on his impulsiveness is very delicate and easily
tripped.

Ruesch helps us partly to appreciate this proclivity by seeing such a personality utilizing *action* as a chief means of
communicating. He doesn't get his satisfaction out of verbal
exchange but out of *behavior*. Ruesch writes:

> The person of action derives no satisfaction from *verbal
> exchange*. The psychopath really has no way of repre-
> senting feelings or thoughts in word or gesture; and if
> he wants to express an inner event he has to resort to
> complicated physical actions which frequently entail the
> exchange of goods, physical contact, or the creation of a
> disturbance. The person of action cannot say, "I dislike
> you"; instead he may break a window or slug another
> person. Nor can he say "I like you"; instead, he may
> shower the other person with presents. His hyperactivity
> is "talk" rather than implementation. Though he appears
> glib on the surface, his use of words does not comprise
> a one-to-one relationship with other events.[47]

In the growing body of research on the psychopath, there
is very little in the way of exploring this very significant symbol aspect of his behavior. It was pointed out above (cf. note
33) that disparity between verbal and performance capacities
might be significant. It is not difficult to see that the child
who cannot trust the words of the parent model will have little faith in symbols and will tend to evaluate his world in
terms of *actions*. The natural corollary of this is that deferring
pressing impulses within (on the basis of acquiescence to
symbols relating to some "future" or to a vague social acceptance) would have little staying value in the face of an action
fulfillment *now*.

Eysenck and co-workers have drawn some connections between introversion and socialization on the basis of their experiments. Introverted subjects are apparently more rapidly
conditionable than extroverts. Their responses after being ac-
quired seem to be harder to extinguish than those of extro-
verted subjects also. It is possible that this kind of individual

difference plays some meaningful part in a greater readiness for socialization.[48]

> Bandura and Walters, commenting on the Eysenck findings, write: Eysenck attributes individual differences in conditionability to variations in cortical excitation and inhibition, which he regards as genetically determined characteristics . . .; however, child-training practices that tend to produce introverted children may also be conducive to the acquisition of self-control, and it is consequently difficult to assess the contribution of constitutional factors to the development of the complex and generalized social behavior patterns to which Eysenck's (1947) dimensions of personality refer.[49]

Two things seem to be most lacking in respect to the sociopath's control: (1) the kind of *primary infant dependency* (*Erickson's "basic trust"*) *which builds up an inner sense of survival-depends-on-other* which evokes anxiety when this relationship is threatened and (2) which is the natural outcome of the first, the *elaboration of a hierarchy of responses* (*strongly reinforced by resolving the anxiety of separation*) *which affords a repertoire of prosocial options sufficiently dominant over more primitive need responses to be elected.* In the sociopath, apparently, even when he seems to be opting for such responses, it is always because he is conscious of this as means to a more basic need satisfaction. Expediency, not the desire to maintain relationship, is his chief motivation.

Mischel and Gilligan set up an ingenious experiment utilizing Grinder's shooting-gallery game to test the resistance of forty-nine sixth-grade boys to the temptation to cheat. The experiment was so arranged that it was impossible for a boy to get enough points to win a prize without cheating on his score-keeping. The boys were also tested on their preferences for immediate rewards of a lesser sort versus longer delayed but larger rewards. It was thus possible to see what correlations would emerge between the preference for immediate rewards and the tendency to cheat.[50]

The authors "theorized that a relatively consistent preference for immediate gratification and an unwillingness to defer or delay the immediate for the sake of larger but later consequences should make it more difficult for a person to observe social prohibitions and restrictions, particularly if violating such prohibitions yields immediate rewards."[51]

The authors reported a significant positive correlation between a preference for immediate reward and difficulty in resisting temptation. They also concluded that the findings "suggest that responses to temptation cannot be regarded simply as a function of internal controls or 'superego strength.' "[52] Evaluation of such responses should include the significance of the reward itself for the person as well as the personal taste differences and the differences in the situation. This necessity of seeing the participant in context must be kept in mind in the evaluation of the control capacity of the individual. The way in which the tempted person construes his context has much to do with his "control." The constant theme of those families with the sociopath is that he construes his world differently as a kind of extension of himself.

Another factor which bears upon the control problem relates to the well-known theoretical point that incompatible positive responses tend to inhibit negative responses. (For example, a strong hunger drive may overcome a child's fear of taking candy from a stranger.)

Bandura and Walters call attention to this fact in relation to the control of aggression. They point out that most of the theory and experiments have been oriented to the inhibitory aspects of guilt or anxiety, assuming that the inhibition of responses is inevitably the result of matching responses with some form of aversive stimulation:

> The development of aggression inhibition through the strengthening of incompatible positive responses . . . has been entirely ignored, despite the fact that the social control of aggression is probably achieved to a greater extent on this basis than by means of aversive stimulation.[53]

Such is to say that the *lack of repertoire* of positive action patterns may have as much to do with the sociopath's impulsive antisociality as a weakness of "control."

Whether from such a learning-theory point of view or from the modified structural perspective of psychoanalysis, control is considered by most theorists to be an amalgam of determinants and forces rather than a single, unitary factor. It tends to be conditioned by many forces, whether conceived as instinctual id, ego, and superego forces or put in emotional and perceptual terms. It involves the whole person and his entire repertoire of possible responses, not just an ego, just a superego, or just a narrowly conditioned pattern. External factors such as stress and peer expectations, as well as inner need and structuring, will also be relevant. The merging of person and situation and control response is more *like* two proximate electromagnets with varying fields of force and variable intensities that finally attract each other than it is like a finger pulling or not pulling a trigger. It is more organismically systemic than mechanical. Nevertheless, it is not accidental that superego lacunae and dyscontrol are so often related, however much it may be true that self-punitive guilt responses and resistance to temptation or control-failure are shown to be related in less than a one-to-one fashion.

There is a type of impulsive lack of control which illustrates this amalgam of forces but which is associated with the presence of an intense superego rather than the near absence of superego typical of psychopathy. Such is to be found in the acting out neurotic character disorder. In such an instance the person is involved in intense guilt anxiety and seeks punishment as a reduction mechanism, and irrational self-destructive impulsiveness ensues.[54]

Examples of psychopathic behavior sometimes reflect the more brutal side, sometimes a less primitive irresponsibility and swindler type.

A recent news article carried the report of two young men who, in collusion with a teen-age girl, enticed another teenage girl into a car, drove her into the desert and smashed her skull with rocks, "Just to see what it was like to kill someone." The pretext: she had turned down one of the boys when he requested a date.[55]

Kisker relates the following case:

Following World War II, a thirty-seven-year-old man applied to a Brooklyn hospital for a medical internship. He showed hospital authorities photostats of degrees from Scottish and German universities and he was given a job. During the next few months he helped deliver several hundred babies. Over a period of five years, he transferred from one New York hospital to another. Finally, after he missed a payment on a car he had purchased, police found that he had never been licensed to practice medicine. Horrified officials of the hospital where he was serving as Senior Resident then learned that he had not even finished high school. In the Army he had been assigned to the Medical Corps, and he had read every medical book he could find. When the war was over, he forged credentials and references and applied to a medical placement agency as a physician. Due to the shortage of physicians, he had no trouble in finding an opening. The superintendent of the hospital where he was first hired said, "He was a very good doctor, and a nice person. He had a marvelous personality and impressed all of us at the hospital." When the self-styled "doctor" appeared in court, he found that the judge had been one of his patients at the hospital only a few weeks before. Granting that the "doctor" was quite an impressive fellow, the judge nevertheless sent him to the penitentiary for a year.[56]

Obviously, there is a world of difference between the two above examples. One is primitive, direct, and death oriented or necrophilic. The second is much more complex, and in many respects, life oriented. The central common factors lie in irresponsibility, ignoring the conditions of community-dependency and norms (though it must be admitted that if the "doctor" had been an artist or a writer he probably would have been lionized instead of penalized). One must remember that the "doctor" was willing to risk the life and health of many patients by setting his own private standards of training, to violate the trust of his patients that he was what he presented himself credentially to be, and, to surrender his internal integrity for "charm." Both personalities represent expansiveness transcending normal lines of social sensitivity and responsibility, an element, as was previously pointed out, sometimes very positive in its aims and difficult to assess, whether it be a touch of creative genius transcending stupid conformity, or sadistic indifference to the conditions requisite for communal life.

Summary

It may thus be seen that the antisocial sociopath reflects a patterning of guiltless (or, possibly, guilt repressed), irresponsibly expedient behavior. It is rooted in an apparent anxiety-deficient expansiveness, which evidence indicates has *possible* constitutional roots and definitely is environmentally influenced by survival figures in infancy. The sociopath's loveless impulsiveness, indifference to consequences, and inability to identify with his victims marks him as a primary object for research and for the reparative concern of those whom he refuses to be concerned about.

THERAPY

Frankenstein believes that the early structured situations producing pure psychopathy are irreversible:

> We maintain that certain structural dispositions, such a predominance of the tendency toward expansion and a defective ability to experience anxiety in an individual with a normal principle of differentiation, may be present at birth. We presume, though it would be difficult to prove empirically, that they have their specific cerebral equivalents. Owing to these congenitally given structural dispositions, frustrating experiences determine the development and the crystallization of the final psychopathic reaction types. *These results of structurization, however, are irreversible.*[57]

The same author admits that where noncongenital psychopathy occurs, there is the possibility of an admixture of neurotic elements which always makes for ambiguity and opens the possibility of reversibility.[58]

The psychoanalytic school is the *most* hopeful in its approach to the sociopath, holding that no functional development is necessarily irreversible if a relationship can be developed. Implicit is the notion that life experiences only *modify* rather than *produce* structure and that the difference between functional psychopathologies is one of *degree* rather than of *essence.*[59]

One of the few therapists to claim some success with adult sociopathic personalities, the late Robert Lindner (a psychoanalyst), qualifies the possibilities for such therapy rather stringently:

> Psychopaths can be treated, if at all, only by the systematic uncovering of the dynamic factors and events which precipitated the condition. *Those in whom the attitudes have crystallized and the patterns have jelled are beyond any therapy.*[60]

Bergler sees the psychopathic personality as a schizoid type, impervious or open to therapy, depending upon the extent to which neurotic components are present. He gives three reasons for the therapeutic inaccessibility of schizoid people:

> The transference repetitions are ineffective; the absence of automatic preventive fear leads to fantastic external self-damage; neurotic masochism is indefinitely maintained because it represents in schizoids a shield and active defense against the deepest "malignant" masochism of pseudocatatonic type.[61]

Cleckley, after long experience, agrees with O'Malley and many others that psychoanalysis of the pure psychopath is most disappointing and largely a failure.[62] Hendricks, reporting on twenty-three cases of psychopathy treated at the Berlin Psychoanalytic Institute, indicates that only one case was considered improved while eighteen left treatment and four showed no change.[63]

Bromberg reminds us that former attitudes toward the psychotic, even on the part of psychiatrists, were that he was untreatable and that as often as not this was a defense on the psychiatrist's part—a way of rejecting the patient. This similar rejection in the case of the psycopath becomes a *raison d'être* for the patient's continued aggressiveness. Bromberg believes that the therapist can overcome this and dissolve the patient's aggressive defenses through group therapy.[64]

Fox believes that a highly unorthodox form of therapy which employs surprise and a relentlessly aggressive but accepting approach has some chance of success:

> Some of the techniques that have worked have begun with the psychologist telling the prisoner the best way to escape and then evaluating it with him, discussing methods of killing his mother [!], accepting a rather extreme homosexual act humourously rather than incarcerating him in solitary, displaying of legal knowledge that structures his situation for him, and engaging in a boxing bout with the psychopathic prisoner. Fairly stable relationships were built after each of these events. . . .
> . . . The therapist absorbs, in the process, the tensions the psychopath needs to dissipate, thereby reducing the need for acting out.[65]

Mr. Fox doesn't say what the mortality rate of such therapists is, but this "punching bag" approach is heroic and novel, to say the least.

Because of the difficulty of holding the psychopath in treatment, an institutional setting or a probationary status that terminates with failure to keep appointments is usually recommended. It is uniformly reported, however, that punishment, per se, is useless in effecting changes (except for the worse) in this disorder.

In the case of youthful sociopaths, much more hope for therapeutic change is held out.

Aichhorn's efforts to treat antisocial "wayward youth" with what he calls a "practical psychology of reconciliation" has had wide appeal and was suggestive of the kind of approaches later employed by Fritz Redl, Wyltwick School, etc. The milieu therapy he instituted had as its aim surrounding the children with staff and environment dedicated not to maintaining protocol but to rehabilitating the children—giving the pupils "experiences which fit them for life outside and not for the artificial life of an institution."[66]

No doubt the sensitive modeling shown in the following

moving protocol was a significant factor in the success of the
school:

> We have an eighteen-year-old boy who had been ex-
> pelled from a military school for stealing from his com-
> rades and who had stolen at home and elsewhere. After
> he had been with us for several months, I put him in
> charge of the tobacco shop. The employees each con-
> tributed a certain amount to buy their tobacco in com-
> mon. I told the cashier to keep an eye on the boy with-
> out letting him know and to report to me when any
> money was missing. Four weeks later, he reported that
> about half the sum taken in weekly was missing. This
> seemed to be the right moment to expose the boy to an
> emotional shock in order to bring about catharsis, al-
> though I had no clear idea how I was going to do this.
> Since I wanted to gain a little time I told the cashier to
> send the boy to me in the afternoon without telling him
> that anything was wrong. The boy came while I was
> still undecided what to do. I wished to keep him with
> me for a while, so I proposed that he help me dust my
> books and keep them in order. What should I do? I must
> proceed in such a way that the catastrophe of exposure
> was unavoidable, his anxiety must be turned into an
> emotional outburst. This sudden change of affect would
> make him accessible to treatment.
>
> The "drama" was played as follows. We began our work.
> I inquired how he was getting along and gradually we
> approached the topic of the tobacco shop. "How much
> do you take in each week?" He mentioned a certain sum.
> We continued to dust books. After a pause, "Does the
> money always come out right?" A hesitating "Yes" of
> which I took no further notice. After another pause,
> "When do you have the most trade?" "In the morning."
> Then still later, "I must look in on you sometime and go
> over your cash drawer." The boy was getting more rest-
> less all the time, but I ignored it, went on working and
> kept coming back to the tobacco shop. When I felt that
> I had intensified his uneasiness sufficiently, I suddenly
> brought the crisis to a head. "Well, when we get through
> here I'll go and take a look at your cash." We had been
> working together for about an hour and a quarter. He
> stood with his back to me, took a book from the shelf
> and suddenly let it fall. Then I took cognizance of his

excitement. "What's the matter?" "Nothing." "*What's wrong with your cash?*" His face became distorted with anxiety and he stammered out the sum. Without saying a word I gave him this amount. He looked at me with an indescribable expression on his face and was about to speak. I would not let him talk because I felt that my action must have time to take effect and so I sent him away with a friendly gesture. About ten minutes later, he came back and laid the money on the table, saying "Let them lock me up. I don't deserve your help—I'll only steal again." He was greatly excited and was sobbing bitterly. I let him sit down and I began to talk to him. I did not preach, but listened sympathetically to what he poured out, his thievery, his attitude toward his family and to life in general, and everything that troubled him. The emotion gradually receded, relieved by the weeping and talking. Finally, I gave the money back to him, saying that I did not believe he would steal again; that he was worth that much to me. I said, too, that it was not a present, that he could smoke less and pay it back gradually. So that no one should know about this, however, he had better put the money back in the cash drawer. I told the cashier that the amount had been returned and that he need take no notice of the affair. In the course of the next two months, the money was actually returned.[67]

Aichhorn's method built on a loving but sophisticated kind of acceptance which waited for relationship before leveling expectations. This is the same priority of ego-before-superego which Redl so explicitly articulates.

His Pioneer House in Detroit was a model of what can be accomplished when the full resources of trained and dedicated personnel are brought to bear on the so-called "psychopathic" behavior of aggressive children. They studied carefully the conditions of person-group and staff interaction and what is necessary by way of exploring and developing a theory about ego-superego control systems to work with such children.

Redl, admitting the necessity for understanding the genesis of aggressive behavior and impulsivity in children, yet stresses the fact that it is not their *hatred* which is the chief problem in working with them. He traces the clinical helplessness of those working with such children to "the decomposition of behavior controls which the piled-up aggression has wrought within the personalities of those children," and "the solidification of some of their hatred into an organized department of shrewdly developed defenses against moral implication with the world around them."[68]

Redl's imaginative approach involved the impact of a hygienically prepared climate which guaranteed protection from traumatic handling by adults, the giving of love divorced from behavioral "earning," tolerance for symptoms and built-in leeway for aggression, a special programming for a carefully studied process of ego support and ego therapy *prior* to any imposition of superego expectation and a clinical grounding of all change objectives in life events in the institution.[69] "Superego repair" followed a carefully analyzed course of objectives and was closely integrated with ego support. Redl, it will be remembered, reports that he *never* found a child totally devoid of superego and doubts that such exists.[70]

Redl did find that in these children superego functions showed distortion of the following sort:

1. "Peculiarities in value content"—often meaning identification with a deviant code.[71]
2. "Inadequacy of the signal function"—often in terms of too weak (low intensity) or too late ("a post-action conscience"—more frequently related to the neurotic child than the "children who hate").[72]
3. "Deficiencies in the identification machinery"—largely because of lack of or inconsistency of early models.[73]
4. "Guilt displacement, model-rigidity, and other superego disturbances"—referring to guilt displaced from the acts initiating the guilt to other acts and, in the case of model rigidity, the ineffectiveness of the superego except unless the situation is directly tied in with the original value-setting models.[74]

The McCords, in their assessment of the Wyltwick Studies, reported significant changes for the better in the milieu therapy of psychopathic children (which they were careful to differentiate from behavior disorders and neurotic and psychotic children). They reported a great decrease in "aggressive fantasies" (The finding regarding aggressive fantasy is not so surprising in view of the widely reported fantasy weakness of the psychopath. Karpman, one of the rare investigators of the dreams of psychopaths, reports: "The psychopath's dream life, like his waking life, is 'of the earth earthly' variety. There is no elaborate or poetic imagery and a minimum of symbolism." [Reported in Maughs, *loc. cit.*]), "a significant increase in internalized guilt," a decrease "in their punitive views of authority figures," and an increase "in positive *ego ideals.*" Two important findings which they stressed are that "the child psychopath's need for love is not extinguished" and that "psychopaths, as children, have no more intense aggressive fantasies than do other delinquents."[75]

Bandura and Walters, in their application of learning theory to aggressive behavior, imply that as our knowledge of the species of parental modeling and the identification process "increases," we may more effectively extinguish and reverse the course of such learning. They point out that rather than "failing to learn," it may be that children are learning too well the deviant behavior that is being modeled.[76] They question the contention that psychopaths don't learn from punishment and point out that, instead, what they have learned of aggressive behavior may be intermittently and vicariously reinforced sufficiently to offset prosocial efforts.[77]

Their exploration of prosocial rewarded modeling through movies raises exciting possibilities for experimentation with institutionalized deviants.[78] Their extrapolations from experiments designed to explore therapist-patient interaction throw light on the possibility for unorthodox forms of relating which may effect changes and which, retrospectively may indicate the reasons for some of the ineffectiveness of previous therapeutic efforts, e.g., the possible *inappropriateness* of unconditional acceptance *for therapy of the antisocial patient.*[79] It is possible that the operant conditioning of psychopaths may hold promise of as dramatic results as some that are just now being explored with long-term psychotics. The authors write:

"The possibility of using planned scheduling of reinforcements for the maintenance of socially desirable behavior in everyday settings has not as yet been fully explored.[80]

SUMMARY

It may be seen from the above that the most critical thing needed is a continuing interaction of theory, experiment, and practice which explores on all levels the significant determinants and change factors. Children otherwise hopeless and headed for a life of adult antisocial sociopathy may well have a chance for rehabilitation. It is too early to assume that any of them are devoid of anxiety or changeless at the core. Redl's work suggests that ego defenses more likely protect the child from value involvements, while his work, the McCord findings, and the new directions for research pointed up by Bandura and Walters suggest that what may now look theoretically irreversible may soon be seen in a more hopeful light.

Chapter VI

NEUROTIC GUILT

I saw . . . structures which are stronger than the good-will of the individual, and one of these structures was the neurotic-psychotic structure.

—*Paul Tillich* (in dialogue with Carl Rogers)

The last chapter dealt with the person who lacks appropriate guilt feeling. We will be concerned next with the person who has *too much* guilt, one who represents a process of guilt carried to the point where it interferes with healthy social living. If the sociopath may be caricatured as a car careening down a hill without brakes, the neurotically guilty person is one whose brakes are dragging all the time, are applied inappropriately and fearfully, or are so sensitive that they take hold dangerously.

Guilt is an element in most pathology to some degree. Even where endogenous elements may be the initial factors setting a psychopathological process in motion, guilt frequently exacerbates the existing problem.

Lorr *et al.*, in a first-order factor analysis of psychotic behavior patterns, recently established *intrapunitiveness* as one of the significant factor groupings in a study which covered a representative patient population.[1] Cattell and his colleagues report *superego* as one of the five significant drive components of personality.[2] The very possibility of internal conflict, in terms of psychoanalytic ego psychology, implies a superego involvement (or its infant precursors).

The "voices" and hallucinations of psychotics frequently make sense when they are understood in terms of the guilt conflicts involved. The psychotic's desperate bid for self-esteem in the face of his own self-judgments often takes the form of an expansive identification with some moral ideal.

Rokeach's study *The Three Christs of Ypsilanti*[3] is especially instructive at this point. Rokeach, a psychologist, placed in the same ward three patients all of whom claimed the same identity: "Jesus Christ." Over a period of many months, as one of the men began to improve slightly, he changed his name from "Jesus Christ" to "Dung." This radical alteration from highest to lowest carries a bizarre note of punitive exaggeration. Its significance is caught best in the patient's own comment that occurred in the discussion about his change of name from "Christ" to "Dung." He remarked: "I know I'm a creature."[4]

Rokeach comments that two of the patients' grandiose delusions were efforts to deal with shame over incompetence rather than guilt, although ego ideals are involved, and the reader will remember our theoretical discussion of these proximate dynamics. Of the patient previously referred to, Rokeach writes:

> The dominant theme is not shame about incompetence but *guilt* about forbidden sexual and aggressive impulses. Leon is a guilt-ridden Christ who strives more to be good than great; he is suffering not so much from a delusion of greatness as from a delusion of goodness.[5]

Anton Boisen's *The Exploration of the Inner World*[6] documents the extensiveness of guilt among 176 psychotics which he studied and is testimony to its significance in his own illness. He writes:

> In our general group (schizophrenics) we find that there are six cases in which there seems to have been an unsuccessful attempt to get away from the sense of personal failure by shifting the group loyalties and associating with bad companions. The great majority, however, have never questioned the implanted loyalties but *have fallen far short in their performance*. Most of them, moreover, take their shortcomings so seriously that they

cannot bring themselves to acknowledge them to anyone else. The result is a sense of isolation and guilt which acts as a barrier between the individual and his fellows. . . . The great majority had thus before their illness been maladapted to their external social environment and *all*, with six possible exceptions, were of those who in the light of their accepted ideals were subject to a serious sense of inner disharmony and isolation.[7]

Freud was the first to see the full significance of guilt in the neurotic process. He focused on the Oedipal conflict as the kernel of neurosis because it is a nodal point (for many if not all) where the infant's psychobiological needs and his first experience of community truly totally conflict: "How do I get what I want? (i.e., full possession of loved object and effective elimination of opposition to that possession) *and also keep what I need* (e.g., *security* against people treating me in similarly rejecting ways, while keeping the *love* of those who protect even as they oppose me)?" This may seem an unusually abstract and abstruse way of putting the problem, but in spite of the questioning whether the focused genital-sexual aspect of the conflict may be nonuniversal, it is true that for every human being, consciously or unconsciously, some balancing out of biological-psychological social vectors (when they conflict) is an inevitable condition of socialization. Freud felt that such conflict had a biological-phylogenetic history and probably, for most people, an ontogenetic (if unconscious) validity.

The fortunate normal is spared the traumatic crisis and rides through it, just as he experiences digestive processes (if he is aware of them at all) as a normal after-meal pleasantness. The unfortunate child, whose biosocial needs are conflicted by anxiety, deprivation, or seduction, experiences trauma or subtraumatic conditioning which produces sufficient anxiety about either satisfaction of physical needs or the dangerous degree of his impulses that he is moved to the development of exaggerated *defenses*. The degree to which these become structured into his character and integrated into a way of life, or the degree to which a response is conditioned and remains relatively autonomous, or an unintegrated symp-

tom, is a current puzzle to clinicians. This is a puzzle compounded by the contention of operant therapists that the
conditioning therapies may remove dramatic, long-standing
symptoms without other symptoms taking their place.[8]

It is the author's conviction that symptoms may be (*a*) very
deeply set by conditioning and integrated into the total personal gestalt or (*b*) less integrated and relatively autonomous
conditioned responses. If one were to employ the iceberg
figure, the alternative might look like this:

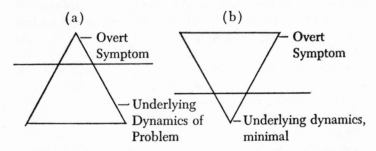

(a)   (b)

— Overt   — Overt
Symptom   Symptom

— Underlying
Dynamics of   — Underlying dynamics,
Problem   minimal

If this is the case, and there is much clinically to bear it
out,[9] it would help to integrate the conflicting therapeutic
findings of the behavioristic and psychoanalytic schools. Every
clinician has known patients with deep and complex intrapersonal conflicts involving almost every aspect of their lives
which tended, however, to be expressed through very subtle
symptoms of brooding depression or ritualistic life patterns,
with little that would stand out in bold relief to "rank" for
reconditioning. It is also obvious that some very bold and ex-
trusive symptoms seem shallow and to be fairly extraneous
and incidental conditioned alternations of the character, with
very little secondary elaboration or reinforcement. It may be
that the greater degree of favorable responses of phobic type
of neuroses to behavior therapy and the greater resistance of
obsessional type disorders to it (as reported by Eysenck)[10]
reflects some such postulated difference.

As guilt underlies and pervades many neuroses, it inter-
weaves itself in such a way that its presence may be evident
in a total sense of worthlessness, an inability to enjoy life, or a

feeling of pseudoexistence more than in florid or precise symptoms. The following poem touches the reaches of such pervasiveness:

ON GUILT

Exiled from the Neuterland
I flee
from one
terra incognita
to the next
forging passports
until I become
a persona ficta
petitioning for an amnesty
from a decree
issued in the Hall of Travesties
for a transgression
of the Code of Allegations
committed by an Identity
I can't remember
in a country
that is
a phantasy.[11]

Where does one attach an electrode to this? How does one "rank" it for reciprocal inhibition? It is exactly at such junctures where the subjectivity of human suffering merges into the parameters of describable pathological symptoms that the sensitive therapist knows he must often operate. He has the same kind of reaction to some suggestions of the behavioral therapist as he might to a patient who said to him, "Hook me up to your machine, Doctor, and cure my unhappy marriage." Does one "cure" a Hamlet? Was his an illness? How defined? Until we include such questions in our therapeutic theorizing, we have ignored the complexity of man and we have oversimplified the task of therapy.

Rather than try to treat the problem of guilt in neurosis in a general way, let us look closely at two of the symptom groupings in which guilt plays a prominent part: Neurotic Depression and Obsessive-Compulsive Neurosis.

NEUROTIC DEPRESSION

The psychoanalyst views neurotic depression as an over-response to a loss. Freud, in his paper "Mourning and Melancholia,"[12] elaborated on an earlier notion of Karl Abraham relating melancholia to grief. The depressed person resembles the person who grieves. He has lost a loved object. In the case of the mourner, the object-love that is lost is an actual external person. In the case of depression, the object lost (in addition to an external loss) is the love of the superego, "self-esteem," the love of the introject. These may be closely interwoven and often are to some degree. However, the normal person is more readily able to accept the loss and its finality and seek new objects. The depressed person continues the "mourning," suffers unusual guilt, feels worthless, and is for a time disinterested in new object relations. Rado once described melancholia as "a great despairing cry for love."[13]

The pathological extenuation of this process in the depressive is believed rooted in his character disposition. (There is disagreement among authorities concerning the inevitability and the degree of physical predisposition in the neurotic depressive. There is much more consensus that the psychotic manic-depressive involves "endogenous" factors, although even here there is disagreement.[14]) The psychoanalyst traces this to the first year of life in which the child, often "orally fixated" and having established a strong dependency upon a loving and warm mother, finds the mother then qualifying the gift of love, food, and "supplies" in some way. The arrival of a sibling may divide the mother's attention, she may seek to control behavior by the withholding of the previously unqualified love, etc. Frustration and rage in the infant ensue. The infant, presumably, is terrified both of his inner mounting rage and his lonely helplessness—his loss of the good mother.

Aloneness (independence) and an all-devouring *aggressive oral rage*, that would like both to incorporate and permanently possess the love object, lie as core fears in the heart of the depressed character. The infant in a sense knows two mothers, the good mother and the bad mother, the one who resolves the inner needs and prevents the inner anxiety and the one who frustrates and rouses inner rage and a sense of helpless aloneness (annihilation). The good-bad mother is incorporated into the ego of the child, and the ambivalent love-hate dynamics typical of the infant-mother relation continue to exist between the ego and the superego.

One sees in the depressive a tendency to *deny* hostility. This is a natural ego defense, where an important need is dependency and relationship. Occasionally, the hostility breaks through and its intensity is apparent. Usually, the hostility is turned on the self; that is, superego aggression is turned against the ego, the "good" introjected parent withholds love from the "bad" child (ego) (which is also identified with the bad parent). (Karl Abraham "showed that self-reproaches are not only internalized reproaches of the ego against the object but also internalized reproaches of the object against he ego."[15]) It is this peculiar combination which makes it possible for this self-hatred to be so powerful, for guilt to be so dominant.

Fenichel writes that "it is, in the last analysis, the 'oceanic feeling' of union with an 'omnipotent' mother for which depressed persons are longing."[16] And again, that all depressed persons "are psychologically in the situation of a narcissistically hungry infant lacking the necessary external care."[17]

The depressive character is marked by dependency on the external object for love and ego supplies, and his self-esteem seems to depend on these. This is often seen in a lack of basic self-reliance, an insensitivity to individualism (his own or others) and a feeling: "You *are* who you love." He tends to resent independence in his love object and resorts to vicarious living through the love object. He tends to relate to the loved object through a kind of servanthood which is manipulative: "I am so good you *must* love me." (I am indebted here to Dr. Philip Bower for some insights expressed in his lectures on the depressive at Elgin State Hospital. He cannot be held responsible, however, for any personal distortions which may have crept in.)

It is the close dependency need and fear of losing the affection (that means self-esteem and protection from inner rage and helplessness) that drives this type of character to identify himself, to affiliate with groups and causes so often. He is a loyal booster, patriot, joiner, and other directed in his givenness to conventionalities. His sexual relationships are often sadomasochistic and his life may be woven around the theme of guilt and suffering, happiness and unhappiness, with a probable pessimism. Such themes are often evident in projective tests.

This "unhappy ending" fear is a recurrent element. For this reason, Gutheil gives the following formula: "$D = S + P$." ("Depression = Sadness + Pessimism.")[18] In other words, some typical human loss (of love or goods) is exacerbated in the depressive personality by the *set* of pessimism: "Here it is again, I am left alone and helpless. It will always be this way."[19]

Freud pointed out that in grief the world becomes empty and that in melancholia the ego becomes empty.[20] Fenichel elaborates on this:

> In the phenomenology of depression, a greater or lesser loss of self-esteem is in the foreground. The subjective formula is "I have lost everything; now the world is empty," if the loss of self-esteem is mainly due to a loss of external supplies, or "I have lost everything because I do not deserve anything," if it is mainly due to a loss of internal supplies from the superego.[21]

It is important to see the close interconnection of object-loss and guilt. Each is a loss of love. The loss is usually related to failure to please the loved object and is oriented to the denied hostility toward the object. The pessimism probably arises from the subliminal awareness that "it must ever be thus," with any objects. That is, "I will always be dependent and hostile and will, no matter how hard I try, always disappoint and therefore lose my love objects — including my own self-esteem."

The efforts to deny such, to deny the hostility and the pessimism may reach manic proportions in the psychotic, but they are often also evident in the pseudoebullience of the neurotic depressive and in the turning of hostility against the self (guilt) to prevent breaking of relationships.

Rosen and Gregory quote one depressive patient:

> It's hard for me to get angry at anybody. Sometimes my mother but not outwardly. If I get angry with her, I feel real bad afterwards—she always makes me feel wrong. I still feel she is my mother and I owe her respect. Everything I do, I'm trying to please her but then I can't. I can't feel like an adult in that household.[22]

Many writers see the impulsive behavior and acting out of alcoholics and addicts as basically efforts to avoid depression by obtaining narcissistic supplies: "Since depressions are states that develop if these supplies are missing, addictions and impulse neuroses, in so far as they still are able to achieve their end, are suitable for evading depressions."[23]

Rosen and Gregory summarize the depressive:

> The major predisposing personality traits are conscientiousness, dependency, inability to express anger directly and outwardly, and intro-punitiveness, that is, a tendency to blame oneself rather than external factors for failures. Depression may be viewed as a turning of hostility or anger against the self instead of outward. The formula for reactive depression is thus self-hate plus an external loss. A tendency to orality may be present: in psychoanalytic theory, pessimism, helpless dependency and loss of appetite (or an excessive appetite) are attributable to oral fixation and aggression.[24]

SUPEREGO DIMENSIONS

If one looks at neurotic depression in terms of our superego dimensions as described in Chapter IV, some of the outstanding elements are these:

Feeling

Respecting *intensity*, the superego feeling consists in an ambivalence between ego and superego (in both directions), which reflects the parent-child paradigm. The intensity of hostility, sense of alienation, annihilation, and depressive loss of self-esteem is a turning back on the ego of the aggressive rage originally felt toward the parent (and now the introjected parent). One would expect it to vary in some proportion with the amount of ego investment (cathexis) in the lost object and the degree of responsibility felt for its loss.

The rigidity of response and lack of *flexibility* reflects the neurotic conviction that love has to be *won* and that failure to get it is a failure of the ego to comply with the conditions of love. Sacrifice, self-punishment, ego suffering, is (as it was for the child) the condition of restored love and self-esteem. It is possible that the expectable spontaneous remission from depression is directly related to the fact that, given sufficient suffering, a sense of equilibration occurs, and punishment, having been endured, is no longer necessary. It has been noted by clinicians that actual physical illness or pain may result in an associated lifting of guilt or depression. Some theories of electroconvulsive therapy resort to a similar explanatory dynamic.

Content

Superego *content,* as has been mentioned, frequently concerns itself with conventional taboos, loyalties, and patriotisms. These may be reflections of the original parental object or of the substitute through whom the depressive is "vicariously living," or the "cause" that functions in a similar way. There may be mood swings between asceticism and abandon, with episodic breaking of taboos followed by much guilt and self-deprecation. Money is frequently highly valued and possessions clung to at the same time that the person may ask very little materially for the self. Love may be conceived as something one passively receives. What is given in the process may be more in the nature of service or devotion than spontaneous love. Pride and self-esteem are associated with compliant goodness more than accomplishment or creativity. There may be devotion to work, but there is little personal investment in it.

Timing

Regarding superego *timing*, one notes the generalization over time. There is a kind of vague pessimistic extension into all futures in the midst of the depression and a sense of the stoppage of time and emptiness of it. Even biological functions seem to slow down during depression. Guilt seems to be less associated with a particular event and more related to a permanent condition of the self.

Control

Respecting effectiveness of *control*, we noted a general acquiescence in the conventions and mores of the persons and groups to which the person is loyal, with occasional episodic outbursts.

Deutsch and Krauss, discussing the distinctions between defense and control structures, emphasize the common belief that

> defensive structures are more likely to develop if the *intensity* of the instinctual drive is so high that the drive seems "uncontrollable," or the reality is so intensely frustrating that there is little hope of drive gratification, or if the instinctual drive is in irreconcilable conflict with another instinctual or derived motivation.[25]

All three of these probably participate in the depressive inclination to *deny* hostility, which eventually breaks through in the face of frustration and then is punitively reiterated in guilt and depression.

The same authors further point out:

> Defensive structures function to *block* immediate or delayed drive gratification, e.g., denial or repression of hostility so that gratification does not occur even when the drive object becomes available again. . . .
> *Control* structures, on the other hand, provide for the possibility of delayed discharge and for the development of motives and techniques of finding in reality the object which permits discharge.[26]

It is evident that the depressive's ego handling of his hostility is more in the nature of a defensive than a control type response. When the denial or repression proves incapable of inhibiting the hostility or aggression the breakthrough is reacted to by retroflexion and guilt and depressive slowdown. This cycle is peculiarly evident in the depressive reaction to manic agitation and discharge.

OBSESSIVE-COMPULSIVE NEUROSIS (OCN)

Example:

A married college man of twenty-eight presented himself to a counselor for help in making a vocational decision. His complaint was that he couldn't seem to "settle" on one academic major or life program. Every time he decided, and began to work, doubts would develop. He was in his third year of college and had changed majors at least six times. Much of his time was taken up with removing bits of glass and nails and pins from streets and sidewalks. He was a part-time government clerk and was also seriously preoccupied with picking up paper clips and rubber bands in the office. His explanation was that "people might slip on them." Before he retired at night, he carefully double-checked all door locks and assured himself that all gas jets were off: "I don't want my wife to get hurt." He said that when he got frustrated, he would go for a walk and daydream about being a Prussian military officer. His Draw-a-Person figures were a large, hulking matron with a big star on her dress and a very stiff-postured, square-jawed Prussian officer with monocle and boots.

His problem is a clear example of many of the following symptoms widely associated by clinicians with the obsessive-compulsive neurotic: repetitive irrational rituals, brooding preoccupation, doubt and dogma, guilt, self-punishment, ambivalence, rigidity, lack of spontaneity, struggles to restrain repressed rage, preoccupation with orderliness, cleanliness, perfectionism, bouts of severe temptation, etc.[27, 28, 29]

The term "obsessive-compulsive" is used because most writers consider it to be one neurotic syndrome made up of varying kinds of cognitive and motor symptoms, with sometimes *obsessive thought patterns* and sometimes *compulsive acts* dominating the picture. Alexander felt that the obsessions concerned essentially the *forbidden wishes and desires* and the compulsions essentially a *reparation* for these.[30]

There is a kind of "asbestos logic" to the symptoms, in that they seem to channel impulses "too hot to handle" by obsessively tossing them back and forth in the mind, or countering the impulses in a behavioral way by compulsive rituals which seem intended magically to "undo" or counteract the impulses, thus reducing the anxiety or at least structuring it in some way.

What are the impulses defended against? Freud believed that they are the sexual and/or aggressive impulses of the Oedipal conflict (incestuous wishes toward the mother and death wishes toward the father, accompanied by castration fear) on the one hand, and the pregenital anal-sadistic impulses toward which the person regresses in his reaction to the Oedipus conflict.[31] This occurs because there had been fixation at the anal-sadistic level in psychosexual development by virtue of parent-child conflicts surrounding excretory behavior and the evocation of defiant emotions conditionally related to expulsive-retentive behavior. Erikson speaks of this as the "crisis of autonomy."[32] Rado contends that the rage generated by this crisis is the core of the OCN problem, but that it need not revolve only around toilet-training. It may, he believes, center on any rage-inducing parental frustration: *"The ultimately psychodynamically ascertainable factor is rage."*[33] The defense against the instinctual rage is "retroflexed rage," that is the rage via superego dynamics, is turned back against the ego and impulses in a self-punitive, restraining, and often sadistic way.[34]

Freud, writing on this mounting intensity of self-hostility that was the result of and the defense against the murderous rage, indicated that the more a person restrains his aggression by way of his superego, the more intense and aggressive his conscience becomes.[35] It is important to see that this retroflexed rage *is* the guilt feeling, the self-punishment, which occurs in response to the conscious or unconscious impulses, which, when conscious, are spoken of as obsessions if repetitive.

The intensity of the rage, and its more or less continuous operation, presents the ego of the OCN with a constant problem of defense. One writer describes the ego as a "football."[36] It is pressured now on one side by the frustrated impulses of the id and then by the punitive retroflexed instinctual rage via the superego. This accounts for the continual ambivalence, wavering back and forth, doubt and obsessive symbolic struggle of the ego in the OCN. As for the infant, it was a question of Can I do as I please with my powerful impulses, or am I under the will of another? Can I trust my own biological signals (i.e., retention, expulsion, etc.) or should I doubt them and depend on external direction? This problem becomes internalized when the superego is established, and central to the conflict is loss of superego love and the infliction of superego rage just as the child experienced (or fantasied) vis-à-vis the parent.

The defenses utilized to protect the ego from these overwhelming pressures from both sides (rage and guilt) or guilty fear tend to be fairly uniform. They work to keep the feelings at as much distance as possible. *Isolation, undoing, reaction formation,* as Freud pointed out,[37] become active following the initial regression to the anal-sadistic level. Intellectualization also becomes a uniquely economical way of defending against feeling, for it may provide a sense of being "involved" with feelings (because one is thinking or talking about them), at the same time that it enables the subject to be planning for and carefully organizing his future so that nothing surprises him. He will have thought it all through and be thus protected against spontaneity or frustrations that might overwhelm him with rage.

The keeping of ego distance from feelings is described by Shapiro as comparable to a pilot who flies by instruments.[38] The OCN generally has good instrumentation and may negotiate rather expertly in most areas, but it is as though all reality were mediated to him indirectly:

> He can fly his plane *as if* he were seeing clearly, but nothing in his situation is experienced directly; only indicators are experienced, things which signify other

things. . . . He relies on rules and principles that . . . feel authoritative and external to his own judgment. A paradox appears in the symptomatology of the obsessive-compulsive. As far as conviction is concerned, he is characterized symptomatically by two outstanding features: doubting and uncertainty, on the one hand, and dogma on the other. Psychoanalysis has already dissolved this paradox by demonstrating a significant relationship between the two: dogma arises to overcome doubt and ambivalence, and to compensate for them.[39]

Isolation serves to protect the ego from the dangerous impulses by keeping apart associations which would be threatening. Freud related the process to the "taboo on touching" in which primitives felt that touching the tabooed object meant death.[40] Since touching for the OCN would be the vehicle of motor expression of his two dangerous impulses (i.e., incest and murder) it becomes an obsessive-compulsive preoccupation to avoid it. The children's rhyme "Touch the crack and break your mother's back" exemplifies this.

The author knew one mother, who, preoccupied lest her small child be contaminated or hurt by germs from strangers, cleansed with carbolic acid all articles (such as doorknobs) touched by guests while visiting. Not only did this compulsion isolate her child from the germs, it also helped to isolate her own consciousness from her hostile impulses toward her child.

Since analysis depends upon a process of "free association" of ideas and feelings, one of the difficulties in the psychoanalysis of the OCN is the effectiveness of his capacity to isolate—to keep threatening associations from occurring. He may be psychologically sophisticated, and talk glibly about what is going on, but it is most often a descriptive, distanced kind of reporting, more appropriate to the analyst than to the patient. It is almost drained of feeling. One analyst interpreted this to his patient: "You keep trying to sit in my chair and join me in looking at yourself. Try to *experience* what you are feeling rather than just describe it."

This isolation extends to forbidden objects, persons, places, and ideas. It would be classified as a phobia if other signs of OCN were not present, as Rado indicates.[41] Kisker also compares the two syndromes: "Just as the phobia is a development of the anxiety reaction, the obsessive-compulsive reaction is a further development of the phobia."[42]

Psychoanalytic study has revealed many of the interrelationships between religious ritual and the OCN's defenses. Divine objects, totems, and words are hedged around with taboos which are violated at the risk of death. Prescribed rituals rigidly guide the believer so that his actions will not endanger him unduly. Freud described this as "manifestation in one's relation to God of the original ambivalence toward one's father."[43]

It was for this and similar reasons that he described religion as a collective compulsive neurosis and obsessive-compulsive neurosis as a "private religion."[44] Ritual is also closely connected with undoing and reaction formation.

Undoing is a "negative magic"[45] which is aimed at abolishing behavior that has just been completed. What Freud called the "dichronous"[46] nature of the symptom, Metzner labels "Januslike,"[47] and Rado designates "oppositional."[48] All refer to the "seesawing" back and forth of ideas and acts, one expressing the impulse, the other the superego opposition to it or "undoing," or punishment. Many of the symptoms of the OCN involve lining up one symbolic object precisely with another (e.g., shoes beside the bed). Rituals may "undo" the impure acts or life of the believer or allay the hostile side of his ambivalence. Verbal rituals undo the hostile impulses that lie beneath the surface of the believer's feelings toward the father-god's demandingness. They are evident in the prayers and psaltery, the invocational and benedictory formulae, and ensure the propriety of the relationship.

Rituals of sacrifice, atonement, lustrations, and baptism may be expected magically to undo the sinfully broken relationship or the proscribed act which has been performed. Incense is burned to purify the air and symbolize a holy presence.

The obsessive-compulsive may be specially anxious even in the midst of such ceremony, for he may feel impulses to blasphemy or obscenity most powerfully in just such solemn moments and struggle with terrifying temptations to laugh at funerals—often just because such solemn routines may evoke his frustration and responsive rage over imposed rules and roles.

The constant preoccupation with orderliness, perfectionism, and cleanliness bespeaks the inner struggle against just the opposite: the anal-sadistic rage that would react against all control and would "smear" all into chaos. Fenichel describes the OCN as one caught in the middle of the formula: "May I be naughty or must I be good?"[49]

The necessity of making sure in advance that there be no error or wrong to have to undo, or to upset the precarious inner balance, makes it very difficult for the OCN to make decisions or to commit himself to courses of action without much pro- and con-ing, careful qualification and planful attention to detail. He is willing to work hard, but his work is often marked by overattention to trivia. Life itself is ritualized into routines.

Reaction formation is the countering of an impulse with its opposite. The impulse "I want to be bad" is experienced as "I must be virtuous." The impulse "I want to be dirty" is experienced as the thought "I must be impeccably clean." This is the preventive system of pharisaism, which by its constant preoccupation with moralism reveals its unconscious eagerness for libidinous or sadistic abandon. When the impulses break through the defenses, as they occasionally do, the threat of moral chaos or intensity of the guilt warning signal is such as to necessitate the doubling of counterefforts. Excessive emphasis on pity, purity, and perfection, on "not letting anyone get hurt," become ego-acceptable reactions to the disguised impulses pressing for expression. No wonder some wit remarked, "When you see someone coming toward you to do you good, run for your life."

Not infrequently, the reaction formation is joined to the defense mechanism of projection. First, the evil impulse is located in some other individual and the reaction is directed outward. This paranoid device lessens the internal guilt somewhat at the same time that it permits the person to vent his sadistic rage "for a good cause." The angry prophet, unmoved by fellow feeling or tenderness, who delights in the destruction of the evil ones rather than bemoans their fate, caricatures this type of defense.

The significance of the foregoing is heightened if it is set over against the following description of the healthy conscience by Rado:

> True to its adaptive purpose, *healthy conscience* effects moral self-restraint and promotes peaceful cooperation and cultural achievement by means of self-reward. It is a beautiful example of autoplastic adaptation. *The appearance of automatized mechanisms of expiatory self-punishment in its organization signifies pathological developments.* Healthy function fulfills its adaptive function smoothly; it has little need for guilty fears and the reparative work of repentance. But with early automatization, conscience grows into an organization dominated not by the healthy mechanisms of self-reward, but by the morbid mechanisms of expiatory self-punishment. . . . A conscience so constituted will diminish rather than increase the organism's capacity for happiness. It is an example not of autoplastic adaptation but of autoplastic maladaptation.[50]

We are talking about healthy dynamics, not ethics. That there are times when ethical social issues have a primacy over individual survival or "adjustment" is not contested.

SUPEREGO DIMENSIONS

If we now look briefly at our superego dimensions in respect to this syndrome, we find the following:

Feeling

In the OCN feeling is heavily oriented to self-aggression. The feeling is negative and intense, largely unmodulated by affectionate warmth, to the extent that psychoanalysts speak of a libidinous inadequacy.[51] The feelings of affection tend to be overtoned by sexual guilt and sadomasochistic meanings. Both rage and affection are kept at a distance by the defenses mentioned and tend to be displaced to intellectual symbols, moralizing, guilt struggles, and automatized discharge devices. There is spasmodic breaking through of the defenses by impulses and motor acts, but these tend to be symptomatic, alien, and countered by self-punishing, undoing, reparative motifs. The *intensity*, though great, is buffered by conceptualization. This necessarily results in rigidity—a planful advance structuring and screening to preclude spontaneity.

Shapiro writes in respect to feeling:

> The superego of the obsessive-compulsive has often been considered to be unusually harsh, and it has also, or perhaps alternatively, been described as inadequately integrated. These descriptions no doubt reflect in part the evidence of more or less continuous tension or worry associated with the sense of "should" that appears to plague these people and from which they hardly seem to escape. Although the phenomena are familiar enough, the explanation seems somewhat different to me. The qualities of "harshness" or "inadequate integration" are absolutely necessary to the whole aim and function of the mode of experience and activity of which the sense of "should" is an aspect. Experiencing a continuous pressure that feels separate from and alien to his own wishes is the very condition that allows the compulsive to feel the presence of a command under which he can serve. [Shapiro speaks in the same article of "a special sort of awareness . . . a watching over himself, a giving himself commands and directives" . . . a "special kind of self-consciousness" . . . "sitting behind himself and directing" . . . "continuous role-playing. . . ."][52]

Content

Whereas there is a sense in which, for the *depressive*, feeling governs content (or at least one gets the impression that pain-carrying has a primacy), in the case of the OCN the impression is just the opposite. Everything is organized to keep the pain of rageful feeling at a distance. As this is sometimes put, the ego of the OCN rebels against the superego, and stands in a kind of isolated ambivalence respecting it, whereas the ego of the depressive is overwhelmed by it, submits *in the hope of winning love* by dependent acquiescence. (It should be remembered that this kind of anthro-

pomorphization of a process is validated to the extent that
ego-superego dynamics reflect child-parent relational paradigms.)

Though the substantival quality of the value contents of
the ego ideal vary as widely as human cultures vary, *in terms
of the dynamic function of the contents,* one would expect
similarity among OCN's in any culture where they might develop. The similarity would focus on details of moralism, duty,
or demand units, according to whatever had been internalized,
and by means of which preoccupation one had learned to
abort impulses conceived to be dangerous, or the rage retroflexed by their emergence.

It is not likely or necessary that there be a total discon-
tinuity between content and feeling. In fact, it is difficult to
conceive of an OCN developing in a culture where aggression
is approved and sexuality casually structured.

Contents reflect a precocious ego realism, a painful preoccupation with the future in such a way that its surprise aspects are minimized and the necessity for spontaneous response is lessened. Side by side with such, it has been noted,
lie magical attitudes that provide a kind of "carbon-dating"
for the emergence of the early ego functions,[53] for example,
the ritual-undoing of proscribed impulses or acts. The illogic
of such rituals to the outsider sometimes verges on the delusional. Yet the OCN is not really deluded. He has a kind of
perspective on his magic. As Shapiro puts it,

> Close examination shows that he never even states that
> he *believes* these things to be true, e.g., that his hands
> are contaminated after forty washings. He never says,
> "I have cancer," or "I have been contaminated." He
> says, rather, that these things *might be* . . . an important
> difference.[54]

Nevertheless, the OCN operates, respecting his magic and
in spite of his perspective, as though it were reality. This
strongly reinforces the behaviorist's assertion that there is at
work here a completely accidental conditioned confluence of
symptom and anxiety reduction.

One important recurring element in the content structure

of the OCN is the degree of perfectionism, such that one might almost speak of a "value acceleration." No matter how fully he seems to comply with superego requirements, the anxiety that motivated the behavior in some measure seems always to remain, hence the pressure to sharpen the criteria and ensure the adequacy. "Just one more time," and any speck of dust or germs will be surely removed. Go over and doubt just once more, and then one can feel *certain* and dogmatic about his conviction. Hence the necessity to examine with focused scrutiny, to reassure oneself once and for all, not only regarding the performance but also the values by which it is enjoyed. The more precise and definitive the theological system, the more necessary it is for doubt to explore all its reaches to exclude any tiny flaw in certainty that may remain. One sees this apotheosized in religious refinements of the law, the "commentaries on the commentaries." It is also to be seen in the traditional law-grace controversy, where the whole question is raised whether man can live in a provisionality accepted by God or must guarantee a *perfect* performance to survive.

Timing

The OCN is preoccupied with time in the future mode. He is constantly concerned to forestall surprise (hence any danger of spontaneity or impulsive response) and to plan for every exigency. His intellectualization provides him with a kind of "prelived" map so that life has more of a *déjà vu* quality to him than to most. This concern accounts for the not infrequent interest of the OCN in timetables, almanacs, etc.

The fact that, here again, he cannot totally preclude surprise often makes him anticipate negative surprise, the projection of self-punishment onto God, fate, or the environment, where it waits to descend upon him for his slightest infraction. Crashes, illness, hell, bad luck—all become vehicles of his anxious self-negation.

The dreams of David, the OCN in the movie based on the story of *Lisa and David*, epitomized the conjunction of time and anxiety. All his ambivalently loved ones had their heads extruding through holes around the perimeter of a huge clock, the hands of which were sharp knives. His rage led to their beheading in the dream. When he began to get well, the shift in ambivalence was symbolized by his successful, but Herculean effort, to stop the hand before it reached his girl friend's head. Thus the OCN's preoccupation with time is to preclude the chaotic effects his rage might have on others or (retroflexed) on himself.

Timing, where it concerns the synchronous control of behavior by way of the integration of value content, feeling, and effective control tends to be good—too good—to the point of absurdity (obsession) and the elimination of the spontaneous. *Hence one can speak of the polar opposite of the sociopathic personality in the OCN.* The former seems almost incapable of applying values to the future. The OCN is overwhelmed by the need to do so.

There is another sense in which it may be said the "timing" is *bad,* in that it is constant. To use an earlier metaphor, it is like brakes that are on continuously. It is perhaps dubious to say that when the car decelerates upon release of the throttle the brakes are therefore "functioning well" under such conditions.

Effectiveness of Control

It is a truism that the OCN rarely does what he is afraid he will do. Though often enough concerned about suicidal thoughts, he almost never commits suicide. The mother obsessed with thoughts of harming her children rarely puts her obsessions into action. The symbolic enactment often, by intellectualization, discharges the impulse, to be followed by compulsive behavior of a *reparative* sort which undoes the evil impulse and usually provides self-punishment.

From the point of view of maturity, rather than social adjustment, or conformity, one may describe the "control" more as a "stalemate." The figure of the ass caught between two bales of hay and unable to move toward either is apropos.[55]

Asocial "compulsions" sometimes classified under obsessive-compulsive neurosis, seem, as Fenichel construes them, to belong rather under *impulse disorders* or instances of these mixed with obsessive-compulsive disorders.[56] Typical of the *neurotic* symptom is the ego-alien quality of the symptom—the pain connected with it. Contrarily, the *perversion* is a symptom that provides satisfaction. Its removal means a loss of pleasure for the subject rather than a freedom from pain. Kleptomania and pyromania, as examples, often involve libidinous satisfactions or orgasms. It may well be that they are conditioned accretions on an obsessive-compulsive personality and are therefore rather highly responsive to therapy.

ODIER

The French psychoanalyst Charles Odier, in his book *Les Deux Sources consciente et inconsciente de la vie morale*,[57] affords the scholar and therapist a helpful comparative study of normal and neurotic guilt. He sees superego as the seat of neurotic unconscious dynamics and contrasts it with the moral conscience which is conscious. Because of his helpful summary, we will take the liberty of paraphrasing and condensing some of the aspects of neurotic guilt he singles out for emphasis. They will amplify some of those we have stressed in connection with the OCN and depressive:[58]

Some Signs of Neurotic Guilt

The *sense of ought* tends to precede any intelligent weighing of the problem and is automatic. Feeling dominates judgment.

The conflict is largely unconscious; there is much latent guilt feeling that seems independent of content.

There is a "blind obedience" to conscience, without questioning, indicative of the "primitive heteronomy" of the child.

The ego has little strength in relation to superego; it is overwhelmed by superego, yet its efforts lead to few conflict resolutions, are "pseudo-moral" and often "ineffectual."

There may be confusion of the personal and the cosmic.

"I think I ought" may be experienced as "God says I
   must."
"Egocentric morality." Obedience is not out of love of
   the good so much as an automatic response to preclude or overcome guilt anxiety.
Pride, fear, defensiveness and preoccupation with moral
   superiority (though often feeling morally inferior)
   may dominate the picture; no self-respect.
Automatic self-punishment in response to guilt anxiety
   (often ineffective and must be repeated indefinitely).
Constant struggles with temptation and preoccupation
   with evil.
Often insensitivity to gross wrongs done but intense
   preoccupation with moral minutiae or imagined sins.
Anxiety replaces genuine remorse.

At the time of this writing, the dynamic and psychoanalytic approach to neurosis is coming under increasing criticism
and challenge by psychologists trained in experimental and
behavioristic methodology. Disavowing the need for or relevance of complex inner explanations of "symptom formation"
they have made impressive attacks both theoretically and
therapeutically on neurotic problems.

The gist of their approach is centered in the conviction that
neurotic behavior is the product of conditioning, the learning
of dysfunctional responses that occurred simultaneously in
connection with the reduction of anxiety, and that the behavior can be extinguished or reciprocally inhibited by the proper
application of learning theory and re- or de-conditioning.

Mowrer, Wolpe, and Eysenck have been in the vanguard of
this movement in varying ways, although it stems from earlier
experiments by Pavlov and Watson in the experimental induction of neurosis in animals, and is prefigured in Jones, Dunlap,
Salter, Shoben, Dollard and Miller, and others.[59] We will look
at the application of this approach as a therapeutic method in
the next chapter. Here we wish to consider briefly one of the
problems it raises for the understanding of obsessive-compulsive neurosis as a guilt phenomenon.

One central feature stands out: a general rejection of the
notion that the symptoms represent the peak of a complex

dynamic process, which continues to operate even if symptoms are removed.

In respect to this, it is known from laboratory studies that what appears to be "compulsive" behavior can be easily produced in animals. Fonberg produced repetitive responses in dogs, under stress conditions (lifting of foreleg and "shaking off") which represented regression to a previously learned way of reducing anxiety.[60] Skinner reports ritualistic responses in pigeons which much resemble "compulsive" phenomena.[61] Such evidence makes it clear that "guilt-dynamics" need not be at work in order for such symptomlike behavior to be present.

Ayllon, Haughton, and Hughes describe the experimental induction of a broom-carrying "compulsion" in a schizophrenic patient by simple operant conditioning.[62] She was offered cigarettes as a reinforcement for carrying a broom. Two board-certified psychiatrists, *unaware of the experiment,* were asked to observe the patient and comment on her behavior. One remarked:

> The broom represents to this patient some essential perceptual element in her field of consciousness. . . . It is certainly a stereotyped form of behavior such as is commonly seen in rather regressed schizophrenics and is rather analogous to the way small children or infants refuse to be parted from some favourite toy, piece of rag, etc.[63]

The other doctor commented:

> Her constant and compulsive pacing holding a broom in the manner she does, could be seen as a ritualistic procedure, a magical action. . . . Her broom would be then:
> (1) a child that gives her love and she gives him in return her devotion
> (2) a phallic symbol
> (3) the sceptre of an omnipotent queen. . . .
> This is a magical procedure in which the patient carries out her wishes, expressed in a way that is far beyond our solid, rational and convenient way of thinking and acting.[64]

This is an embarrassingly precise way of clarifying the critique which the behaviorists are leveling at the clinicians. It can be said that several of the symbolic meanings attributed to the patient's behavior might normally, in such circumstances, be supportable. It is possible, of course, that the reinforcement value of the cigarettes accorded with a "phallic" significance. However, the danger of surplus meaning and the lack of necessity for it in at least *some* symptom behavior is evident.

As soon as the reinforcement for the behavior was completely withdrawn, i.e., no more tokens or cigarettes were given for broom-carrying, the broom-carrying ceased. The "symptom" extinguished.

The authors of the article just referred to draw the conclusion that such "symptom" behavior continues to be expressed because it is reinforced by persons in the environment, *not* because of some "guilt or other feelings, the existence of which is questionable at best."[65]

It could be pointed out that this may well represent the kind of "inverted iceberg" symptom previously referred to—a largely peripheral and attenuated, symptomlike conditioned response which has a life cycle concordant with the externally rewarding environment.

Let us, however, assume that the inner drive is not for a cigarette or the tokens which will be exchanged for the cigarette, but that it is a drive for perfection, for self-esteem, for approval from without and within to counter a constantly present and often reinforced anxious neurotic conviction that one is "worthless," "dirty," or "evil." Now let us assume that acts or impulses which heighten this drive happen one day to include one which *reduces* it markedly. That is, some ritualistic act or obsessive thought pattern serves by isolation, distraction of attention, self-punitive significance, or whatever mechanism, to reduce the guilt anxiety. It then tends to be a response set available whenever the anxiety is restimulated. The removal of such a symptom by some counterconditioning would not resolve the underlying drive for perfection or self-esteem.

It is exactly this which is at issue between the learning theorists and the psychoanalysts in the argument over symptoms and the nature of neurosis: whether symptom removal solves the "underlying problem" or whether the symptoms *are* the "underlying problem," which dissipates when the symptoms are removed.[66]

Metzner, in a comparative evaluation of Wolpe and Dollard/Miller, raises some technical questions about the application of learning theory (based on animal experimentation) to complex human behavior.[67] He speaks of the possible "spurious precision" which such applications may entail, and he adds:

> It is noteworthy that the most successful cases of the application of learning theory to treatment have usually involved well-defined, objective, visible behaviour deficits. A general theory would require extensive consideration of (1) how "stimuli" are organized, i.e., of perception, its distortions and idiosyncracies; and (2) how "responses" are organized, i.e., of behavioural sequences, of goals, strategies and interactions.[68]

It is conceivable that a therapist, asking the patient to picture in fantasy the anxieties he feels about perfectionism and superego demands, by reciprocal inhibition and relaxation therapy might decondition guilt anxieties of a neurotic quality. This would border on a kind of personality modification Mowrer warns against.[69] It also would seem to raise major questions about the interaction of patient-therapist value systems that will be raised as an issue in the next chapter.

As Metzner indicates, the successful treatment of obsessive-compulsive neurosis by conditioning therapy has been largely in respect to "well-defined, objective, visible behaviour deficits."[70] To what extent this complex neurosis is "nothing more than its symptoms" and to what extent its symptoms run through the whole fabric of a subject's personality are still highly conjectural. Eysenck and Rachman allude to cases in which *the nature of what the symptom is a defense against* must be known in order for symptoms not to recur after conditioning therapy, and they cite cases of such remissions because of inappropriate applications of method by therapists preoccupied only with motor symptoms.[71]

O. H. MOWRER

O. H. Mowrer has been an active pioneer in the application of learning theory to the problem and treatment of neurosis. We will consider his therapeutic approach in the next chapter. The point to be made here is that he sees neurosis (and psychosis) to be the result largely of a "learning deficit." That is, whereas the Freudians, Dollard and Miller, and (he contends) Wolpe see neurosis as the process of *excess* learning of a fear response to a drive stimulus (such as sex, aggression, etc.), which fails to extinguish, Mowrer believes neurosis is the result of a *real guilt anxiety* which results from the subject's failure to learn to abide by moral cues.[72] He thus suffers from conscience-pain which is justified according to Mowrer and which he needs to respond to by way of a behavior change in the direction of more moral behavior.[73]

Mowrer makes the point, in a number of approaches,[74] that the problem is not that of an unadaptive *surplus* of learning which needs to be extinguished or inhibited, nor that of impulses freed from repression (caused by the surplus superego learning), but *one of learning to adjust to the conscience-demand and its reality-oriented adaptive cues.*[75] He is concerned, in fact, lest both Freudian modification of superego demand (with implicit freeing of repressed impulses) and Wolpian deconditioning should produce sociopathic personalities.[76]

It is this author's conviction that Mowrer has made a major contribution to psychology and psychotherapy in forcing consideration of the importance of values and of real guilt (remorse) in human behavior, normal and pathological. It is also held, however, that he has enthusiastically *overstated* the case and thereby compounded the confusion. This will be considered under four headings: (1) Mowrer's caricature of Freud, (2) Mowrer's moralistic view of neurosis, (3) Mowrer's legalism regarding guilt structure, and (4) Mowrer's forced artificial value dichotomy (guilt is all good or all bad).

1. *Mowrer's Caricature of Freud.* Freud's essential position was that in the process of moral training the neurotic suffers conflict about instinctual impulses. He is made fearful of these through a combination of circumstances which are usually: parental threats of severe punishment or loss of love (rejection, "annihilation")—or sometimes imagined threats of this type which may be cued off by sensitivity to parental anxiety —because of expressions of sex or aggression. Such fears result in repressions of the impulses from conscious control and heightened defenses against them which are activated and reinforced as the superego develops and the child identifies with parental values and attitudes toward instinctual expression. When these parental attitudes are harsh (and even when it is just the anxious withdrawal of precarious love) the superego relationships tend to reflect this harshness, sense of alienation and/or loss of self-esteem or self-love.[77]

The result, as we have seen, in the case of the depressive and OCN, is an anxious ego trying to control the organism without adequate representation of all the impulses (because of repression), often functioning as a slave to a tyrannical superego or impulsively rebelling and then submitting to punishment as a way to restoration.[78] The picture is of an ego that is weak in its harmonizing of its impulses and values and spending far too much of its available energy in defense operations and symptomatic behavior.

Freud's objective in psychoanalysis was to form an alliance with the patient's ego to bring about *awareness, autonomy of control*, and a *balance of instinctual and social (superego) forces* which afforded optimal life, fulfillment and satisfaction for the person as he conceived his personal needs and the real physical and social world.[79] This meant frequently the analysis and melioration of a tyrannical superego and the freeing of neurotically bound impulses. The objective was *not* an unleashing of unrestrained instinct on the world or indifference to the values that made human community possible. Some patients and some analysts chose to pervert Freud's intention to such ends, but this was not Freud's intention. He desired to enable the patient to "become his best self, what he would have been under the most favourable conditions." Again, "we want nothing better than that the patient should find his own solutions for himself."[80] Freud's intention was that by freeing the patient to ego control and awareness of impulses he might be more integrated, more *consciously moral* on an adult basis, instead of steering his life on the basis of a frightened acquiescence in infantile fears and parental hegemony.

Freud made it clear that neurotics were kept anxious, guilty, and restricted by compulsions and depressions because of their fearful overresponses to their sexual and aggressive impulses which were defensively avoided rather than consciously related to. One of the chief means of defense was superego punishment and it was also, often unconsciously, the active source of repression and the preventive force against reality exploration by the ego.

For example, the OCN, afraid of his sexual and aggressive impulses, instead of discovering the real intensity, limits and significance of these, shuts them off, compounds their significance, and learns to manage them not by ego-aware sublimation or direct expression but by pitting his superego against his impulses in a gigantic symptom struggle, keeping them at a distance through isolation, repairing them by undoing, and converting them into compulsively expressed opposites. The result is a stifled anxiety-ridden and rigid existence void of spontaneity and joy—"respectable" (in a puritanic, legal sense) but *ruined* for the kind of autonomous, ebullient maturity of which a human being is capable, and conscious underneath of a self-condemnation, no matter how punctilious his behavior or how orthodox his dogma.

Now how does Mowrer react to Freud's effort to redress the imbalance of the personality? He indicts Freud as "the 20th Century equivalent of the Devil, thinly disguised."[81] He interprets the task of the psychoanalyst to be: "To align himself with and to speak for the instincts, in opposition to the moral or pseudo-moral forces within the personality which have instituted the repression."[82]

It *is* the task of the analyst to strengthen the person's ego as he weighs these matters and to help the person's courage as he compares what has often been forced on him as "moral reality" with what he *himself* can see in the world of human social living. It is *not* his task to side either with the patient's id or his superego but to strengthen the ego such that it can resist superego sadism and reality-test the values so that he can act congruently with those he is convinced are genuine rather than rebel blindly or acquiesce blindly.

Mowrer writes as though Freud were unaware of the fact that some superego values are worthwhile and realistic. But, as Hartmann summarizes:

About the "necessity" of moral codes . . . [Freud] repeatedly and clearly expressed his opinion. He realized the integrative function that such codes and standards have for the individual. "Conscience" was, for him, a "necessity: [its] omission the source of severe conflicts and dangers. . . ." More than once, he traced the "necessity" of moral codes to the fact that human society could not live without them. He called the superego a highly valuable possession for human society. In another connection, he showed how the development of the superego can lead to a reduction of the external means of coercion used by society. He noticed "with surprise and dismay" that "so many people obey only outer pressures," instead of developing their own moral standards. He was obviously far from being a moral nihilist.[83]

How Mowrer, if he ever read *Civilization and Its Discontents*, can write, "Freud . . . did not take guilt seriously"[84] is incredible. Mowrer writes, "Psychoanalysis is not messianic but demonic." Yet is there not something also demonic about ignoring the distinctions Freud established between real and neurotic guilt, ignoring the *fact*[85] that Freud admitted the relevance (though he did not emphasize the importance) of real guilt, and then, by denying the distinction, turn the clock of history back by confusing the two?

2. *Mowrer's Moralistic View of Neurosis.* Mowrer writes, "Neurosis . . . is just a medical euphemism for a state of unacknowledged and unredeemed real guilt."[86]

It is this author's belief that the problem to which Mowrer is calling attention is that real guilt cannot help being present in every neurotic. This is easy to agree with. However, rather than admitting that *real guilt and neurotic guilt react with and reinforce each other,* Mowrer would burden the already burdened sinful neurotic with the conviction not only that he is wrong in having violated some genuinely held value but that he is as worthless and despicable and worthy of self-hate as he feels he is. It is difficult to imagine even Mowrer reminding a neurotic depressive who is morose over some loss that he *deserves* his anguish. A suicidal neurotic may not need this kind of assistance. It is quite a different thing to bear the guilt of an act one has committed than to have added to it the overwhelming "I told you so" of a sadistic superego (reflecting unsolicited parental judgments on one's infant instincts). One might wish Mowrer had more readiness to qualify such remarks as:

> Conscience, that is to say the capacity for self-blame and self-punishment, is a marvelous human and social invention which has the highly adaptive function of causing us to "tramp on ourselves" in order that others don't have to do this for us.[87]

One may agree that restraining brakes on a car are a good thing without believing they need to be so tight as to drag all the time or be applied so harshly that they dash heads.

3. *Mowrer's Legalism Regarding Guilt Structure.* Mowrer's legalism reaches its climax in a near "quantitative" view of the relationship between suffering, punishment, and forgiveness, which bids well to reinstate a spiritual calculus:

> It should be noted that in the situations which one encounters "clinically," social (i.e., interpersonal) punishment is often unnecessary. This is the case (a) when the erstwhile offender has already "done penance" in the form of the suffering inherent in "mental" disease and (b) when such a person resolves to "make-up" in some way, in the future, for the negative, destructive things he has done in the past. This is probably what we really mean, or ought to mean, when we speak of "forgiveness." The suffering which the neurotic has, in one way or another, already experienced surely earns him some "credit" [*sic!*]; and we [!] ought also to be willing to give him the benefit of the doubt (at least a time or two) by agreeing to *let* him "work out" his own salvation if he

wishes to, instead of having it occur entirely on a retrib-
utory basis. Thus, forgiveness in this sense involves both
giving credit for the self-inflicted punishment which is
always a feature of neurosis and functional psychosis
and giving the individual a "second chance" to be cooperative, helpful, constructive, good.

. . . As long as an individual is defiant and unrepentant,
his conscience continues to "hurt" him; when he comes
to terms with conscience, and with the external community which it represents, the hurting stops and life's zest
and meaning return.[88]

To the *theologian,* such a quote shows a reaction not only
against "cheap grace" but against *any* grace. It puts a price
on readmission to the community from which the sick person
feels alienated. Gracious love has a right to expect and encourage reparative responses when forgiving love is extended.
It does *not* demand these as the *price* of forgiveness.

To the *psychiatrist,* such a quote carries the veiled message:
"No matter how sadistically self-destructive your superego, no
matter how distorted your values vis-à-vis reality, no matter
how cruelly they may have been imposed on you by a neurotic
or psychotic parent, they are *right* and it is appropriate that
you should suffer so, regardless of the nature of your sin.
Acquiesce in this punishment, reconfirm your guilt, and then
you will be well."

We do not wish to fall into the same excess of exaggeration
that Mowrer does because we believe that he is calling attention to a critical matter. It is, however, important to clarify
what this author believes as a violence both to theological
and psychiatric reality.

It is not surprising that Mowrer sees himself at odds with
Calvinists and with Freudians for their insistence that "salvation" and "health" are *given,* not earned.[89] Both these depth
orientations to human brokenness recognize that the individual who has become hopelessly lost in self-condemnation,
who feels self-alienated by a superego which condemns him
regardless of what he does (no matter how hard he tries,
sacrifices, atones, purifies, compulsively works at acceptance,
or at rightness through effort), that *such* a person can only

discover wholeness, peace, the *capacity* even to love by *ex-periencing* the unqualified acceptance and affirmation of his being in all its self-hate. Such affirmation of the self-that-is, even when it is rebelling and hating, *especially* when it is, is alone what enables the "wayward" violator of community positively to want and affirm others rather than brokenly acquiesce in a power struggle and ambivalently knuckle under with unconscious moralistic hatred. Mowrer's legalism, for all its worthwhile calling of attention to the necessary connection between genuine grace, responsive reparative behavior, and real guilt, is so patently contradictory to theological and psychiatric history that it vitiates the corrections it would rightly make. Not only with the OCN, but *especially* with the neurotically depressed person, the deep conviction that he is loved, he is worthful, only when he is jumping through some extraneously imposed moral hoop is what feeds his inner despair and undermines the reality and inner genuineness of his manic flights into "goodness."

4. *Mowrer's Forced Artificial Value Dichotomy.* It seems fair to say that had Mowrer taken a less disjunctive approach to the problem of guilt, he might well have made his point without so much theoretical fallout. He has pressed the issue courageously to make his point, and debt is due him for this. Yet he has gone too far.

It is not necessary to declare that *all* guilt is real in order to clarify the contribution of value systems to human society. Neither is it necessary in order to show that the real infraction of core values held by a neurotic or psychotic will produce or contribute to his illness by heightening his neurotic guilt and reinforcing his sadistic self-rejection and alienation so that he thinks of himself as beyond humanity, a beast, "R. I. Dung" or reactively, "Jesus Christ."

It is possible to make the case for a modest, tonic anxiety as a healthy and necessary reality factor in life that keeps us from walking off cliffs or putting our hands in propellers, without at the same time sanctioning a parental program of cautious overguardedness, germ-watching, and panic induction. The point should be clear: real guilt, moral remorse about the violation of the genuine conditions of human community, should be present and recognized in a socialized human being. It should function in advance as a warning signal and in retrospect as conscience-pain if it is ignored. Its warnings and pain should be heeded as implying attitudes *and* behavior. Both minister and parishioner, psychiatrist and patient, should be crystal clear about its reality and inevitability if a shared system of values is to have any substance in a culture.

Having granted the above, it is equally necessary to grant what Mowrer seems bent upon denying: that some people—many people—are, in the process of growing up, under the tutelage of parents so anxious about instinctual (usually sexual and/or aggressive) behavior that they impose an oppressive instinct-fear on the child, punish his spontaneity and autonomy, encourage repression and dissociation, reward excessive compliance, and promote deceitful harmony at the price of unconscious self-contempt through superego identification. Because the child experiences the pseudoquality and often brutalization in such value training, his ambivalence and rebellion may be the price he has to pay to maintain his "autonomy" and what sanity he has.

Any therapist who approaches such a patient, and any pastor who approaches such a parishioner, will have to keep clearly in mind the fact that *there is probably a mixture of both neurotic and normal guilt in all of us to some degree.*

To treat *neurotic* guilt on a confessional, reality basis is to reject the counselee and to identify with his tormentors, internal and historical. It is to deepen his despair and self-hatred. It is to compound his confusion, minimize his autonomy and maximize either his acquiescent self-abasing conformity (in his desperate effort to extort "love" and "acceptance") or else to maximize his rebellious, self- and other-destructive acting out.

To treat *real* guilt on the other hand as *neurotic* and something "that cannot be helped" is, as Mowrer makes clear, to cut the very nerve of humanity, to cauterize moral sensitivity, and to undermine human community and the hard-won values of the human race in the name of science. Any therapist who is so eager to eliminate the very possibility of guilt that he sedates the genuine conscience of a person or his anxiety about violating what he sincerely holds to be the conditions of human life is himself reprobate and as much in error as though he were to sever nerves to eliminate pain.

Summary

We have attempted in this chapter, by the exploration of two paradigmatic neuroses, to elaborate some of the ways in which neurotic guilt manifests itself through superego sadism, ego impoverishment, lowered self-esteem, symptomatic defensiveness, futile, repetitive efforts at reparation, etc.

We have briefly alluded to the growing question raised by learning theorists and behavioristically-oriented psychologists of the interrelationship and possible identity of symptoms with underlying neurotic dynamics. It was felt that this issue may be ultimately resolvable through a dimensional approach to symptoms as more or less attenuated or deeply rooted aspects of the personality.

The last section explored and presented a four-part critique of the guilt theory of neurosis proposed by O. H. Mowrer, contending in essence that his caricature of Freud, his legalistic moralism, and his forced dichotomy of guilt as either all real or all neurotic and false does violence to the facts and fails to recognize the interweaving and interacting nature of real guilt (remorse) and neurotic guilt.

Chapter VII

THE PSYCHOTHERAPY OF GUILT

Psychotherapy must be a therapy of grace or it cannot be therapy at all.[1]

—Paul Tillich

The effort to provide a therapeutic experience for a guilt-laden person involves several implicit value judgments: It presupposes a judgment about the technical and moral competence of the therapist to deal with the problem, a judgment that the type and goals of therapy are appropriate, and a judgment whether health values take priority when these seem to conflict with other values.

For centuries ministers and priests, often with misplaced confidence and authority, have dealt with guilt problems and value crises. As often as not, their efforts to work confessionally and theologically with neurotic guilt exacerbated the problems.

Psychotherapists, utilizing the insights of Freud and the psychoanalysts into guilt dynamics, have, with some rare exceptions, looked with disdain at such blundering crudity in the handling of guilt. They reflect the view that only the person skilled in the dynamics of unconscious behavior can hope to free a person from rigid superego shackles and that theologians are, like typhoid Mary, more contaminant than therapeutic.

It is only recently that extensive research and thought have been dedicated to the systematic exploration and empirical validation of the role of guilt and value dynamics in therapy outside, that is, of psychoanalytic circles. Mowrer, for a time, was almost a lone pioneer.[2] C. Buhler,[3] D. Glad,[4] W. Wolff,[5] P. London,[6] W. Glasser,[7] J. Drakeford,[8] and others in increasing numbers have turned their attention to the issues. One sees not only a technical concern but also a growing humility about the adequacy of the psychotherapist in terms of his competence to wrestle with value problems, subjectively and objectively.

Bugental speaks of accepting "the guilt of being a therapist" and adds "that there is guilt for our failure to be all that we can be as therapists to these people who come and give us their lives and trust."[9]

Goodwin Watson writes:

> The illusion that our art transcends morality has kept us from forthright study of the ethical and religious disciplines. We psychologists would take a dim view of any experts in philosophy and religion who might hang out a shingle to practice psychotherapy. We would deplore their lack of training in our discipline. My thesis is that scholars in religion have a right to take an equally dim view of most psychotherapists. Psychotherapists operate on unexamined premises concerning life's meaning and values.[10]

To speak lightly of "competence" in the role of therapist to the guilt-laden and the person in conflict over life's values is to risk either presumption or ignorance, or both. It is perhaps because of this that knowledgeable clerics are studying psychology and alert psychotherapists read Tillich and Buber.

The therapeutic "surgeons" most familiar with guilt know that what looked at first like a well-localized operable tumor has turned out to be a deeply enmeshed growth whose fibrous roots in even the healthiest of men extend so far into vital organs as to make some reaches of it seem irremovable. None of the honest surgeons claim to be totally free of what they seek to heal in the patient. Even to speak of *values,* in the normative sense which transcends mere assertion of taste, is to embroil oneself, except for the most fatuous, in the guilt of nonrealization. Only the flip dismiss all of this tension as neurotic. So competence here would seem to carry humility as one of its hallmarks. Hopefully more exacting criteria than humility may be discerned.

THE THERAPEUTIC PROCESS

Research on therapeutic technique has begun to reach a level of precision that holds out hope for an eventual clear description of and understanding of the process. If this is too utopian, at least it promises to permit evaluative sampling and comparison of the various therapeutic options in terms of effectiveness and predictability.[11]

The range of therapeutic theories is staggering. Robert Harper's survey, entitled *Psychoanalysis and Psychotherapy 36 Systems*,[12] gives a hint of the size. The approaches vary as widely as Whitaker and Malone's "experiential therapy," with its emphasis on id processes,[13] to Ellis' rational therapy, focusing on rational self-talk;[14] from Rosen's authoritative and directive, sometimes muscular role-playing,[15] to Roger's congruent therapy.[16] New ones appear frequently: "integrity therapy," "reality therapy," "actualization therapy," etc.

Similarities in the diverse approaches are coming under scrutiny. Even within the subjective-objective extremes of existentialist therapy as opposed to manipulative operant conditioning, research is beginning to isolate some common patterns which seem to pervade all successful therapy. Some of these reflect patient and therapist environments,[17] some of them patient-therapist expectations and hopes,[18] others the curative implications of novelty, persuasion, and influence.[19]

Some interesting paradoxes appear. For example, just as an emphasis on the manipulative reinforcement units of speech are being recognized as highly relevant factors in therapeutic change, with overtones of the therapist as a kind of "reinforcing machine,"[20] attention is simultaneously focused on the critical importance of the therapist being able to do this because of his role as an identification model who evokes certain expectations in the patient.[21] Thus a Carl Rogers, who abjures all manipulation, is shown to be (however unconsciously) involved in "selective empathy," unwittingly rewarding and punishing the client's responses.[22] Thus also, a Skinnerian therapist, highly conscious of this aspect of his therapy, at the same time may be unaware that his responses have reinforcement value because of his quasi-magical position as a "scientist" or the degree of hope brought to the situation by his patient.[23]

TECHNIQUE AND RELATIONSHIP

Other developments that command attention relate to the interaction of theoretical technique and the personal relationship existing between the therapist and patient. Fiedler's studies, for example, seem to indicate that more important than the type of technique used by the therapist is the degree of experience and expertise in the relationship he develops with the patient. He found that there was more similarity between therapists in widely divergent theoretical positions, e.g., Freudian and client-centered, than between experts and novices using the *same* theoretical techniques.[24]

As Glad has pointed out:

> That therapy method makes little difference in the generalized outcome of "success" has been widely heralded in both clinical and research publications. . . . Only when the additional question "Success of what kind?" is raised, does it become plausible to consider the special influences of particular methods.[25]

Glad's point becomes more definitive in respect to the conditioning therapies. Eysenck and Rachman's position, like that of Wolpe, focuses largely on symptom therapy and the external signs of neuroses.[26] As they continue to expand their approach, however, one can see an increasing involvement in more subtle inner meanings of "symptom" and greater complexity of what is "ranked" for therapeutic extinction or desensitization.

Mowrer makes the very trenchant criticism that, just possibly, the deconditioning of symptoms (which may be the major signs of guilt) may actually reflect participation of the therapist in the sociopathic deterioration of a patient.[27] One need not go so far as to agree with Mowrer's contention in the same article that neurosis "originates . . . in palpable deviant conduct." It is possible to see it as a reflection of infantile superego tyranny (perhaps exacerbated by deviant conduct) which nevertheless needs more reparative work than symptom removal—reparative work that may not seem necessary when only symptoms are removed.

Truax, in perhaps the most recent research report on psychotherapy at the time of this writing, indicates that there is no automatic value to be gained by psychotherapy as such.[28] Evidence shows that a person may be made better *or worse* by psychotherapy depending greatly on the therapist's capacity to provide central therapeutic elements of "empathy," "non-possessive warmth," and "genuineness."[29]

He tentatively hypothesizes that counselors possessing the above attributes act as positive reinforcers and evoke high levels of positive feeling in the patient, thus heightening the patient's positive self-reinforcement, and decreasing patient anxiety.[30]

Truax writes:

It might be tentatively proposed that these three "therapeutic conditions" have their direct and indirect effects upon patient change in the following four modalities: (1) they serve to reinforce positive aspects of the patient's self concept, modifying the existing self concept and thus leading to changes in the patient's own self-reinforcement system; (2) they serve to reinforce self-exploratory behavior, thus eliciting self concepts and anxiety-laden material which can potentially be modified; (3) they serve to extinguish anxiety or fear responses associated with specific cues, both those elicited by the relationship with the therapist and those elicited by patient self-exploration; and (4) they serve to reinforce human relating, encountering, or interacting, and to extinguish fear or avoidance learning associated with human relating.[31]

It is further evident that changes occurring in therapy (as in marriage) may look and feel different from the "inside"

than from the outside. Feifel and Eells analyzed the percep-
tions of both patients and their psychotherapists at the conclusion of therapy concerning the changes that occurred and
what was thought to be helpful. Sixty-three outpatients and
twenty-eight psychotherapists participated. The open-end
questionnaire provided some of the following major findings
and conclusions:

> (a) Therapists stressed changes in symptomatic relief
> and improvement in social relationships, whereas pa-
> tients focused on self-understanding and self-confidence;
> (b) patients underlined the opportunity to talk over
> problems and the "human" characteristics of the psy-
> chotherapist as helpful, and the therapists highlighted
> therapeutic technique and support to the patient as most
> beneficial.[32]

THERAPEUTIC EXPECTATIONS

It is clear from the data that a great deal more governs the
outcome of therapy than technique and the expertise of the
therapist. The prognostic expectations of the therapist, the
hope and trust potential or LOA (level of aspiration) of
the patient, the placebo effect, the "demand character" of the
situation, as well as spontaneous (and "unspontaneous") remission have to do with outcome.[33] The patient's "need to
change" and the therapist's capacity for empathy are both
related to therapy length and success.[34]

INSIGHT

There is a growing skepticism about the degree to which
therapeutic change is a result of patient *insight* as contrasted
with the degree to which insight follows changed behavior
(manipulatively conditioned by the therapeutic interaction
and the therapist reinforcement).

The traditional psychoanalytic position has been that there
was a direct relation between lack of insight and the presence
of symptoms. This was not generally cognitive awareness in a
simple labeling sense but deep emotional insight achieved

through a process of analytic transference. It is generally held by psychoanalysts that symptom removal unaccompanied by insight will result in further symptoms replacing the original one.

Learning theorists are making a strong case for the position that symptom changes may be quite independent of insight in that they may be removed without the necessity of insight[35] and that, in some instances, insight *follows* rather than precedes symptom removal.[36] The latter point, as Saslow notes, had already been recognized by some psychoanalysts (Alexander and French). They found:

> that changed behavior on the part of the patients they were working with led to less frequent repression of early events in the person's life. Significant traumatic memories were recovered better, and various kinds of dream material of significance to the early history were communicated for the first time, only after new and improved behavior had already occurred.[37]

Saslow concludes that the evidence from behavioral modification data indicates there is no reason "to think that the sequence of insight (into early problems and early difficulties) and behavior alteration *must always go* in one direction."[38]

Jay Haley, standing rather obliquely to both conditioning therapy and "insight" therapy, interprets the changes in therapy to be the product of a forced choice imposed on the patient in a game of studied "one-upmanship." The therapist, functioning in terms of a quasi-hypnotic role, confronts the patient with an ambiguous and paradoxical situation which forces him, in order to maintain the "illusion" of his autonomy, to choose the direction posed for him by the therapist.[39] Haley has isolated one of the important "game" elements in psychotherapy. Whether it is as neat as he pictures it, or, pictured correctly, whether it is to be employed as unqualifiedly in the manipulative way he construes it is conjectural. One is tempted to speculate that Haley's approach would be effective as long as a Parent-Child complementarity existed (using Berne's terms),[40] but that movement toward Adult-Adult therapeutic objectives would backfire.

It should be remembered that the question of the manipulative role of the therapist must be related to the immaturity,
dysfunctionality or pathology (however conceived) of the
patient. In a classical sense, the therapist implicitly is often in
the position of standing *in loco parentis* for a patient who has
lacunae in this area. He wants and often needs guidance, modeling, values, perspective. More and more it will be seen that
the morality of the therapist will be construed not in terms of
manipulation or no manipulation, but whether the manipulation is *necessary* (in view of the patient's needs and abilities),
whether it moves the patient toward greater *autonomy, health,*
and *freedom,* or whether it moves him toward dependency
and automatism; whether it removes symptoms at the possible
expense of the total self, or whether the *total life needs* are
kept in perspective in the process of symptom removal.

It is not a question of manipulative influence (every parent
must operate this way in the early life of his infant). It *is* a
question of whether the parent-infant paradigm is admissible,
and if so, a question of *responsible* influence, the degree to
which this influence is used to move "infantile residues" in a
patient toward adult autonomy, and the degree to which the
patient's autonomy is included in the process *at the earliest
possible moment.* Any therapist who ignores these elements is
irresponsibly playing with human life, no matter how altru-
istically he rationalizes his behavior. If Berne and Rogers are
right, it may be that no person is so void of adult, autonomous
potentials that he needs to be manipulated like an infant.
Shostrom contrasts the "actualizer" with the manipulator.
This is a concept much more appropriate to the therapist and
expresses what we have been emphasizing.[41]

SYMPTOM REMOVAL VS. CHANGED LIFE

Psychotherapists may be divided into roughly two major
groups in terms of therapy goals:

1. Those who see their task essentially one of removing
obstacles to health and symptomatic evidence of these, and

2. Those who see a further task—that of helping the patient

move toward meaningful values which go beyond mere "health" values (e.g., "self-actualization"). Here the issue is more a question of how broadly one interprets the term "health"—as narrowly as "symptom-free" or as expansively as to include one's total value system, world outlook, religion, etc.

In Shostrom and Knapp's terms, this is the issue of "cure" versus "growth."[42] Rieff makes a strong case for the notion that Freud's objective was not even cure but rather a higher level of analytic consciousness: "Freud's object was personal capacity, not general cure. Moreover, one will not lead to the other. Cure is a religious category."[43] Rieff recognizes this as a source of confusion for Freud's followers and a major reason for the defections of Jung and Adler.

Tillich assessed this as an unresolved problem in Freud—a dichotomy between his ontological and existential position; namely, that Freud was seeking to cure people of disease while not believing a cure was possible in theory: "In popular terms, his pessimism about the nature of man and his optimism about the possibilities of healing were never reconciled in him or in his followers."[44]

This crucial problem of the *goals* of psychotherapy is, as several such writers have seen, the point at which psychotherapy and religion merge in their confrontation of the phenomenon of man. It is possible that Freud (as Rieff interprets him) and the action therapists (with some exceptions, e.g., Perry London)[45]—in their resistance to "depth" and "value" implications of symptoms—are more honest in clarifying the limits and limitations of psychotherapy than the neo-Freudians and humanistic therapists who would intrude a religious perspective (even if a humanistic one) and value emphasis; especially when these go beyond clearing the way for health to spell out what health should include (e.g., meaning, self-actualization, etc.).

There is, however, a fair case to be made for the point that health *is* more than the absence of symptoms and does have a *plus* quality however difficult of definition or description.

One can sense the subtle inclusion of this plus quality in Nunberg's description of the aim of psychoanalysis as: "A simultaneous increase in the mobility of the id, in the tolerance of the superego, and in the synthesizing power of the ego."[46] Ego-superego synthesizing presumably includes goals of community which in some measure transcend sheer id fulfillment. It is not likely that therapists of any persuasion are going to be able to eliminate this issue, however they define it.

Shostrom and Knapp see a demonstrable value shift in most advanced patients in therapy. They write:

> What are some of the value orientations that distinguish the advanced patient from the beginning patient? In general it may be said that he is more time competent (Tc) and is thus capable of more effective use of his time, being primarily present oriented versus past or future oriented. He is more inner-directed (I) and thus able to direct more effectively his own life, relatively independent (compared to the beginning group) cf peer pressures and urgings. He tends toward greater affirmation of self-actualizing values (SAV), behaves with less rigid adherence to his own particular set of values (Ex), shows greater sensitivity of responsiveness to his own needs and feelings (Fr), displays greater freedom to react with spontaneity (S) and shows more self-acceptance even with his own weaknesses (Sa). Persons more advanced in therapy tend to view man's essential nature in constructive terms (as contrasted with a view of man as "essentially evil") (Nc); they have a greater capacity for transcending dichotomies (Sy), are better able to accept aggressive tendencies rather than repressing or denying them (A), and are more capable of developing intimate contacts (C). In short, they are depicted as more self-actualized.[47]

One can scarcely avoid the aspiring, open-ended and growth-oriented quality of the adjectives describing these value shifts in therapy. At the same time, if such expectations are applied to the action therapies (conditioning) it is dubious whether mere symptom removal can be equated with such criteria.

VALUES IN THERAPY

Such an effort to explore empirically value shifts in therapy exposes a vast and new area of research. It has long been the

concern of people going to therapists that they might lose
their identity. The disavowal of this by the therapist who
claims neutrality and the objective of simply helping the person achieve a better balance among the resources already
resident in himself has not always been convincing, nor has
research into what happens in therapy borne out the picture
of a neutral therapist respecting values.[48]

One study by Rosenbaum *et al.* indicated that failure to
progress in therapy was related to religious belief, indicating
that the more religous patients were less likely to benefit from
psychotherapy.[49] As Glad intimates, it is possible that the
hiatus between the values of the religious patient and many
an agnostic therapist might account for this, and he conjec-
tures whether "a therapist with a religious value system might
be much more effective for such people."[50]

Glad has emphasized the fact that "psychotherapy theory
is essentially a value system"[51] and that "each theory is a
value system about the nature of personal maturity."[52] His
studies make a fair case for the position that the values and
goals of the therapist have a great deal to do with the values
and goals ultimately adopted by the patient in the course of
therapy. This position is being borne out again and again in
various studies.[53]

As Glad makes clear, one therapist might hold as a goal
for therapy (especially the Sullivanian interpersonal therapist)
adjustment to the social milieu, while a Rankian therapist
might emphasize the unique *creativity* and acceptance of difference by the patient and the acceptance of guilt over failure
to conform to social expectations. Maximizing different values
would lead to different therapeutic objectives.

We have already mentioned the "selective empathy" dem-
onstrated in the client-centered therapist. As for the psychoanalyst's efforts to preclude value influence of his patient (by
means of his own analysis, etc.), J. R. Reid comments:

> However well-analyzed the analyst himself may be and
> however well he may understand his own unconscious,
> and finally, however well his analytical incognito is pro-
> tected by transforming himself, for therapeutic purposes,

into a kind of impersonal radar screen that will help the patient orient himself socially in relation to his own unconscious projections, however well these conditions are fulfilled and maintained in the analytic situation, it remains undeniable that in a hundred ways, both gross and subtle, the analyst will inevitably show his moral colors and what side he takes on many a controversial issue about the rights and wrongs, the goods and evils, in some problematic area under analysis.[54]

It is widely held now that the evidence supports the unavoidable value-influence of the therapist. The degree to which he accepts, articulates, and heartily espouses or minimizes this aspect of his influence becomes now the critical issue, to be returned to in connection with the *content* aspect of guilt therapy.

The foregoing general remarks about current therapy, sketchy as they are, serve to elaborate the complexities of any effort to carry on the therapy of guilt. The following attempt to present a more concrete approach to the problem of guilt therapy should be considered qualified by the previous remarks and with full awareness of the rapidity of current change in this field.

Special Elements in the Therapy of Guilt

Therapist Values and Objectives

The first responsibility of the therapist is an articulation, at least for himself, of his own values and value goals respecting his world view, the therapeutic process, and his particular responsibilities to any patient who comes.

That the blind don't lead the blind very well has been philosophy enough to make wise the analysis of the analyst. Yet it goes farther than this. The therapist whose *only* objective is "freeing the patient" may be unleashing irresponsibility. On the other side, the therapist confident that he knows the values a patient needs for living *his* (the patient's) life, and prepared to play the role of conditioning authority, should be sure that he has worked through the implications of the world he is imposing, the meaning for him of human freedom and the motivation of his possible manipulative proclivities. There is an awesome irreversibility in some "utopias," Russian, Skinnerian, or otherwise. The degree to which a therapist envisions freedom in relation to responsibility to a world, as well as to the patient's self, will have much to do with the direction toward which he works in therapy: freedom *to* choose, or freedom *from* choice.

The therapist may frankly avow only a *health* ethic in relation to therapy attempting to isolate the problem at hand as a surgeon attempts to decontaminate the scene of the operation from outside influences, or he may believe that this is an unrealizable objective, that the values are internal to the operation and not separable from health.

Whether he restricts his objectives to an isolated health ethic, working for internal balance and function (e.g., making a neurotic thief a "healthy" thief), or whether his value goals for the patient reach beyond the patient to a wider frame of reference and objectives, he must also decide whether he will attempt openly to manipulate, condition, or "one-up" his patient in the desirable direction, or will seek instead to minimize this aspect of his influence, democratizing the problem of goal choice.

How the therapist looks at guilt will itself heavily determine his approach. Whether he sees all guilt as pathological and something to be eradicated, whether he sees it in its varied nuances and with varying relevance for health, or whether he sees its absence as a dysfunction to be corrected will influence his goals. He may take an existentialist approach and hold guilt to be an unavoidable *given* for all men, or he may assume the stance of some conditioning therapists who consider it an unwarrantable fiction. In one case, he will take the guilt seriously and communicate with the patient about it; in the other case, he will handle it as a trivial irrelevance.

Therapy involves a constant interplay of sensitized listening, diagnostic projection and "fitting," of awareness of relational processes and changes and of therapist influence on these as he reacts to the patient. These may be subtle and out of focus at any particular time, but they seem to be present to some degree in any therapeutic process, even if attention is essentially directed to congruent participation, as in Rogerian therapy. As this process goes on, the therapist, like an ice-skating teacher, will be making some tentative observations— at first usually to himself—about where this particular person needs most to change: whether he takes the social curves too fast, lacks moral leg muscle, can't see the holes in the ice, needs to revise his skating rules to fit the rink he is on, needs his self-confidence heightened, requires temporary support, etc.

Therapist Attitude

The single most critical factor in relating to the guilt-laden person is *acceptance*. For real or neurotic reasons, or *both*, he cannot accept himself, he is suffering from a sense of alienation and lack of love or punitive rejection from his own super-ego. Probably the most commonly approved canon of therapy is acceptance of the patient *as he is*, without judgmentalism on the one hand or tacit approval on the other, with the possible specialized and highly structured variants on this mentioned in Chapter V concerning therapy of the sociopath. (Although many will come seeking judgmentalism or approval from the therapist, wanting to play games of "Kick me" or "If it weren't for mother," etc.) This acceptance means an openness to the person, whatever he presents. It means recognition of his feeling and sensitivity to its meaning for him, whether this is a profound depression, an anguished neurotic self-laceration, or a realistic assessment of values violated or unfulfilled. Theologically and psychiatrically this is a *sine qua non* of a therapeutic relationship.

Carol Murphy reminds us that a sinner "is a very lonely man." She asserts that the job of the therapist is not to reinforce the rejection of one part of the personality by the other but to seek to establish an "unalienable relationship" in which the rejecting and rejected aspects of the self may be looked at, understood, and more meaningfully integrated or changed. She would "shift the question of sin from being solely a matter of conscience to being a question of isolation or alienation," and adds:

Is there not a morbid or neurotic kind of conscience? Mowrer would say "No," if by neurotic conscience is meant one that is "too strict" and must be mollified by psychoanalysis. But I believe a definition of a morbid conscience can be made in the light of the preceding description of the role of alienation. The distinction between morbid and healthy conscience is not between strict or lenient but between *rejecting* and *accepting*. For example, a morbid conscience will consider sexuality as such to be sinful—it thereby rejects and alienates a portion of the personality. The healthy conscience will accept sexuality as good and holy and therefore to be handled only with reverence. Obviously, this may result in a stricter standard of conduct than the conscience which devalues the source of sexual expression. A healthy conscience, in short, may often say "No" to many kinds of action, but never to persons.[55]

There is a danger of equating acceptance with approval. Some patients and counselees will so equate them. Only the subsequent therapy will clarify the distinction. The person in the company of a good therapist will feel he is being encouraged neither to "live it up" nor to "go on suffering because he ought to." He will sense that here is someone who will stand beside him, *with* him, in his very human dilemma and try to help him make sense out of all the conflict and find ways to live more fully and less destructively toward himself and others.

Carol Murphy, again, writes:

A rejecting society will produce a rejecting conscience, and this will in turn be rejected by the neurotic person, whose unconscious will contain both the rejected impulse (as Freud thought) and the rejected conscience (as Mowrer thinks). The proportion between these two repressions will vary among different types of disturbance, and, just as repressed impulses tend to be irrational and childish, so the repressed conscience will tend to be an irrational and childish taboo. As an extreme example of alienation, take the case of a woman, committed to a mental hospital, who had tried to kill herself and her children. Her children died, but she herself survived, with total amnesia for the tragedy. She had rejected the fact of what she had done and therefore also rejected her sense of guilt. But it was her guilt that made the

memory of the deed unbearable. Mowrer would say that
a Freudian therapist would try to minimize her guilt
feeling in order to restore her memory, while the religious therapist should enable her to acknowledge and
confess her guilt openly. The important thing to bear
in mind, however, is that the patient cannot endure her
memory until she can endure her guilt, and she cannot
bear this unless she is assured of real acceptance on the
therapist's part. Whatever may be the place of atonement and restitution in therapy, this basic acceptance
comes *first* before confession is possible.[56]

All else that happens in the therapy of guilt is subordinate
to the accepting relationship. It is possible for a person to
eliminate a guilt feeling by going through an act of restitution—paying a price. A therapist may sit as a judge and encourage such behavior. There is much of this in the approach
Mowrer emphasizes. Restitution is not trivial, it is critical.
But it leaves the transaction on a payment level unless it is
the free loving act of an accepted person.

As E. M. Pattison has shown, payment to *win* love from another whom one has wronged, from one's parents, or from
one's superego is, if it is simply a mechanical rite, a neurotic
mechanism based on "the punitive model of forgiveness, which
is not forgiveness at all, but only the payment of a price for
narcissistic gratification."[57]

Even in successful cases of reduction of guilt feeling, this
may lead to lowered self-esteem, the sense that one's acceptance and hence *worth* lies not in the affirmation of one's
being *as he is* but in one's capacity to bribe a favorable response out of another. Love becomes no longer a basic condition of life that is a *gift* but an exaction from life which one
extorts. It is probably the fact that the neurotic was never so
accepted and loved as an infant, so that he developed the
neurotic stratagems which get him social approval but not
genuine self-love. *Any therapy that sees his problem only in
terms of social approval or good behavior or sides with his
superego and assumes that the internalized parent was "right"
will never get to the deep hostility and ambivalence nor beyond it to the unloved rebelling self which is waiting to be*

loved unconditionally and independently of jumping through moral hoops for its raisin.

In its most elaborate caricature this is just what *religious sacrifice* represents: placation of the angry god. It is what Pfister refers to as a *synthetic* (as opposed to analytic) solution of guilt.[58] It is irrationally ritualistic, and it reveals the thinly veiled conviction that God's love is not a reliable *given* in life but something extorted or manipulated—that his true nature is wrath and that he needs to be cajoled if we are to escape his cruelty. One finds this attitude not only toward the god but also his father in the religious neurotic.

Perhaps only on the basis of a dramatic history such as religion has provided us can a sufficient magnification of this subtle guilt problem enable us to see its ramifications. Ritualistic religion may be, as Freud saw, simply a neurosis writ large.

E. M. Pattison makes the helpful suggestion that guilt may be understood on the basis of two models, a *punitive* model and a *reconciliation* model.[59] You don't *buy* a parent's love through capitulation or self-punishment. Yet this is what the infant and the neurotic are often convinced of: *Love is the result of my being good enough. Yet psychologically the opposite is true. I can only be "good enough" if I am loved enough.* The whole issue of law and gospel is caught up in these alternatives. That they are not totally separable is known to both theologians and psychologists, but how they interact is not so widely known, and certainly many details remain a mystery.

When love is not experienced as *gift*—i.e., when one is never loved *in spite of* one's wrong, a tremendous ambivalence develops, a secret repressed hate and a fearful, abject and dependent "love." This is the "goodness" that secretly always wants to be something else. It is grudging goodness that cannot endure someone else's not being "stuck" with its limitations: "Everyone *has* to conform because *I* have to." This is neurotic goodness. It is joyless, or whatever "joy" it knows is the product of a secret pride and self-righteousness. It is legalism, and it spawns legalism, conformity, and manipulative goodness. It is not free. It fears and resents freedom.

What genuine guilt (remorse) cares about is that *a personal relationship has been broken, love has been wronged.* The sadness that ensues is normal and natural, as when a friend has gone or been injured. What *neurotic* guilt cares about is that the self may be punished or love must be recovered. It is narcissistic and concerned about this punishment more than reconciliation with the other.

Acceptance is the affirmation to another that there is love which is given in spite of guilt, unqualifiedly. The result is that the person feels that there *is* hope of human relationship and even of self-acceptance, so now he can face his guilt in all its rawness and seek to do something about it.

It is after this primary acceptance has been proffered by the therapist and experienced by the counselee that the more difficult work of guilt therapy begins.

The process of receptiveness on the part of the therapist evokes more openness in the counselee. He normally moves into further catharsis of feelings, confession, exploration, penitential and restitutional affirmations and a sense of relief, whether in a religious or a secular setting. If some such sequence does *not* occur, this in itself is a signal to the therapist.

The therapist will be alert to whether the counselee tends to be preoccupied with egocentric anxieties and guilt avoidance through superego stratagems (pseudoconfession, compulsive-ritualistic confession, "masochistic surrender," "scapegoating," "atonement," "undoing," "sacrifice," "reaction formation," rationalizations, etc.).[60] He will note to what extent there is a genuine concern for the values involved, whether the conflict is largely conscious or contaminated by much symptomatic material that seems unconscious. Is this person preoccupied with simply fearful inhibiting or is there a spontaneous quality about the moral feeling? Are the concerns marked by automatic self-punishment and self-contempt or self-toleration? Is the mood one of heteronomous servility or autonomous control? Does the effort to deal with guilt realistically and restitutionally bring relief or does the guilt continue as a kind of free-floating entity? If so, this may indicate either a displacement, a pseudoconfession that will respond to continued exploration, or it may reflect deeply entrenched neurotic guilt that demands extensive therapy.

It is this judgment which is most important. The therapist will probably in most instances be able to encourage the genuine efforts to do the "grief work" of guilt and help the person to some restored self-esteem through confession and restitution. If, however, he is convinced that this is essentially a repetitious neurotic pattern, he will refuse to be continually drawn into this artificial relief cycle and will proceed (if prepared by training) to challenge the neurotic defenses and move ahead in therapy, or (if not prepared by training) will refer the individual to appropriate intensive help.

Superego Dimensions

In making the above judgment, a guilt-value "diagnosis" may be in order in terms of the superego dimensions articulated in Chapter IV. Such a "diagnosis" would rarely be conveyed, at least at the outset, to the patient or client, but it would help to establish some of the goals of therapy.

Feeling

Is the effect appropriate? Does the "punishment" fit the "crime"? Is this a person who is never right, sternly self-rejecting and neurotically demanding? Or one who, confused by an identity crisis, is seeking a new value orientation, or one who has impulsively jeopardized important values and is searching for acceptance, forgiveness, renewed relationship?

Is the feeling depressed, with a mood of apathetic self-dejection, little or no outgoingness, and reality-oriented but overactive self-hate? Is it related to repressive object loss? Is it marked by suicidal hints or references?

Or perhaps this is an anxious, voluble, and compulsive speaker, perfectionistic in his goals, overassiduous in his ambitions and discontent with any of his achievements, fatefully searching the future and preparing for it, incapable of relaxing, or, of enjoying deserved rest, inflexible in application.

Is this a person capable of affirming his good points or

successes even as he speaks unhappily of this present condition? Is his feeling alleviated by self-reflection about its appropriateness or inappropriateness, marked by authenticity and an outgoing concern that is not too obviously a reaction formation or a social role? How does the feeling fit the *content* of thought?

Such questions are not intended to be prescriptive or exhaustive but *suggestive* concerning the feeling level of self-judgment: inexorable, oppressive, and unhopeful in the depressive; rigid, unspontaneous, ambivalent, automatic, and future-scanning in the compulsive; ineffective, absent, or manufactured in the sociopathic personality; appropriate, congruent, and painfully present but productive of change and motivationally significant in the normal. Obviously these are extremes, purer in form than the usual fact, but suggestive of a dimension. They help the therapist determine priorities, enable him to assist the counselee to sort out his genuine guilt from neurotic feelings, and to evaluate, and act on, new insights and authentic imperatives.

Content

The point at which guilt therapy relates to *content,* or the substantives of the superego system, is currently a focus of theoretical conflict. It promises to continue to be as long as the future remains open for man.

If we speak of these substantives as *values,* we normally mean some judgment about what is "good, right and desirable," with a certain degree of "commitment" to the judgment.[61] This degree of commitment obviously varies tremendously from value to value and from time to time regarding the same value. (This is why we have distinguished between feeling and content.) In fact, our attitude toward some values may be that they are good for all men *but* ourselves, or that they should be desirable *for others.* Weisman emphasizes the importance of early evaluation of a patient's perspective re values: "To understand the nature of a patient's conflicts, the analyst must appreciate his style of life and his singular set of acceptances and ideals."[62]

These values or judgments about social reality, which reflect the accumulated experience not so much of our own ego (though it is a factor) as that of the race before us and the culture of our childhood, reflect and structure our own identity and, depending upon the extent of our integral identification with them, serve as cues for feeling and action responses. They are the substantives to which the sense of "ought" attaches in varying intensities.

Cumming and Cumming write:

> Values are an intrinsic feature of all societies; they are learned in the give-and-take of interaction and they shape our goals and give us hope, solace and a meaning for life. In spite of the fact that they are part of the warp and woof of everyday life, however, they are abstract, symbolic, and almost uncodified. In fact, in homogeneous societies, an oblique reminder, such as "it's not cricket," is sufficient to remind us that a norm has been infringed; the norm itself need not be specified.[63]

This observation concerning what is "cricket" derives its importance from the fact that such a phrase evokes the *feeling* response of superego without specifying, but only implying, a *content* which, articulated, might in itself carry little weight.

Most therapists tend to agree that dealing with values in therapy is unavoidable. The *way in which* the values are dealt with is the focal issue, an issue most sharply put in terms of the question: *To what extent, if ever, does the therapist intervene with his own values?* Various answers are reflected in different psychotherapeutic schools. We shall try to represent a few samples:

1. *Maintain Maximum Neutrality.* This is the classical psychoanalytic approach. Heinz Hartmann reflects it in this remark: "While *the analyst learns to keep his personal values from intruding into the analytic situation,* this does not generally lead to the detachment of his interest from moral concerns."[64] And again, "The analyst, even more than the non-analyst, will be wary of claiming the authority of psychoanalysis for what he realizes to be his personal moral codes."[65]

Weisman, in like vein, writes: "Indoctrination is anti-analytic, although axiological objectives are often served by semi-analytic methods."[66]

This very effort to maintain an analytic neutrality about value persuasion is often misunderstood and brings the analyst under frequent criticism. One reason, of course, is that by helping the patient trace the genesis of his value system (Weisman writes: "The analytic adventure in self-exploration includes questioning the very motives and acceptances, values and ideals, that the patient seems to regard as reliable guides to an uncertain world. Because what is accepted as real may be simply unchallenged illusion, his respectable codes of 'oughts and shoulds,' duties and obligations, may conceal self-deception, defeat, and surrender of responsibility."[68]) it is possible for the patient to assume the artificiality of his values or to assume the analyst's neutrality is a secret connivance with his violation of those values. This may or may not be the case. As analysts are quick to point out, it is a fallacy to substitute causal explanations for moral justifications.[67]

Carl Rogers, while of a phenomenological persuasion theoretically, and differing markedly from the psychoanalytic technique, reflects a similar concern for neutrality on the part of the therapist concerning the counselee's value content. His articulated concern is that the therapist reflect, and help the client reach his *own* awareness of, the existing value conflicts and choices he has to make, with every confidence that the client can and should make these decisions out of his own resources. He envisions the role of the therapist to be more that of a participating liberator rather than a teacher —one who releases inner values rather than imparts them from without.[69]

2. *Assert a Moral Code.* Such an approach (typical of traditional authoritative and priestly counseling) may take a stance like that of O. H. Mowrer, who seems at many points to assume some universal status, if not parochial legalism, regarding existing Western ethics.[70] In the effort to emphasize the significance of real guilt as a factor in psychopathology and to redress what he believes is a psychoanalytic bias

toward id-release, he gets into a rather uncritical box. It is one that precludes criticism of possible unhealthy superego dynamics or contents and that favors an alliance of the therapist with the patient's values, with very little insight into the question of their genesis or appropriateness.

Other therapists reflect a similar approach concerning therapist intervention and intrusion of his own values, while assuming different stances regarding existing cultural mores and/or the patient's identification with these.

Albert Ellis feels free to assert what he believes is his scientific or rational morality and to educate the patient out of his "superstitions" into an enlightened position vis-à-vis sex mores, God, etc. He does this bluntly, didactically, and authoritatively.[71]

M. Brewster Smith presses for an explicit avowal of values by the therapist. He believes that one can leave mental health neither to the Rousseau-like view that benign inner forces will unfold themselves nor to the view that the existing cultural mores are ultimate. He believes the psychologist has a place in the battle with the humanist and the theologian and should be explicit about the values that he believes are health-supporting, even though the existing state of the discipline does not permit him to claim finality for these. He does not see the therapist as a fanatical persuader but as a responsible participant:

> When his role as ... therapist vests him with more direct and personal responsibility for goal setting, he will not hesitate to act in terms of his convictions about what is desirable in the relationship, and of the best knowledge and wisdom he can muster. But he *will seek to move such relationships in the direction of increasing the responsibility of the other party for choosing his own goals.*[72]

Perry London, quite explicitly, sees the psychotherapist in the role of a "secular priest" whose job it is to hold out to his patient a "secular salvation" in view of what he considers to be the abdication of this arena by the religionist:[73]

Then he would fulfill a role more like that of a priest than of any other professional, but he would be a secular priest, whose justifications are not in a theology revealed from heaven, but one discovered or intimated in the laboratory. The genesis of his consideration would then be the nature of man, and his gospel the fulfillment of that nature, its decalogue the medium of behavior—and all preached from the altar of science.[74]

The largess with which some of these views dispatch the agonizing history of morals and imply a "scientific" way out of the value dilemma is startling and reveals, as nothing else, the metaphysical restrictions of many behavioral scientists and the possible *un*readiness of many a therapist to clarify the guilt problem for his patient.

3. *Make Qualified Affirmations.* C. M. Lowe recognizes the dilemma of values in therapy and the unavoidable immersion of the therapist in particular value commitments. Rather than imply that there is an ethic that is derivable from science, he opts for the frank recognition of value biases and open avowal of therapist identifications:

> We would suggest that, as psychologists familiarize themselves with the value orientation under which they operate, they confess their philosophic biases and then turn those biases to fullest advantage by being of professional assistance to the special interest groups with which their values coincide. . . .
> We conclude that differences in value orientations cannot be resolved, each orientation having adherents whose beliefs should be respected. We suggest that each counselor have an understanding of the values both of himself and others and that his values be known by all who are personally affected by his professional behavior.[75]

The above seems to this author a more honest position for the psychotherapist, and a frank recognition of his existential involvement in the whole human value predicament. In view of the fact that research indicates movement toward therapist values on the part of patients who improve,[76] it would seem fair to let a would-be patient choose a therapist who agrees somewhat about the direction his life ought to take. This is certainly more to this author's value taste than trying to brainwash a patient into the belief that the therapist's values are scientifically derived and their incorporation the *sine qua non* of mental health, much as both might like this to be the case.

Leary's,[77] Perl's,[78] and Shostrom's[79] emphases on elaborating the polarities and patterns of life in such a way that a balancing response in the counselee is evoked are reminiscent of Jung's concepts of personality. They suggest a balancing, offsetting role of the therapist regarding values, the exposing of eccentricities and distortions in such a way that life is experienced as a shift within a spectrum rather than choice of total disjunctives. This may be more realistic than some of the more dramatic goal-choosing that often plays into megalomanic tendencies or immobilizes the person by the extremities demanded.

Donald Glad makes a strong case for recognition of the long-range goals and values that seem indigenous to particular therapeutic systems and for the interdependence of theoretical goals and technique that make it possible to derive subsidiary decisions regarding intervention from the long-range goals. With these concerns in mind, he analyzes four therapeutic approaches (psychoanalytic, interpersonal, dynamic-relationship, and client-centered). He defends the position that patients reflect the thinking of their therapists concerning their problems and adjust in the therapist's idiom:

1. Psychoanalysts enhance a genital-parental integration by selective response to the sexual and transference symbolic aspects of the personality.
2. Client-centered therapists promote emotional understanding, self-acceptance and awareness of others by providing emotional empathy to the client.
3. Interpersonal therapists facilitate skill in social relations, consensual validity and interpersonal security by responding to such interpersonal aspects of the client.
4. Dynamic relationship therapists nurture pride and satisfaction in one's unique autonomy by accepting and encouraging the uniting and separating gestures of the client.[80]

The foregoing options (by no means comprehensive) suggest the wide variety of basic issues that emerge the minute one faces guilt therapy in respect to content. The general direction they point to indicates the possible dangers inherent in a therapist who is too self-confident of the impeccability of his value goals. The issue of whether therapists, wittingly or unwittingly, manipulate patients toward their values seems no longer to be the question. It is widely agreed that most of them do. The real problem is what these values are, how clearly they are stipulated, the degree to which the patient's health and autonomy are related to other values, and *the extent to which the patient's identity is put before the coercive enthusiasm of the therapist.*

As psychologists continue to explore and discuss the various value positions they hold, it will hopefully become more evident which orientations allow the optimum balance between the individual's health-autonomy-identity-fulfillment and society's rights (that is, the recognition of the conditions which allow health-autonomy-identity-fulfillment for all individuals). A pathology of whole societies is conceivable, as Fromm has so well argued,[81] and a perpetual function of thought will be to measure the conditions that may make for harmony in a particular historicogeographical era against long-range potentials and the good of men yet to come. (This issue is sharpened by the assertion of some writers that the therapist should represent the norms of the community [even if not his own] on behalf of reflecting "reality" to the patient: "While professionals often disagree with many of the norms of the larger society, it seems more ethical to equip the patient for the general culture rather than to teach him eccentric or minority values."[82]) It, at this level, becomes an issue of theological and philosophical proportions, invoking the most diverse and extensive myths and symbols by which man lives and has lived. Because the best intentioned of such efforts is always parochial in its parameters to some degree, Tillich has emphasized the critical importance of what he calls "the Protestant principle" as a means by which structures are constantly challenged in the name of optimal process and new structures.[83]

All individuals experience some value conflict. The degree to which such conflict is considered normal or neurotic is to some extent itself a value conflict among (hopefully) normal therapists. How much should the individual's values serve his own needs and how much should they serve society's (or the therapist's)? As we tried to show in previous chapters, pathology may lie in either the individual or social extreme. Buhler points to the *enormous range of choices* in competing values and the *rapidity of change* as sources of value conflict and calls for a more inclusive value theory.[84] Obviously this age-old hope is not about to be quickly or finally realized, no matter what scientific resources are brought to bear upon it. As Matson sees so well, science itself may pose a bigger problem than it solves.[85]

The necessity of values as binding goals in an individual's identity is well established by writers such as Buhler, Lynd, Erikson, Wheelis, etc.[86] The long thread from private need on out through society's (mankind's) needs to religious faith of some sort (whether secularly or ecclesiastically conceived) is an unbroken (though occasionally unseen) one.

Philip Rieff[87] has distinguished between the therapeutic vs. the salvatory nature of therapy. The former is an effort to clarify the magnitude of the problems and to delimit the scope of the values being served by the counseling, attempting to restrict the limits of the problem in the name of functional efficiency and realistic modesty—much as a surgeon (however much he may hope for and strive for the total health of his patient) may feel obligated to restrict himself to the minimal field of a patient's diseased organ. The analogy suggests the appropriate parallel: the surgeon is most dangerous who believes naïvely that a little tinkering or excision will solve everything or that "health" is reducible to his canons of function alone.

Buhler formulates the general principles that "most modern psychotherapists have in common":

1. Present-day psychotherapists strive to help the patient to a better understanding of himself in order to help him to *face and accept reality* as it is and to *master his own life* better than he did before;

2. Most modern psychotherapists want the patient *to work through his problems by himself* as much as possible, with the therapist being mostly an intermediary in the process of self-understanding, rather than a teacher or a knowing authority;

3. The present-day therapists base their work mostly on their *personal relationship* with the patient and on the *interpretations* that they give to the patient's motives, development, affects, and behavior;

4. The therapist's training, experience, and personality that determine this procedure may vary greatly. But regardless of their theoretical bias and their therapeutic approach, they will have to help the patients to cope with their lives, with the goal of *functioning better than before*, of *mastering their lives*, and of conceiving of *life as worthwhile*.[88]

The same author concludes her survey with the assertion that value intervention appears warranted in the following five situations (we condense):

1. When a patient has seemingly successfully worked through his problems and when he should begin to bring acknowledged new values to materialization. . . .

2. Situations in which the analyst would undermine his own *integrity* and *feeling of self-esteem* if he avoided taking a stand in certain matters that concern the welfare of mankind and of society. . . .

3. A . . . situation . . . in which a *change of direction* of the patient's goals or behavior seem acutely indicated. . . .

4. A . . . situation . . . may arise in connection with choices that have to be made. . . .

5. The situation, which is bound to arise specifically in our work with children and adolescents or younger and inexperienced people, a situation where a therapist switches knowingly or unknowingly to the role of *educator* . . . where he has to *introduce and to emphasize values* that the less mature person has not as yet conceived.[89]

The author makes plain that the above list is not presented as a system, nor is it intended to reflect completeness.

One may in all fairness pose the question of therapist readiness for dealing with all value orientations. A man might feel quite ready to attack or seek to guide a patient through complex religious problems (with which he was quite unfamiliar) who at the same time would be quite critical of a colleague doing heart surgery whose training had been almost entirely in obstetrics. Glad and others raise this as an important question in dealing with values.[90] It is heightened by the growing acceptance of manipulation (We call attention again to the fact that this is an unfortunate term. It may be accurate as it applies to some therapies. Probably, however, most therapists in using it would qualify it somewhat to approach Shostrom's term "actualizor."[91]) as a *raison d'être* of therapy and the growing sense that it is *only* a question of *what kind* and toward what goals.[92]

A focal problem for any therapist who works with patient values is the *maintaining of patient self-esteem* at the same time that guilt-producing material is being explored.[93] There is a tendency for such a patient to settle into neurotic patterns of self-disparagement, depression, and hostility. One of the points at which a therapist may feel obligated to intervene didactically is where he finds the value contents *preclude* self-esteem, where, for example, the religious adherent has so focused on his *sinfulness* that he has failed to accept the grace note of *forgiveness and love* indigenous to his own faith and to incorporate these as a basis for self-love. Glad calls our attention in this regard to some important questions H. S. Sullivan proposes the interviewer must keep in mind. The answers to these form guidelines for the therapist in this touchy area:

> What does the interviewee esteem and what does he disparage about himself?
> To what experiences is the patient's self-esteem particularly vulnerable?
> What are the characteristic "righting movements"—security operations—which appear after the patient has been discomposed?
> How great are the interviewee's reserves of security? . . .
> *How well is the person's life justified?* Can he express estimable things about himself? Has he tried actively

to accomplish worthwhile purposes? Does he have secret shames and regrets?[94]

While these are essentially *feeling* elements they govern
greatly the therapeutic assessment of value content and especially those *ways* and *times* in which reconsideration of
these becomes appropriate.

Sullivan's sensitivity is especially pertinent to the problem
of reexamination of content (which is tantamount to questioning the wisdom of identification figures) in such a way as
to avoid attacking or overwhelming. He suggests for example:
"I have a vague feeling that some people might doubt the
utility to you of the care with which your parents, and particularly your mother, saw to it that you didn't learn to dance,
etc."[95] (This as an alternative to "Your mother really loused
you up!")

To repeat, one cannot introduce processes of value change
and criticism aimed at the establishment or integration of contents without menacing self-esteem and risking exacerbation
of guilt. Therefore knowing how to maintain self-esteem and
even to make it a companion motivator in value therapy is
imperative.[96] This is where Carl Rogers' sensitivity to patient
autonomy in the determination of the direction and rate of
change highly commends his counseling theory.

Space does not permit the adequate exploration of the many
nuances that pervade individual superego content problems
and their unique organizational patterns. The scholar interested in pursuing these factors in detail will find a valuable
treatment in Heinz Hartmann's *Psychoanalysis and Moral
Values.*[97] Hartmann's discussion of the *genetic determinants
of values,* of *value agglutination* and *irradiation,* of *therapist
involvement in the valuing process,* and of the *normalcy of
the guilt dynamic* are imperative reading for the guilt therapist. Hartmann, speaking of the clinical assessment of moral
stability, indicates that in addition to the possible emergence
of earlier superego elements during regressive processes, it is
necessary to assay the following:

> There are different degrees of reliance on the accepted
> codes that have to be considered; also differences as to

the degree to which principles tend to be carried out in action. It is most important to evaluate the moral equilibrium as to its reversibility or nonreversibility and its vulnerability in the interplay with other factors. Practically, and theoretically, the most relevant aspect is the constancy or dependability of morality vis-à-vis reality, mostly social reality, and vis-à-vis opposing pressures from within. That is its "autonomy," which is in some ways comparable in its definition to the secondary autonomy of the ego.[98]

Hartmann alludes to what he calls "the transvaluation of moral values" which occurs in everyone's development.[99] It is the process that Piaget has explored so fully in his studies of the movement from a familial to a peer code. The degree to which this normal process can be built upon and extended in therapy may well relate to the extent to which ego processes have matured or have been too heavily dedicated to defensive or rigid structuring. Hartmann speaks of the "generalization," "formalization," and "integration" of moral values as processes in which ego-superego functions merge, adding:

One can say, I think, that in what one may call the moral "codes" the influence both of the superego and of the ego, particularly of the integrating and differentiating functions of the ego, are traceable. Thus we will expect to find in every system of moral values elements which directly correspond to the pressures and to the aims of the superego, and others that show the influence of the ego.[100]

The psychotherapist is faced with the problem of helping the patient achieve a balance between the *integrative* function of the ego as well as its *adaptive* function. This means a knowledge not only of the general culture and the private environment of the patient's early life but also of the genesis of his particular interaction with these and the unique way he has adapted in accordance with the vicissitudes of his instinctual development. He needs to know how the patient reacts when he faces conflicting instinctual, superego, and external demands. He must help the patient explore and find what values are real *for him* and mobilize the energies to act on them. He will tend to focus the patient's attention on the

positive ego gains inherent in his values rather than on the
obligatory superego aspects, helping him to see how his values
serve his needs and fulfillment rather than concentrating
only on the ways they oppose these.

Hartmann reminds us that, though the psychoanalyst may
put the patient's health first *in therapy*, he need not consider
psychological health the highest ethical value in a scale of
values and he should not *equate* health values and moral
values, even though these may and do overlap at many
points.[101] He will also have to guard against the patient's
identifying with his efforts toward moral neutrality (vis-à-vis
the patient) as a paradigm for the patient's attitude toward
all values.

Timing

In a major sense the problem of treatment of superego
timing in therapy is an aspect of the general problem of ego
integration and adaptation. It is brought to attention, however, because it may be timing of the *application* of values to
behavior, or the *cycle* of the guilt dynamic, rather than the
inappropriateness or unrealism of the values which accounts
for dysfunction.

Patients may develop a cycle of behavior in which the value
system tends to be brought into decisions essentially only *after*
the fact. That is, the subject concentrates so exclusively on his
pleasure needs that other values which may contradict these
and even serve his long-range interests are not given consideration but only come in as instigators of self-punishment
in a *post hoc* fashion. Many a counselee is quite blind to such
a cycle and, however repetitive his "impulsive" behavior, may
fail to find the time elements and sequences consciously until
they are brought to his attention by the therapist. Even then
they will seem unrealistic to him unless the therapist calls
repeatedly to his attention, especially in more vital transference relationships, the way the timing operates.

The reader will recall our discussion of Joseph Finney's
concept of timing in Chapter IV as he compares it with the
feedback cycle. The guilt process may be effectively intact,

but not operative as an adequately effective warning system, only as a punishment system. Such a dynamic, as Freud has shown, may actually be associated with criminality.

Children who have not had satisfying training in experiencing delayed gratification or whose waiting was rarely rewarded, or who often experienced long-delayed punishment, may experience confusion or repression around timing.

Kurz and his colleagues made a study of the relationship between the ability to make judgments about the passage of time and the capacity for impulse control as measured by the Rorschach test. They found that persons with low M and high sum C responses "cannot tolerate delays" and find waiting uncomfortable and time dragging.[102] It is conceivable that such persons tend toward the sociopathic end of the spectrum and that, where guilt processes are operative, even the prospective pain or anxiety regarding future guilt or punishment are not sufficient to overcome the need for tension release or even add to it.

Redl emphasizes the fact that any effort to appeal to superego values as a basis of motivation in the case of a person with a weak ego tends to evoke heightened anxiety and panic. He stresses the importance of strengthening the ego of the patient before attempting superego therapy.

Redl and Wineman write:

> The normal reaction to guilt would be along the lines of *insight* into the nature of the offense, *self-recrimination to the point of stir-up into change of self, gestures of appeasement toward victims* of the guilty action, *attempts at restitution of damage,* some *marginal defensive actions like avoidance of guilt-raising persons or places,* and, most of all, if intimate ties are in the picture, *a need to confess and "settle" bad feelings with people* who count in one's life or their substitute.[103]

The above is a helpful capsule guide for the therapist in exploring and suggesting ways for a guilty person to set ego goals for the resolution of guilt and guilt-producing behavior. Yet, as Redl points out, such measures are often inappropriable by the person whose socialization patterns are disturbed or undeveloped.

Lacking such ego resources, Redl and Wineman found children whose guilt was aroused resorting to sulking silence and hatred, aggression, irritation, and scapegoating. He found it necessary to help the children improve their reality testing and discrimination in order to discover their previously unnoticed position as "links in a causal chain" or the "fast evaporation rate" of their memory for such participation.[104]

In discussing the time factor, Redl and Wineman emphasize two elements in their children's constant "war" with time: "One is their great difficulty in making any distinction between what we might crudely term the 'subjective experience' and the 'objective measurement' of time,"[105] the other concerns what the authors call a "severe disturbance of these children's relation to the future, including their own."[106] Deferring something in time was experienced not as delay but outright refusal. The children "had not developed much of a realistic concept of 'themselves in the future' so that there was little to appeal to, one way or another. What 'ego ideals' they were swaggering around with, if existent at all, were totally delusionary."[107]

Control

Control is essentially identified with the "power function" of the ego. Redl and Wineman write: "The task of an ego that is in good working order is not only to 'know' what reality demands are, but also to exert some force, so as to influence behavioral strivings in line with that knowledge."[108]

The ego psychologists, discussed earlier in Chapter IV, see behavior as the amalgam of *all* the structural aspects of the personality. The therapist therefore will be interested in the degree to which dysfunctional behavior is a reflection of imbalance in the direction of id or superego domination, ego weakness, rigid defensiveness, value inadequacies, poor superego signaling, etc. He will be interested in the degree of frustration tolerance the person is capable of, the point where it breaks down and the response of the individual when it does. He will want to know how the patient copes, what defenses are employed, whether the person retreats, fights, or

seeks sympathy, and whether he experiences repeated failure
and lowered self-esteem or whether he rigidly inhibits satisfaction of needs and ends up with guilt aroused by hostility over
his frustration.

Control may be partly effected and self-esteem maintained
or restored by use of typical operations which Weisman calls
"superego strategies," routine devices for allaying guilt, shame,
and depression:

> For such purposes, patients make use of superego strate-
> gies, some unwittingly, others at self-conscious, ritualistic
> lengths. A few of these strategies are *confession, mas-
> ochistic surrender, scapegoating, atonement, undoing,
> sacrifice, reaction formation,* and *excuses, apologies,* and
> *justification.*[109]

The therapist will be alert to analyze such strategies to try
to determine their relative effectiveness, significance, and salu-
tary or deleterious quality. He will seek to help the patient
develop perspective about them and replace or deploy them
by means that heighten his autonomy, authenticity, responsibility, and fulfillment.

Control may be functionally bound to a few models. That
is, the person may function well in the presence of persons
who act as surrogate parents but be almost helplessly the
victim of impulse where such are not present. This is sometimes spoken of as "model rigidity."[110]

The therapist who attempts a neutral attitude toward patient values in the attempt to affirm patient autonomy may
find the patient "interpreting" this neutrality as a model and
identify with what (he thinks) is the analyst's indifference to
acting out of impulses contrary to his own (the patient's)
values. He may also resist what he thinks are therapist values
in a rebellious acting out. Either way the therapist will find it
appropriate to interpret when he feels the patient can handle it.

A person already guilt-laden does not respond well to more
guilt should a counselor appeal to his conscience. He may
acquiesce in a self-punitive identification with a punitive
counselor, but it is ego-deflating, reduces his sense of auton-

omy and self-esteem, and mobilizes neurotic defenses. It is far better to try to help him bind his values to his wishes and needs, helping him to see ego gains in new behavior patterns. Thus Bellak and Small write:

> The consensus of learning theorists is that motivation is most successful when it is positive. Drastic forms of punishment tend to spread effects over the entire learning situation which produce inhibition and unresponsiveness. This finding is of significance in psychotherapy where *we rarely attempt alleviation of symptoms by appealing to the superego for punitive motivation, but rather to the ego for more positive realistic satisfactions.*[111]

It is extremely important when trying to help a patient with control problems to help him break the cycle which, because it keeps repeating itself, lowers his self-esteem. If the therapist can help the patient explore concrete life situations or habit patterns and find new ways of *acting* which can be practiced and which are viable enough to be achievable, taking into account the patient's abilities, success in such areas may become a powerful reinforcer.

The author recalls a suicidal and depressed woman who was quite intelligent but very self-deprecatory. She felt worthless and that life was useless. She had a very modest desk job, was divorced, and had to support three children. She had only a high school education and felt hopeless about the future. After considerable therapy, since she was quite able and energetic it was suggested that she might think of a night-school class as a way to better her possibilities. This was seized upon and became a first step toward radical change. Fearful at first and unsure of her abilities, a few good grades reinforced her self-confidence and enhanced her confidence in therapy and the exploration of new options.

Often people involved in sexual acting out are seeking reinforcement for self-esteem rather than just a sexual experience. If their interpersonal values are such that guilt ensues, the behavior actually lowers the self-esteem and the guilt necessitates the search for a new episode. Helping them explore and accept their positive transference feelings and also to find that these may be compared and related to their sexual feelings, and helping them discover the *fact* of their existing controls in a scarce therapeutic relationship, may enable them to discriminate nuances of feeling that were previously fused and confusing guilt-arousing.

Bellak and Small mention ways of increasing self-esteem to heighten control by suggesting that the counselor may point out the positive features in the person's life (these should be well-established ones drawn from the patient's own reports). This includes recognition of accomplishments such as the patient's ability to tolerate many difficulties and that he has managed to do something *rational* about his problem. Without being phony or Pollyannaish it is possible to convey the message: "Your situation is understood" and, implicitly, "You have basic resources and can be helped to utilize these."[112]

Tarachow makes the point that the process of analysis itself confronts the patient with a new kind of value system. He experiences the fact that what he thought was all bad in himself may be experienced as worthful to the analyst: "Just as religion must offer its avenues for aggression, so must psychoanalysis. The patient has one set of values: we must offer him another. We value his aggression and his love."[113] This can be effected by focusing on milder or socially approved expressions of threatening drives.

Some patients become very distressed about the possibility of losing control and acting out some aggressive or sexual fantasy. Weisman points out that the fantasies may be interpreted to the patient as his attempts "to maintain control" rather than indications that he is about to act on them: "Thus the analyst helps the frightened patient to summon up personal responsibility by recognizing that his apparent fears are expressions of his capacity to control."[114]

Weisman further suggests that in the case of the obsessional patient who is afraid of losing control and acting on some destructive fantasy that "it is altogether proper to point out that this phantasy is itself a protection against feelings he fears even more—tenderness and love."[115]

The more a patient's problem tends to shift from overcontrol toward sociopathic undercontrol of impulse, the more likely it is that one is facing a problem of lack of identity, model absence, and lack of clarity about roles and commitment to these. To the extent that such is the case, the therapist may need to function more authoritatively in limit setting, reflecting reality gains, and functioning as an ego model. He will try to relieve hostility without letting himself or society become unchallenged scapegoats and restricting himself only to the most crucial areas in limit-setting (to mobilize the least rebellion).[116]

Eric Berne's treatment verbiage may be helpful in enabling a patient to develop some ego distance from his problem and therapeutic perspective. Where he can visualize his impulsiveness as "child" and his lacunae in role identification in terms of a distorted, absent, or maladjusted "parent" as well as see his "child's" magical fantasies, he has some chance of gaining an "adult" stance toward these.[117]

It should be remembered that what may be an *apparent lack of control* can be content poverty. To this end, Cumming and Cumming write:

> Since values are formed through the same processes in which skills are learned, those who lack skills are likely to have confused, disorganized and amorphous norms and values. In fact, in at least a third of mental hospital admissions, we find an association between skill deficiency and value deficiency, inasmuch as there is a group of patients marked by occupational failure, unstable marriage, and petty, often impulsive, crime. Such patients are often misunderstood; for example, they are described as "unable to postpone gratification." The ability to postpone gratification, however, depends on a clear hierarchy of values; that is, giving up a present gratification in order to have something more valuable in the future requires that we be able to choose between objects or goals. Amorphous, disorganized value structures do not give us this ability. Impulsiveness in persons from deprived backgrounds may more profitably be thought of as an ego deficiency based on inability to hierarchize values than as either excessive strength of id impulse or weakness of superego.[118]

Pastoral Counseling of Guilt

The church in its efforts to counsel the guilty person has gone through a cycle. At first it resisted secular therapy as something alien. Then it was seduced to it as the answer to everything. Lately, a more sophisticated generation of pastoral counselors is emerging which is growing in its ability to live "on the boundary" and to draw from, and hopefully contribute to, both the secular and religious community.

We have not chosen to deal here extensively with the peculiarly religious therapy of guilt: examination of conscience, repentance, confession, request for forgiveness, penance, restitution, etc. These are important in the handling of real guilt insofar as they take it seriously, deal genuinely with estrangement and reconciliation, and work with the parishioner. These are dealt with in the classical literature of the church and in many helpful current books available such as those by Sherrill,[119] Roberts,[120] Tournier,[121] McKenzie,[122] Belgum,[123] Drakeford,[124] etc., and it is assumed the reader will avail himself of these. It is *not* assumed that this area is unimportant.

Real guilt demands and deserves being faced, shared, and made up for insofar as possible. Any estrangement from life's reality, or breaking of the bonds of its wholeness, is sin, and it is always toward God and man, even if the only man "around" is one's self. Manipulating self-esteem or attacking guilt symptoms, without also dealing with *existential* guilt, is irresponsible.

The minister, as he comes to a greater sensitivity about neurotic guilt and neurotic religion is, or should be, more able to do honest business with it and also to be more ready to take seriously genuine guilt and contrition when he sees it. He will refer more wisely when he refers, and he will deal more meaningfully with those he should continue to counsel. Moreover, he will be prepared to relate in a team fashion with a psychiatrist or psychologist.

As we have tried to indicate, the difficult problem is the mixture of real and neurotic guilt. Sometimes the unresolved real guilt inflames the neurosis and almost always the inverse is true.

The pastor will be alerted to neurotic possibilities if he finds that helping a person face his real guilt (and helping him *find* it, often beneath some sham guilt) is not effective, but discovers the parishioner can't accept his forgiveness, or that it has only a momentary effect. He will note whether the person is preoccupied with punitive rather than reconciliation aspects of religion, is self-contemptuous in his relation to God, uses religion as essentially a pacifier for narcissistic fear, sees the gospel only as sin machinery or God as a defense against his own sexuality or aggressiveness or is occupied with pseudo-confession. All these suggest the need of intensive therapeutic work that may go beyond the average pastor's expertise.

It is *existential* guilt that the pastor should always be able to help the parishioner with—enabling him through acceptance and a similar theological frame of reference to interpret his sense of guilt regarding his life, fulfillment, self-actualization, and faithfulness to God's creative purpose. The more sensitive he is as a counselor, the more ready he will be to help the parishioner disentangle neurotic projections from authentic aspects of religious experience. They will be able to explore together the ways in which even restitution or "good works," that attempt quite concretely to make up for or undo wrongs to fellow humans, may be mechanical and egocentric.

The pastor familiar with guilt dynamics will be able to help people explore and understand the phenomenon of forgiveness and being forgiven. Even this, as Pattison so well articulates, has its pathology. Forgiveness, he says, may be construed and carried out as a "duty" done in pride and condescension. Again, it may be too eagerly extended by a masochistic person who denies or minimizes the other person's guilt.[125]

In his work with the parishioner, the pastor can help him interpret the existential situation in such a way that he sees God's purpose and concern is not the mechanical resolution of guilt-feelings or playing little moralistic games with his creatures, but the exciting creative business of *living* and *loving*. He will help him see that God has already affirmed his forgiveness and reconciling love and that the job of the guilty person is to get beyond his anxious game of trying to win acceptance or achieve some pseudoinnocence and to "accept his acceptance," accept the fact of his creaturely guilt and its forgiveness, and get on with productive participation in the work of the world. As Fromm sees so well, much guilt is a pseudoguilt, a kind of displacement of one's real guilt over lack of productivity, a failure of responsibility to participate in creativity.[126]

The most important task of the pastoral counselor, perhaps of any counselor, is to help the counselee shift his concern from guilt feelings to what he genuinely *is* guilty of and to help the person explore and find ways of making value decisions about his life and acting on these. This means accepting responsibility for his life and authentically affirming it, moving toward self-actualization. This does not deny guilt, it accepts its reality, and redirects it toward channels that produce more lasting self-esteem and minimize not only the tendency toward, but the necessity for, self-punishment.

In the effort to achieve the above, the therapist may find that neurotic stratagems are too deeply embedded. The religious symbols may be captive to strongly reinforced guilt dynamics, defense mechanisms, and superego strategies—even the "confession" may be phony, the concern for love a reaction formation, and efforts at restitution manipulative. He may have to refer to a more skillful therapist who can deal with the neurotic structures.

The secular therapist, on the other hand, may find that he is unprepared to deal with the symbolism and frame of reference of a person's life without jeopardizing the patient's identity. He may solicit a pastoral counselor's help in existential aspects of guilt or refer the patient for continued counseling on noogenic levels more familiar to another counselor and the patient.

Chapter VIII

GUILT AND THE RELIGION OF LOVE

If you know something, then you know something about God.

—*Paul Tillich*[1]

Up to this point, we have concerned ourselves chiefly with those elements which may run across many cultures—especially those in which the family approaches the autonomy it has enjoyed in Western civilization. We have attempted to deal with the structures and processes through which the dynamics of guilt operate and to explore the manner in which these interact with the superego somewhat independently of the particularities of its contents. We have tried to emphasize the intrapsychic functions as much as possible and to show the way in which the familial enviroment is incorporated into these varying processes, dependent upon both parental uniqueness and individual projections. We have also sought to elaborate normal patterns and the pathological syndromes that may emerge from these interactions, as well as some treatment approaches appropriate.

We wish now to face a few issues that have been critical in both the formation and treatment of guilt in the entire sweep of the Judeo-Christian tradition and its current contributions to the human scene. This may seem too vast a scope to encompass in a chapter or a book. It is; yet epic views must be *more* rather than *less* attempted as life's complexities and dissociative forces accumulate. The likelihood of public error seems to this author to be greatest when, in the name of whatever sophisticated tentativeness, individuals timidly hold back their private integrations of data.

Whether or not some scholars have been correct in relating the word "religion" to the Latin root *religare*—binding together—the attempt is indicative that religion for mankind has long been associated with a critical ego function. It is this function which above all others is indigenous to the survival potential of the ego, vis-à-vis reality—namely, its *binding capacity*.

Freud, in spite of his view of religion as a mass neurosis, gave reluctant recognition to its potential for binding anxiety for mankind.

> Nor may we allow ourselves to be misled by our own judgments concerning the value of any of these religious or philosophical systems or of these ideals; whether we look upon them as the highest achievement of the human mind, or whether we deplore them as fallacies, one must acknowledge that where they exist, and especially where they are in the ascendant, they testify to a high level of civilization.[2]

However one evaluates it, there is much to support the notion that the ego devoid of some deep (articulated or unarticulated) religious perspective is given to panic or depressive despair in moments of ontological reflection. Progoff makes the point that religion is a dominant factor in social cohesion.[3] As Paul Tillich put it: "Finite being includes courage, but it can not maintain courage against the ultimate threat of nonbeing. It needs a basis for ultimate courage."[4] Courage need not demand security or life. It does want death to be *meaningful*.

The title of this chapter was chosen deliberately in the face of current eagerness on the part of many theologians to disavow "religion." To say this is not to ignore the weight of Bonhoeffer's assertions about "mankind come of age"[5] nor to discount much of the healthy insight that such concern entails. It is, however, a necessary recognition that what goes under the rubric of "religion" historically is critical to any dis-

cussion of guilt. It is also a personal caveat: the author does
not believe religion is a "totally" removable organ from the
human social body. It is disguisable, modifiable, capable of
displacement and distortion, but it is more like lung or brain
tissue than it is like an appendix or even a limb. Its *total*
excision means the death of man as a spiritual being.

To say this is to mean by "religion" two elemental things:
(1) a center of valuing (that is, that value—God, god, gods—
by which all others are measured and to which ultimately
they are conceived to be subject) and (2) that integrative
view, perspective, or explanation which (for the person or
persons, privately or corporately) "binds together" the world.
(Loder has a stimulating discussion of the binding capacity of
internal images. He writes: "Through an internally 'conceived'
concrete conformation of sensory-motor and intrapsychic stimuli (the image), there is created for consciousness an internalized essentially private, pattern of symbols, pictures, sounds
and sensations of all varieties. It is this partially 'open' incom-
municable image of one's self in the world that integrates
one's personal past, his present environment, and his intention
into a single moment of understanding."[6]) This may be as
distortedly broad as the Communist or Nazi ideology; it may
be as varied as a Buddhist, Christian, or other (including scientific) world view and centering of values. But man will be
informed by myth and ritual and symbol as long as he confronts history, within and without; even if it is an inverted
religion of existential atheism where the ego has *become* god,
creating worlds seriatim, moment by moment. That man is
most deluded about religion who thinks he lives without it.
He has simply repressed the reality of his finitude and ultimate dependency.

Teilhard de Chardin espouses a Logos-like principle in his
Omega point which informs and structures the vast evolutionary processes of life. He writes:

> Neither in the play of its elemental activities, which can
> only be set in motion by the hope of an "imperishable";
> nor in the play of its collective affinities, which require
> for their coalescence the action of a conquering love,

can reflective life continue to function and to progress unless, above it, there is a pole which is supreme in attraction and consistence. By its very structure the noosphere could not close itself either individually or socially in any way save under the influence of the center we have called Omega.[7]

The superego becomes the dynamic point of impingement of this structuring Word on the self. Through its internalized images and vision of the world it provides a monadology for the self as an existing *part* as it appreciates its connectedness to the system-gestalt of the universe. Here the overagainstness of the All is experienced and must be affirmed or denied by the ego.

The Judeo-Christian religious tradition has been germinal in a positive *and* a negative way in both the formulation and the treatment of guilt. This tradition has been that of a *familial* religion (patriarchal, father-son, holy mother, etc.). It has been interfabricated with intimacy, tenderness, wrath, punishment, acceptance, rejection, filial love, and concern. In both its highest extremes and most degenerate excesses, it reflects the optimal and the minimal in human health and sickness as these express themselves in family process. This is supremely evident in its handling of guilt.

This author concurs with Freud's *psychological* premise in his book *The Future of an Illusion*[8] that religion is essentially a projection onto the cosmos of familial structure, that God is projected father (psychologically), and that this basis of trust is the sustaining, binding meaning that makes religion crucial to man. It is *not* agreed that this *explains away* God. (Cf. J. E. Loder, *op. cit.*, for an excellent discussion of Freud's efforts to reduce metaphysics to metapsychology.) It is perfectly possible that the way in which the intelligent power who is the Ground of Being made himself known, *revealed* himself, was by making man biologically dependent upon human parents and prone to such projection. Psychological explanation does not account for ontological reality, however much it may throw light on it. Freud's argument may as well be applied inversely, to the effect that his negative father feelings stimulated him to want to *eliminate* a cosmic father.

My concern here is not to attempt a religious apologetic. That has been done more adequately by others in other settings. It is articulated here to clarify the seriousness with which I take the religious symbolism and to make apparent my particular religious position. The author sees himself in the mainstream of the Judeo-Christian tradition and, incidentally, resistant to the superficial aspects of the current "God is dead" theology. The resistance arises from a conviction that this trend in theology (when it goes beyond a commentary on relevance to reach a symbolic and epistemological nihilism or reductionism) is an effort to *depersonalize* and *defamilialize* the theistic projections and symbols of the Judeo-Christian tradition in an effort to be more "scientific" and neutral in its conceptualizations. It is contended here that *exactly the opposite* occurs. That is, that the familial biological dependency of man, out of which his trust and his tendencies to project a cosmic parenting figure emerge, is exactly the "scientific" phenomenon (the *given* in our world) which irreducibly confronts us. It is the nature of the creative intelligence pervading all phenomena, and constitutes the sufficient symbolism by which man can meaningfully order his relationship to the cosmos, including other men.

It is also in my thinking the only symbolism that provides the polar meanings out of which man's own identity and the nature of a theology of sonship (e.g., Jesus as "a man for others") emerges. It is no accident of unsophistication, immaturity, or primitivity that such personal and familial symbols pervade the entire spectrum of the Judeo-Christian writings and traditions up until the last decade and that Jesus and the principal prophets resort to such symbolism in a repetitive way to convey the essence of their religious insights.

It is possible that the underlying and perhaps unconscious motivation for the "God is dead" theology is pride, man's continued infantile desire to replace the father (God) and to be *more* than son and creature and, further, extrapolation from the Oedipal aggression incident upon man's socialization —his murderous wish to eliminate the father as an obstacle to his incestuous fusion with nature (an escape from the anxiety of freedom) as he experiences such security in the mother figure. (This may be the symbolism of the angels who are placed by God to prevent Adam's return to paradise.)

This return to mother to escape reality (and father, god) is possible to conceive incestuously or idolatrously. The Biblical writers frequently equate idolatry and harlotry. In any case it is a "disobedient" regression from responsible mature growth.

Modern man's ego makes a binding effort to unite himself directly with reality (seen in reverse forms in his regression to orgiastic rites, chemical religions such as LSD, etc.) and represents a shortcut which would seek to leave out father as a necessary polar element in the male-female (androgynous) fundaments of self which constitute the irreducible minimum poles of complete personality.

These poles constitute in the father, on the one hand, the movement toward aggressive autonomy and actualization of potential, independent of the gestalt of existence and attempting to maximize uniqueness. In the "mother" pole is evident man's rootage in nature, his absolute dependence upon the processes of life which produced him and which nourish him, as well as recognition of the commonality of his existence with the rest of life which evokes tenderness and identification with suffering and helplessness. Without both of these elements of autonomy and dependence, he is less than fully human, and indeed it is these dynamic polarities which constitute his creativity and his possibility of true self- and other-consciousness.[9]

There is an interesting parallel in the dissolution of the early psychoanalytic triumvirate: Freud emphasized *sexual love* as the libidinous mortar of psychic reality which bound man together internally and also to external reality. Adler countered with the belief that man must recognize *power, strength,* the capacity for *autonomous individualism,* as this basic force. Jung insisted that both of these must be adjunctive to a more profound process of *individuation* and integration which works toward wholeness in the personality. So neither binding love nor differentiating power but *both*, cohering in a polar but dynamic continuum, constitute the total psychic reality. (The religious fervor of the disciples of these three men heightens the comparison.) The reader will recall our remarks about the power-love problem in superego development in Chapter III.

It is no accident that as man takes the computing machine as psychological model, reflecting more and more the machine-like nature of the world which he has invented, his theology at the same time mirrors a depersonalizing proclivity.

Some thinkers see the movement away from personalizing projections to be a healthy trend toward mature autonomy. This is true respecting impersonal phenomena. Yet psychiatry failed when it was impersonal with *people*. Our question is this: Is a universe that produces persons impersonal in its depths? Is it to be understood "impersonally"?

Fromm is Biblical in his contention that man *moves away* from incestuous mother-earth ties, by means of obedience to a patriarchal tribal god, and *toward* a status of autonomy in which he argues with his god, like an equal, and demands that God keep his covenants of justice. It describes the movement toward universalism, and away from fearful dependence toward psychological freedom, similar to the movement within the child toward adulthood.[10]

Fromm tells a Talmudic story of God's children arguing with him and defeating him, indicating their complete autonomy or at least equality, whereupon God smiles, adding, "My sons have defeated me." Fromm comments: "The very fact that man has made himself independent and does not need God any longer, the fact that having been defeated by man is precisely what pleases God."[11] That this religiopsychological movement warrants the abandonment of ontological religious claims is a different and much more complex question.

All of this, of course, comes down to the question whether reality itself is *personal* in *at least* the minimal human sense or whether to speak in such terms is itself a delusional or illusory extrapolation from the accident of personhood in the evolutionary process.

Teilhard de Chardin, in his book *The Phenomenon of Man,* after tracing the development of evolution as an emergence of consciousness ("a noogenesis rising upstream against the flow of entropy"),[12] says, "The only universe capable of containing the human person is an irreversibly 'personalizing' universe."[13] He makes bold to identify: "The palable influence on our world of *an other* and Supreme Someone . . . is not the Christian phenomenon, which rises upwards at the heart of the social phenomenon, precisely that?"[14] This is not a matter of logic alone but substantively a matter of faith, and we will leave it there.

Historically, the binding efforts of the human ego, as they have taken religious form, have moved in the arena of personal projections. God has been conceived in personal, essentially paternal terms, and the way in which man has related to him has tended to follow lines which correspond to his ego-superego relationship. These latter have been institutionalized and unconsciously projected in myth, rite, and theology.

Oscar Pfister, a student of Freud, himself a psychoanalyst and at the same time a Reformed pastor in Switzerland, has traced many of the nuances of this aspect of the Judeo-Christian tradition in his book *Christianity and Fear.*[15] In this work he has shown the way in which the mainstream of the Hebraic imagery concerning God was reflective of a fear-laden, child-parent, ego-superego relationship. This was a relationship in which acceptance and the possibility of trust in the powerful parent figure depended for the child (and subsequently for the believer) upon adequately satisfying the superego codes (parental expectations), and, when these were violated, making appropriate sacrifice or restitution and thus "synthetically" restoring the relationship.

Guilt in this context was a (negative) *raison d'être* of the religion and of the ritual and constituted the fear base that activated the need for the religion. It also provided the structure from which the ritualistic resolutions of guilt that dominated the religious approach to the deity emerged.

Pfister's work makes the point, not new in itself but psychologically put, that the significance of Jesus was to elaborate a new sense of relationship with the father-God by his evidencing and asserting the accepting love (*agapē*) of the deity toward man *independently of man's rituals or superego strategies aimed at overcoming the projected alienation.*

This constitutes recognition of the Christ event as *the cosmic enactment, in a paradigm sense, of the fundamental core reality upon which all subsequent healing and psychotherapeutic relationships rest: acceptance and affirmation of other life,* the proffering of loving concern that seeks to understand and help, independently of what, at first, the one who needs help can offer or do or be.

Pfister points out that this affirmation constitutes the *analytic* resolution of guilt for man which opens him to freedom, autonomy, and the kind of maturation which allowed the fulfillment of his potentials and the enrichment of his personal and social life. This religious event paved the road for the *normal* rather than the *neurotic* overcoming of guilt conflict, moving the issue onto the domain of love and freedom rather than fear and sacrifice. Man was to conceive himself as a forgiven and accepted child of God freed for fullness of self-realization and other-concern, whose guilt should thereby be turned to remorse for violating an accepting love, rather than a fearful anxiety in the expectation of primitive sadistic wrath. This cannot be stressed enough. It is the separation of normal and neurotic guilt for the first time in religious history in such a profound way (though this is foreshadowed in some of the prophets and writers like Hosea, etc.).

This "analytic" conception cuts through both the atonement theories which persevere in projecting a hateful vindictiveness onto God (in which Christ is a "sacrifice" to appease his anger) and also the kind of psychoanalytic critique made by Theodor Reik, namely, that the idealism is too high and that man, "the moral climber, "can only be rescued from a destructively extreme ethic ("The ardent love of virtue is as murderous as a fanatic hate of vice") *by lowering his ideals.*[16]

Pfister traces the way in which the hopeful and ego-supportive perspective of the Christian message was gradually displaced by a new legalism and a reassertion of a guilt-laden, fear-filled kind of expectation toward the creator and religious-ritualistic effort to manage this regression. Even in the efforts of the Reformers, he sees its continued activity and the failure of the church to fulfill the indigenous message that lay at the heart of its "good news."

Pfister, in his discussion of Luther, makes it plain that this first of the great Protestant Reformers did not escape from fear in his religious experience. As is widely known, his early years in the priesthood were filled with fearful experiences as was his childhood.[17] "Fear fantasies of the devil, of demons and of ghosts were part of his mental pabulum as a boy."[18]

Nevertheless, Luther achieved a great measure of success in overcoming fear in his experience of the significance of justification by faith, as set forth in the writings of the apostle Paul. Pfister writes:

> Solvents of fear in Luther were the feeling that he was in the hands of an unconditional and everlasting grace, triumphing over the continuing sinfulness of man; and, in connection with this feeling, the elimination of various compulsion-neurotic traits from his idea of the Deity, in which process the overemphasis made on the magical quality of the sacraments necessarily became somewhat weaker, while stereotyped rites ceased in prayer and liturgy. Fear was further alleviated by the belief in the anticipatory mercy of God and by the reliance upon his help in every distress, physical and spiritual, temporary and eternal. These elements are calculated to win love and consequently to overcome fear; but . . . they were balanced by the sinister characteristics attributed to God —the predestination which condemned the vast majority of mankind for all eternity, the small number of the elect, the power of the devil, and the horror of the last judgment and of hell. Most of the fear fantasies remained in force, and the same was true of the fear factor in symbolic actions and of the painful elements in Luther's theory of the sacraments, even where they had not yet received the sanction of the Church.[19]

Luther, according to Pfister, considered fear entirely normal and even necessary and regarded it as a significant part of education into religious belief, at least in the early years.

As for John Calvin, his system of fear repulsion depends entirely upon the grace of God as it is reflected in the doctrine of election; thus, Pfister indicates, Calvin goes one step farther than Luther in removing even the merit of fear as a condition for election and God's free grace.

Nevertheless, Calvin is not free from fear. Pfister speaks of "the diabolization of Calvin's idea of God, tracing it back to his relation with a tyrannical father—or rather to a projection into God of the characteristics which Calvin hated and feared in his father."[20]

Calvin does not fail to see God's grace and love, but it is an ambivalent sight:

> Calvin makes the fight for the honor of God the sum total of Christian duty, a psychologically necessary reaction to his secret diabolization of God. This action is an overcompensation, like, for example, hand-washing compulsions, fanatical truthfulness. It balances an impulse of an opposite character rejected by the conscience, in this instance, hate of his father.[21]

Pfister credited the Reformers with the replacement of the Roman Catholic legal relationship between God and man by a system of dogma which repelled fear through stressing the exclusive efficacy of the divine grace (to the exclusion of human merit achieved through good works in the form of faith, ritual, or charity). They rediscovered the vitality of personal faith in the intense experience of grace and love which for a time put an end to the Catholic fear-compulsion motif that prevailed.

It was not long until the Reformers, however, had reintroduced elements of fear into even the Protestant faith by virtue of the fact that they soon veered away from the freedom of faith and conscience and got to the place where they were substituting, in a sense, a new orthodoxy of the Bible instead of churchly power or papal authority. *The religion of love soon became the obsession again of a dogmatic kind of structure which made it a fear-producing process in the lives of many adherents.* Love became the victim of neurotic guilt.

Pfister symbolizes in his life the happy confluence of the authentic aspects of the Christian faith and the conceptual critique of psychoanalysis which permits the differentiation of normal and neurotic guilt. It is such a combination that enlivens a genuine concern for objective values optimal for human community, a genuineness and integrity freed of a fearful and stultifying subjugation either to parochial codes or conformist demands.

The Oxford scholar Roy S. Lee, in his book *Freud and Christianity*,[22] has called attention to the same issues that dominate Pfister's writing in a little different idiom. He points out that Christianity, as Jesus intended to convey it, is essentially an *ego religion* rather than a superego religion.

What does this mean? It means that in spite of the fact that the Judeo-Christian tradition has long allied itself with the guilt-oriented superego restraints against man's impulse life (which become codified and institutionalized in religious structures) in a real sense this is a violation of the much larger ramifications it should have for mankind. The best in this tradition has never allied itself solely with a code morality or a superego-oriented conception of man's relationship with God. Much attention is now being drawn to this matter in contextual and situational ethics.

Many aspects of the tradition emphasized the goodness and beauty of creation, unmodified by later strictures upon how it is to be utilized or enjoyed. There is a kind of joyous celebration in the creation and in man's instinctual life (such as his sexuality in The Song of Songs) which simply does not lend itself to the kind of asceticism which often has been attached to it by some obsessive-compulsive priests and scholars. It is a pre-Freudian recognition of the value of the *id*. Moreover, the highest prophetic note in the writings of the Old Testament and in the teachings of Jesus clearly transcend code strictures and obviously accept the code violator in the community of love as an effort to restore and retrieve the violator, even in the face of religious professionals who seek to impose the superego strictures of the religious apparatus as a vehicle of control and domination. The ego religion of Jesus is one that

expresses an inherent sacramentalism: the notion that *no as-*
pect of life, however humble, sensuous, biological or abstract,
is separate from the presence and purpose of God. The implicit corollary is that God sets himself over against no part of
life (of the id, ego, or world) which is in accord with the
constructive will of love and creative fulfillment.

Lee points out that the figure of Mother-Church may be
construed, as in the human instance, like a "good" or a "bad"
mother. The bad mother keeps her child dependent and helpless and protects it from reality. The good mother is, quite to
the contrary, a *bridge* to reality. She encourages the autonomy
and independence of the child. No conception of the church is
defensible which sets it over against God's creation.[23]

When Freud, in his preoccupation with the reestablishment
of man's wholeness, saw the avenue to such wholeness through
the attack on a religiosity (which in the Victorian era was an
ascetic repression of man's sexual and biological fulfillment)
he struck at this one-sidedness and dissociative, illness-induc-
ing "morality," and pejoratively labeled religion as a mass
neurosis because it set man over against himself. It opted for
one part of man at the expense of the rest, was a religion of
alienation while proclaiming the overcoming of alienation.
However he interpreted it, he was right in challenging this
distortion of religion and morals, and though he may have
fallen into a too narrow metaphysical critique of religion-as-
illusion, he was certainly truer to the inner core of the Judeo-
Christian tradition than was the one-sided Victorian domesti-
cation of the Christian institution of his day.

O. H. Mowrer, in his book *The Crisis in Psychiatry and*
Religion,[24] attacks both Freud and Protestantism together for
what he feels is a demonic defection from the code morality,
which Freud attacked and Protestantism challenged in the name
of a graceful God who accepts and loves even the most wayward sinner. *Mowrer is correct in lumping depth psychology*
and Protestantism together as forces that recognized that
man's deliverance lies not in the intensification of his guilt,
nor in increasing the strictures against his instinct, but rather
in the confidence that there is a loving acceptance that frees

man to explore and integrate the totality of his being: this by
bringing to bear both upon his obligations and upon his instinctual drives the integrative forces of hopefulness working
within himself and in a community of acceptance, which are
unable to operate in a context of alienation, conformity, and
fear. What is needed is not, as Mowrer would indicate, a new
legalism, but rather, a new integrative commitment (transference, faith).

Eckardt writes:

> Mowrer conceives the failings and aberrations of the
> psychoanalytic enterprise as a cancer that has permeated
> and made worthless the whole. His polemic zeal and
> doctrinaire presumptions conceal from him the truths
> that there is more than one way of adjudging guilt and
> of holding people responsible for their actions; that any
> human life involves an incredibly complicated melange
> of culpability and non-responsibility; that personality
> disturbance assumes an infinite variety of forms, and is
> much more than the paranoia which Mowrer over-
> stresses; and that, indeed, an unreserved and unilateral
> attribute of blame may compound, not responsibility,
> but its opposite.[25]

As the Christian faith, at its best, *and* psychoanalysis consistently have made clear, morality (which includes the total
human being and maximizes his potential for living in loving
community) depends much more radically upon his experience of and capacity for a relationship, and the ability to
project the experience of tender concern, than it does upon
the *content* of a rigid code. Indeed, a code that spells out in
detail the requirements and necessities of love *may* be most
lovelessly and ruthlessly applied, either to one's self or to
other persons. The Inquisition is a case in point. What is
needed is a liberated, autonomous love ethic which is humani-
tarian and aware of the existential need for decision, trust, and
faith. Such must be the visceral core of any ethic that involves
man's living with other men and sharing a concern for their
life alongside a concern for his own.

It is certainly conceivable, if not elementally apparent, that
there may be a code eventually arrived at which reflects em-

pirically the universal conditions under which maximum love and mutuality and potential fulfillment for all men are realizable. However, if such is ever developed, it will have to transcend the inner contradictions all codes to date have contained between law and spirit. (Bonhoeffer: "Wherever there is still a weighing up and calculation of guilt, there the sterile morality of self-justification usurps the place of the confession of guilt which is made in the presence of the form of Christ."[26]) Meanwhile, all men, religionists as well as behavioral scientists, must commit themselves to mutual exploration for the values that maximize man's humanity and for a cooperative effort to find ways to implement these on a personal and social scale in therapy and institution.

One of the most perplexing problems inherent in an effort to deal scientifically with the very human and subjective as well as mythical aspects of man (incorporated in his religio-ethical history and reflected in his ongoing existence in his superego content), is the clarification of those levels of his life which lend themselves to purely empirical research and those which demand a personalistic, often mythical and quasi-artistic, intuitive appropriation.

Joseph Royce has helpfully pointed out the *two directions* which man faces in this kind of struggle.[27] On the one side, he indicates, man's reflective functions and *signs* point ever more precisely and sharply toward a language and logical structures which can be related to empirical processes and carefully measured and detailed in the scientific fashion. At the same time, man faces outward toward a vast and mysterious complexity of *myths* and *symbols* which predated his scientific enthusiasms and methodologies and continue to inform the meaning of his life and even of his scientific venture. It is from this direction that many of his aspirational and commitment intentions evolve, and it is from this direction that perhaps most of his deep nuclear values take their strength. So long as man joins both these traditions and interests in himself, he cannot even scientifically consider himself from the purely empirical side, and he is always confronted by the fact that he *is* more than he can measure, and usually far more than he can master.

Tillich[28] has captured this distinction in his differentiation of the *essential* and *existential* aspects of man's life. Man is in his *existence* something that he, in his best moments, is aware he in his *essence* must not be. In its broadest form this is the arena of guilt. Theologically this difference has been explained in terms of "Fall." That is to say, man is estranged from God, and, whatever else this means, it means that he is estranged from his optimal self or the potential ideal which God intended in the creation. His self-realization in this context means movement toward God, toward the *ideal* and the *reality* which lie in him potentially. This is sometimes abetted and sometimes obfuscated through the medium of his human father, who becomes dynamically for him a model of God and his ego ideal.

The symbol *God*, psychologically, may be said to be *idealized father*. In other words a symbol for that *essential best* toward which life seems to be evolving and, in the family, that goal toward which the offspring dynamically move. The fact that this existential father is fallen too, and less than ideal, helps to account for the projection of this ideal out beyond him onto the cosmos. At any rate it is the theological dimension of man's movement toward his *essence*. It is the prescientific and symbolic form of the directional vector in an evolutionary process which Teilhard de Chardin would call the Omega point. In the Old Testament, and early development of the Judeo-Christian tradition, this symbol was invested with many of the wrathful narcissistic and destructive meanings that existential man's projections entailed. The emergence of the Christ figure in Jesus of Nazareth represents the theological corrective which the Christian church contends is the essence of what is meant by *essential* man: *man in whom the potential and the actual are fully integrated, whose male-female, penetrative-receptive, aggressive-tender impulses are healthfully balanced and whose identity is love.* Bonhoeffer recognizes this convergence of Christ and essential man in his remark: "What must be recognized as guilt is not the occasional lapse of error, or transgressions against an abstract law, but the defection from Christ, *from the form which was ready to take form in us and to lead us to our own true form.*"[29]

With this corrective to the essential nature of the *imago dei,* freeing it from the ambivalent projections of pre-Christian man, the symbol "God" for the first time became the true north for man's moral navigation. As Pfister showed, even this corrected symbol continues to be a symbol invested with neurotic meanings by alienated man. The history of the Christian church reflects the confusion as well as the healing potential of the Christian understanding of guilt. It is only with the advent of the insights of psychoanalysis that we now have adequate tools for the severing of the interwoven and confusing meanings of normal and neurotic guilt. Thus we see that *sign* and *symbol* are beginning to merge and that the common concerns of science and religion reveal themselves in the effort to bring together *essential* and *existential* man.

On the one side, there is a danger of religious pride. It is the danger that the theologian will authoritatively demand that *his* God symbol, as he understands it in Christ, is *unequivocally* normative and uncontaminated by ambivalence and hostility through his projections. All we can hope for is that the history of the church and his inner honesty will humble him to explore through the lens of science the elaborate glosses he has painted over his own psychodynamic behavior, religiously rationalized.

On the other side, the side of the scientist, is the danger of another kind of pride. This is the pride that refuses to humble itself to explore the meaning that mankind for millennia has projected into the symbol God and to comb patiently the many nuances that the religious community has found in the meaning of *agapē* as the loving conditions for community. There is the danger that some unphilosophical psychologists will use their scientific prestige to substantiate an unexamined ontology or theology in the name of a "scientific" ethic or that well-intentioned men will, in the name of community stability, promote a parochial ethic and a restrictive view of the human being which will fixate man at a narrow and conformist level of socialization.

Tillich most effectively illustrates the way in which the foregoing sign-symbol parameters of man's life are bound in religious experience. He writes, for example, of what happens to the term "father":

> Religious symbols are double-edged. They are directed toward the infinite which they symbolize *and* toward the finite through which they symbolize it. They force the infinite down to finitude and the finite up to infinity. They open the divine for the human and the human for the divine. For instance, if God is symbolized as "father," he is brought down to the human relationship of father and child but at the same time this human relationship is consecrated into a pattern of the divine-human relationship. If "Father" is employed as a symbol for God, fatherhood is seen in its theonomous, sacramental depth.[30]

A central problem in both the understanding and the therapy of guilt is the development of optimal *autonomy* in the person which is free of selfish indifference to others on the one hand and, on the other, an optimal sense of *responsibility* to the conditions of human community—a responsibility free of rigid conformity or subjection either to others or to the superego in a masochistic or self-hating way. Such responsibility ideally nevertheless will be deeply enough ingrained that the person will be a "man for others," that is, sacrifice his life for the community, if need be, rather than surrender his identity and self-esteem based on love. This is one of the central significations of the cross in Christianity and in the Judeo-Christian tradition is usually the ultimate test of "character" —yet it is a noncompulsive love, spontaneous and free, characterized not by enthusiasm for suffering but by ultimate concern that transcends suffering. This ideal balance of self-other is the zenith point of socialization and perhaps Teilhard de Chardin's Omega or end point toward which the creation groans. It is probably what Freud would have liked to see the ideal ego achieve and what Jung aspired toward in his concept of individuation. It is clear, however, that Freud, because he saw the individual so oppressed by civilization, became the champion *first* of the individual's fulfillment and seemed only secondarily interested in community. He would further have seen as illusory any nonrational commitment.

Weisman polarizes sickness and responsibility.[31] Yet he does this in a way that avoids the pejorative iconoclasm of writers like Szasz, Glasser, Mowrer, etc. It is both an approach sensitive to the demonic transpersonal dimension of evil and one that also avoids the dangers of legalism, self-righteousness, and conformist ethics. Weisman differentiates among the various dimensions of the existential event of sickness: "In the *impersonal* dimension, being sick means to have a *disease*. In the *interpersonal* dimension, being sick signifies a *crisis*. In the *intrapersonal* dimension, being sick is the result of *conflict*."[32] Weisman then goes on to add: "Even if his physical condition quickly returns to normal, being sick may provoke an interpersonal crisis and a persistent unresolved intrapersonal conflict."[33]

Weisman is sensitive to the existential ramifications of "sickness" and to the paraclinical as well as the clinical evidences of dysfunction:

> Sickness tends to take over the patient's entire existence. In the course of many progressive, unremitting, and demoralizing sicknesses, the dignity and privacy of *being responsible* is transmogrified into bare existence and impersonal survival. The diversified mental stage characteristic of the intrapersonal and interpersonal dimensions are reduced to whatever their equivalents are in the impersonal dimension. The sick person then becomes an object, to be manipulated by forces beyond comprehension and control. When this happens, motivated acts do not press for fulfillment, the inner spur to achievement becomes blunt, and the external world offers neither a residue of incentive nor a source of consolation.
>
> . . . The day by day reckoning of sickness is determined by the way it prevents healthy concordant conduct. The least part of the healing function of medicine is to restore only physical competence, without necessarily reinstating purposeful behavior; the largest—and most laudable—part is to help replenish and encourage the sense of being responsible. This aim is often overlooked because doctors, too, suffer from their own polarizations. As a result, one version of organic meaning, one kind of objective meaning, and one polarity of sickness are emphasized while the others are ignored or are assumed to be self-corrective. Physicians can not become so ab-

sorbed with visceral disorders that they ignore what people do with their healthy organs and functions, nor can psychoanalysts concentrate so exclusively upon skewed intrapersonal perspectives that they overlook the manifold interpersonal and impersonal forces that bear down upon any member of our society.[34]

These comments about the three dimensions of the sickness-responsibility continuum throw a light upon some of our earlier remarks concerning pathology. If one is concerned only with a narrow physical view of illness, then health becomes simply a matter of restoring physical function and freeing the individual of symptoms; if illness-health is conceived on a larger scale, then different expectations concerning responsibility arise.

Let us imagine, for example, an ambitious man whose ambition is built around grandiose self-demands and goals that lead to destructive competition with his peers with guilt anxiety over his efforts to eliminate them, all of which add up ultimately in his case to a massive heart attack. A person preoccupied only with the *physical* dimension of illness will be concerned with the repairing of the damaged heart.

If, on the other hand, one's conception of health is a total functionality of the psychophysical organism in its system interaction with the environment, then one may also be concerned to deal with the angry interactions with the other persons in the environment and the broken relationships that had a part in producing the heart attack and involved the person in real guilt. Such a therapist would go beyond physical repair to encourage the repair of the *estranged relationships* through confessional openness, penitential seeking of forgiveness, and efforts at reparation.

On a deeper level, if one were convinced that much that led to the situation involved *intrapsychic* conflict in the person— for example, neurotic guilt, low feelings of self-esteem, and compensatory grandiosity of goal-setting, he would not be content with either of the first two measures alone. Thus it may be seen that dysfunctionality in *any* of these aspects of the person's life constitutes a kind of sickness—disablement.

In the first case, responsibility on the part of the patient may involve turning his life over to the surgeon and passively awaiting his guidance and care—responsibly doing nothing but to acquiesce. This is somewhat similar psychologically to what the operant conditioners expect and require of patients.

In the second case, we can see something similar to what Mowrer, Glasser, Drakeford, and others are working toward, that is the repair of the *interpersonal* dysfunction and restoration of the social relationships. This is the assumption of responsibility for one's participation in the breakdown or estrangement and continuing involvement by restoring the relationship where possible. This deals with the real guilt and helps to restore self-esteem and reduce anxiety.

The third dimension, however, may still be left untouched. If the person has yet to deal with long-standing neurotic conflicts focusing on feelings of inadequacy, compulsive needs to redress those by grandiose attempts at success, etc., more is still needed before one would say this person is "healthy." The assumption of responsibility in this third instance may be more demanding than any of the previous instances. It means taking up the task of exploring one's life with a therapist and working at insight and control such that one may be freed from neurotic guilt and have his self-esteem heightened through transference interactions in the therapeutic relationship, clarification, analysis of defenses, setting of more realistic goals, and such other objectives of psychotherapy. Religion would go one step beyond and say that man is never whole until he is holistically integrated in the depths of his being with the core of reality and ground of his existence, God.

Heinemann's transient phrase "To be human is not a fact, but a task,"[35] captures the focus of both Christian and existentialist concern. However, much life is conceived as a "gift of grace" or an experience of "thrownness" and "Dasein," both traditions emphasize the common *task* element that devolves upon man. This *task* involves *authentic living, acceptance of the irrational dimension of life, facing the anxiety of non-being, and taking symbolism seriously.*[36] It is worthy of note that each of these involves an important personal aspect of superego dynamics and an appeal to *responsibility,* the responsibility to accept the human task, "to be human"—a task one is not likely to resonate to unless some real hope and some powerful modeling images penetrate despair and energize motivation. It is at this point that the integrative and transcendent myths and symbols of religion go beyond existential analysis and stimulate human hope.

The germ of this hope is contained in the Christ event which amplifies and elaborates the fundamental father-God ego ideal and reinforces the primitive mother-trust. It is the confrontation of primary anxiety by the possibility that behind and beneath all is *agapē* and that at some Omega point in the future this *agapē* will be even more fully realized. As Weisman puts it:

> In a sense, to believe in agape is to believe that, in spite of interminable discord and despair, no one is ever beyond redemption, and no dilemma is beyond hope. Conflict has a solution; paradoxes make sense; suffering has significance—particularly at those moments of bewilderment, loneliness, and irrationality when a drastic antidote is needed.[37]

The Christian faith at its best has always been existential, confronting man with his finitude, the reality of anxiety, the necessity for decision, the unavoidable fact of freedom which means he can choose to face life authentically or seek to escape it, but that he cannot *not* choose—that this is the worst of choices and that it will not protect him from the fact of death or despair. It also redeems him from his proclivity toward making a fetish of innocence or his own moralistic perfection his god. It turns his head from its drooping preoccupation with a misused past to face the possibilities of present and future.

In Elliott's words:

> What gives anxiety its bite is that the future is open and unknown, filled with possibility, decision and risk. What gives guilt its bite is that the past is closed and known, filled not with possibility but with the fixed tortuous path of decisions made.
> The past cannot be changed but it can be redeemed, it can become a gift rather than a curse to one in whom

grace works the power to accept his past as his own and himself as forgiven. The healing mediated by a pastor or helper to one burdened by guilt roots in the acceptance of guilt as real, leads often through the uncovering and confession of the real guilt concealed beneath the masks to which guilty feelings have attached, and leads to the knowledge that in true confession one has already received forgiveness. Such help can be mediated by a pastor or helper who knows that his own life stands under grace and forgiveness.[38]

One may discern in Judeo-Christian thought, as Pfister clarified it, a movement from guilt anxiety oriented around an emphasis on the fearful negative toward the positive, from essentially critical, restraining, punitive, and sadistic (superego-) elements of the relationship to God toward the essentially positive, affirming, and accepting (superego+) elements of the relationship. This is a trend that moves from a response to anxiety oriented around escape, cajoling, theologizing, sacrifice, and legalistic legerdemain (typical of fawning before a hated, terrifying, and whimsical parent) toward a response to anxiety oriented around something quite different: *authenticity*. Here the emphasis is on unrealized being, unfulfilled potential. *No longer is guilt a preoccupation with damnation from a projected tyrant. It is not even the threat of the loss of innocence or ensuing punishment or infractions of holy codes. It is rather concern to live up to the great potential given to one by the source of life. Responsibility is shifted from neurotic perfectionism to realistic creative participation in the expansion of love and growth of life.*

The first movement was one of terror before projected hatred. The second is one of love toward a projected love. Even negatively, the moral anxiety is in the second case a remorse over failing the love that has been given—it is awareness that one has lost or misused in the face of the fact of death so much potential for fulfillment and authentic life. As Buber put it, "Existential guilt occurs when someone breaks an order of the human world whose foundations he knows and recognizes as those of his own existence and of all common existence."[39]

Put another way, one may see this development as *from* an infantile concern about rejection and punishment by the parent (God) *toward* an awareness that the *motive* behind anxiety, behind discipline, even "punishment," behind preoccupation with values and guilt is not to terrify, destroy, or be cruel but is a *shaping process*—the end of which is love and the concern for full realization of potential.

Tillich speaks of the wrath of God as follows: "In showing any man the self-destructive consequences of his rejection of love, love acts according to its own nature, although he who experiences it does so as a threat to his being."[40] There is a *"theoprojective" reversal* in the fundamental view of the parent (projected-into-God) concept. No longer is the parent-God conceived as power which doles out love if you fearfully acquiesce, but as *love which is and grants power* and seeks its responsible expression in life. Discipline is to effect the restraint of power that is unloving, destructive. *Normal guilt (remorse) is this ontological psychic fact of creative internal restraint at work in the universe.*

The infant immaturely may say in effect, "I want love (lust, pleasure, irrespective of community) with no constraint, unrestrained by power (parent, God, rules)," and "I want power unrestrained by love (power that doesn't have to take account of others or their pleasure and fulfillment)." In a sense guilt anxiety is reality (God) saying to the infant: "It isn't that kind of universe—you have to have *both*. Integrate these in some kind of authentic whole—bring together the love and power of your id with the love and power acting through your superego introject (symbols of first community). This is *your* task as ego—to decide, choose and risk." This is the ego religion of which Lee speaks: not id *versus* superego, but id *and* superego in harmonious integration. This is fulfillment of the self in the context of fulfillment for all, autonomy in the context of freedom for all, love in the context of justice, therefore responsibility. Not "If I keep the rules, *then* I will win the favor of a tyrant," but "Since I am loved, therefore I will participate in the conditions of love."

The Christian religion at its best has been an ego support

(by way of sustaining hope, providing symbols capable of binding anxiety and providing noogenetic structures). At its worst, it has been an ego weakener (by disparaging instinct or uncritically reinforcing superego functions, however parochial or sadistic). New emphases in theology, reinforced by psychological knowledge, enable us to confront and expose the ambiguities implicit in the indiscriminate exploitation of guilt by religion—an exploitation of man's moral anxiety that grew partly out of its own power needs, partly out of ignorance of psychological distinctions, and partly out of unconscious rationalization of its "sincerity."

Tillich writes: "The courage to face one's own guilt leads to the question of salvation instead of renunciation."[41] *Ultimately,* man discovers that deliverance from guilt comes from without—it is not the product of inner struggle alone. The question of guilt confronts man most profoundly with the paradoxical core of his own nature. That which drives him on toward an endless goal of self-growth, authentic actualization and self-affirmation, may, when out of balance, be as destructive as it is creative. Unless the orectic foundations of self-love have come from without and been internalized, his "self-actualization" may lead to other-annihilation. If experienced distortedly, he may annihilate himself.

Without original dependency and trust, he will never be capable of autonomy and self-trust. Yet even these, extended inordinately, betoken a pathological unrealism. To face one's own guilt is to see its interfabrication with the guilt of all and the futility of the passion for innocence. The very height of authenticity demands self-awareness of *in*authenticity. Guilt points beyond itself to forgiveness, estrangement beyond itself to reconciliation, both of which are gifts, not extortions. "Though I give my body to be burned, and have not . . . [love], it profiteth me nothing."[42]

Man cannot save himself or others by anxiously renouncing the desires that lead to his guilt, nor can he be fully man by renouncing his guilt for his desires. He is the endless recipient of that which is beyond him, or . . . of *Him* who is beyond, who *is* the love that both restrains *and* reconciles.

It is possible that guilt is the shadow that reveals the light behind man that is also within man. A light beclouded in his *existence* but by the variety of its refractions pointing beyond itself to his *essence*, and beyond that to its source—a source most clearly seen in the man Jesus, the man for others, in whom essence and existence united. Tillich once said, "Man is the question, not the answer."[43] Perhaps he is both.

Chapter IX

EPILOGUE: Some Speculative Propositions About the Implications of the Guilt System in Man

1. The experience of guilt is *an affective phenomenal witness to the continuing unfolding of the evolutionary principle:* life moving toward some "Omega point," an ego ideal beyond the existential present, *life seeking to be more than it is,* acting out some indigenous meliorative principle. Sometimes this is unconscious, sometimes self-conscious; occasionally it is gross and punitive, at other times almost defunct, but, overall remarkably flexible and durable.

2. The guilt dynamic, in its broadest sense, is *the psychic "law of gravity" of human community.* It is what permits affective fealty to common values, uniting otherwise disparate men, often with deviant interests, around shared internalized goals.

3. *The guilt dynamic is an important basis of hope.* Through the ego ideal, the internal presence of unrealized but potential images or fulfillments, the ego is motivated to endure present deficiencies and difficulties by imaging for itself future self-esteem. This tends to be underlined by the *defects in hope* which accrue in guilt pathology, i.e., the pessimism and despair of the depressive, the doomlike expectancies and anxious scanning of the future by the obsessive-compulsive, and the seeming inability of the sociopath to imagine a future vividly enough to warrant the restraint of present impulse.

4. *It is through the guilt system that the possibility of freedom and self-transcendence are realized.* By fantasying the self in evaluated interaction with other selves, under the scru-

tiny and judgment of an idealized internal audience (visual and auditory), the self is simultaneously experienced as subject and object.

5. *It is the presence of the guilt dynamic in man which accounts for the initial emergence and projection of the concept of God.* In classical terminology, it is this biosocial dynamic which accounts for "revelation." God made himself originally known to men by creating man biologically dependent in the familial triad. This is to say that *theology has its roots in the biology of the human family. It is also fulfilled in the historical event of Christ the Son faithful to God the reality who is love.*

6. *It is out of this system that authentic selfhood emerges.* It is only through the experience of "Fall," of despair and anxiety over the disjunction of essence and existence, the discovery of alienation, that man learns to know his true finitude and his genuine dependency on the life beyond him. As that life freely proffers him acceptance and love in spite of his alienating wishes and acts, he discovers the courage both "to sin boldly" (because his private "goodness" is no longer the center of his anxious living) and "to believe boldly." His moral power will arise not from perfectionistic struggles or inhibitory flights into "innocence" but from acceptance of the love that transcends his condition, that affirms him and calls him to spontaneity and freedom. It is out of his response to this love that his true personhood emerges.

NOTES

CHAPTER I. GUILT: WHY SO IMPORTANT?

1. Pierre Teilhard de Chardin, *The Phenomenon of Man* (Harper & Brothers, 1959), pp. 280–281.
2. Sigmund Freud, *Civilization and Its Discontents* (London: Hogarth Press, Ltd., 1951), p. 123.
3. Ernest Jones, in *Proceedings of the International Conference on Medical Psychotherapy* (London: H. K. Lewis & Co., Ltd., 1948), Vol. III, p. 26.
4. Helen M. Lynd, *On Shame and the Search for Identity* (Science Editions, John Wiley & Sons, Inc., 1961), p. 18.
5. Erich Fromm, *The Art of Loving* (Harper & Brothers, 1956), p. 7.
6. Paul Tournier, *Guilt and Grace* (Harper & Row, Publishers, Inc., 1962).
7. Clara Thompson, *Psychoanalysis: Evolution and Development* (Hermitage House, Inc., 1950).
8. Patrick Mullahy, *Oedipus: Myth and Complex* (Hermitage House, Inc., 1950).
9. Oscar Pfister, *Christianity and Fear* (London: George Allen & Unwin, Ltd., 1944).
10. Theodor Reik, *Myth and Guilt* (George Braziller, Inc., 1957).
11. John C. Flugel, *Man, Morals and Society* (International Universities Press, Inc., 1945).
12. Carl R. Rogers and B. F. Skinner, "Some Issues Concerning the Control of Human Behavior: A Symposium," in Walter D. Nunokawa (ed.), *Human Values and Abnormal Behavior* (Scott, Foresman & Company, 1965), pp. 122–139.
13. *Ibid.*
14. *Ibid.*
15. *Ibid.*
16. *Ibid.* (Italics not in original.)
17. *Ibid.*

18. *Ibid.*

19. Sigmund Freud, *Group Psychology and the Analysis of the Ego* (Bantam Books, Inc., 1960).

20. David Riesman, *The Lonely Crowd* (Doubleday & Company, Inc., 1953).

21. Erich Fromm, *Escape from Freedom* (Farrar & Rinehart, Inc., 1941).

22. William H. Whyte, Jr., *The Organization Man* (Simon and Schuster, Inc., 1956).

23. Erik H. Erikson, *Childhood and Society* (W. W. Norton & Company, Inc., 1950).

24. Florence R. Kluckhohn and Fred L. Strodtbeck, *Variations in Value Orientations* (Row, Peterson & Company, 1961).

25. *Ibid.*, p. 28.

26. Pfister, *Christianity and Fear.*

27. Roy S. Lee, *Freud and Christianity* (London: James Clarke & Co., Ltd., 1948).

28. Heinz Hartmann, *Psychoanalysis and Moral Values* (International Universities Press, Inc., 1960).

29. Abraham H. Maslow, *Toward a Psychology of Being* (D. Van Nostrand Company, Inc., 1962), p. 192.

30. O. Hobart Mowrer, *The Crisis in Psychiatry and Religion* (D. Van Nostrand Company, Inc., 1961).

31. William Glasser, *Reality Therapy* (Harper & Row, Publishers, Inc., 1965) and John W. Drakeford, *Integrity Therapy* (Broadman Press, 1967).

32. Eric Berne, *Transactional Analysis in Psychotherapy* (Grove Press, Inc., 1961).

33. Anton Boisen, *The Exploration of the Inner World* (Harper & Brothers, 1936), pp. 24–25.

CHAPTER II. The Guilt Process:
Some Questions and Assumptions

1. Paul Tillich, *Systematic Theology* (The University of Chicago Press, 1951), Vol. I, p. 62.

2. Medard Boss, *Psychoanalysis and Daseinsanalysis* (Basic Books, Inc., Publishers, 1963), p. 270.

CHAPTER III. Superego Formation

1. Avery D. Weisman, *The Existential Core of Psychoanalysis: Reality, Sense, and Responsibility* (Little, Brown and Company, 1965), p. 190.

2. Sigmund Freud, *An Outline of Psychoanalysis* (W. W. Norton & Company, Inc., 1949), Ch. 1.

3. Sigmund Freud, *New Introductory Lectures on Psychoanalysis* (W. W. Norton & Company, Inc., 1933), Ch. 3.

4. Sigmund Freud, *The Ego and the Id* (London: Hogarth Press, Ltd., 1927), p. 39.

5. *Ibid.*, p. 41.

6. *Ibid.*

7. Freud, *An Outline of Psychoanalysis*, p. 98.

8. Freud, *The Ego and the Id*, p. 44.

9. *Ibid.*

10. *Ibid.*, p. 45.

11. Cf. Joseph Sandler, A. Holder, and D. Meers, "The Ego Ideal and the Ideal Self," in *The Psychoanalytic Study of the Child*, ed. by Ruth Eissler, *et al.* (International Universities Press, Inc., 1963), Vol. XVIII, pp. 139–158.

12. Cf. Gerhart Piers and M. B. Singer, *Shame and Guilt* (Charles C. Thomas, Publisher, 1953).

13. Cf. Berne, *Transactional Analysis in Psychotherapy.*

14. Flugel, *Man, Morals and Society,* pp. 34–39.

15. Donald MacKinnon, *The Violation of Prohibitions in Solving of Problems* (Harvard University Library, 1933).

16. Flugel, *Man, Morals and Society,* p. 107.

17. Karl Abraham, "The First Pregenital Stages of the Libido," included in *Selected Papers*, 1927.

18. Sándor Ferenczi, *Further Contributions to the Theory and Technique of Psychoanalysis* (Basic Books, Inc., Publishers, 1953), p. 267.

19. Melanie Klein, *The Psychoanalysis of Children* (Hillary House Publishers, Ltd., 3d ed., 1965), pp. 197–198.

20. *Ibid.*, p. 180.

21. *Ibid.*, p. 195.

22. *Ibid.*, p. 184.

23. *Ibid.*, pp. 24, 239.

24. Melanie Klein, in *Proceedings of the International Conference on Medical Psychotherapy* (London: H. K. Lewis & Co., Ltd., 1948), Vol. III, p. 54.

25. Bronislaw Malinowski, *The Sexual Life of Savages* (Eugenics Publishing Co., Inc., 1929), pp. 6–8.

26. Klein sees the Oedipus complex rooted much earlier in childhood and evident much earlier than Freud. Her observations (at this point seemingly supported by Kinsey's findings) are that "the genital impulses set in at the same time as the pre-genital ones and influence and modify them and . . . the genital stage merely means a strengthening of genital impulses." Klein, *The Psychoanalysis of Children,* p. 192. For Kinsey reference, see Alfred C.

Kinsey *et al.*, *Sexual Behavior in the Human Male* (W. B. Saunders Company, 1949), p. 176.

27. Klein, *The Psychoanalysis of Children*, p. 195.

28. Silvano Arieti (ed.), *American Handbook of Psychiatry* (Basic Books, Inc., Publishers, 1959), Vol. I, p. 817.

29. Erich Fromm, *Man for Himself* (Rinehart & Company, Inc., 1947), p. 144.

30. *Ibid.*, p. 145.

31. *Ibid.*, p. 147.

32. *Ibid.*, p. 149.

33. *Ibid.*, p. 157.

34. *Ibid.*, p. 158.

35. *Ibid.*

36. *Ibid.*, pp. 158–159.

37. *Ibid.*, pp. 159–160.

38. *Ibid.*, p. 165. (Italics not in original.)

39. John G. McKenzie, *Guilt: Its Meaning and Significance* (Abingdon Press, 1962), pp. 43 ff.

40. Fromm, *Man for Himself*, p. 167.

41. David P. Ausubel, *Ego Development and the Personality Disorders* (Grune & Stratton, Inc., 1952).

42. *Ibid.*, p. 8.

43. *Ibid.*

44. *Ibid.*, p. 8.

45. *Ibid.*, p. 51.

46. Cf. Anna Freud, *The Ego and the Mechanisms of Defense* (International Universities Press, Inc., 1946), p. 133.

47. Ausubel, *Ego Development and the Personality Disorders*, p. 57.

48. *Ibid.*, pp. 58–59.

49. *Ibid.*, pp. 60, 61.

50. *Ibid.*, p. 62.

51. *Ibid.*, pp. 48–102, 392–459.

52. *Ibid.*, p. 442.

53. *Ibid.*

54. *Ibid.* (Italics not in original.)

55. *Ibid.*, pp. 442–443.

56. *Ibid.*, p. 443.

57. *Ibid.*

CHAPTER IV. SUPEREGO MATURATION

1. Paul Tillich, *Theology of Culture* (Oxford University Press, Inc., 1959), p. 141.

2. Cf. Roger Brown, *Social Psychology* (The Free Press of Glencoe, 1965), pp. 350–417.

3. Albert D. Ullman, *Sociocultural Foundations of Personality* (Houghton Mifflin Company, 1965), pp. 229–257. (Ch. by U. Bronfenbrenner, "Freudian Theories of Identification and Their Derivatives.")

4. Flugel, *Man, Morals and Society.*

5. Hartmann, *Psychoanalysis and Moral Values.*

6. Edith Jacobson, *The Self and the Object World* (International Universities Press, Inc., 1964).

7. *The Psychoanalytic Study of the Child* (International Universities Press, Inc.).

8. Jacobson, *The Self and the Object World.*

9. William McCord and Joan McCord, *Psychopathy and Delinquency* (Grune & Stratton, Inc., 1956).

10. Sigmund Freud, *Collected Papers,* ed. by Ernest Jones (London: Hogarth Press, Ltd., 1953), Vol. IV, pp. 30–59.

11. Sigmund Freud, *Group Psychology and the Analysis of the Ego,* in James Strachey (ed.), *The Standard Edition of the Complete Psychological Works of Sigmund Freud* (London: Hogarth Press, Ltd., 1957).

12. Freud, *The Ego and the Id.*

13. Freud, *New Introductory Lectures on Psychoanalysis.*

14. Sandler *et al.,* "The Ego Ideal and the Ideal Self," in *The Psychoanalytic Study of the Child,* Vol. XVIII, pp. 139–158.

15. Jacobson, *The Self and the Object World,* Ch. 6.

16. *Ibid.,* p. 76.

17. *Ibid.,* p. 101.

18. See J. C. Flugel's discussion of the sources of moral conflict in the ego ideal in *Man, Morals and Society,* pp. 58 ff.

19. Hartmann and Loewenstein, "Notes on the Superego," in *The Psychoanalytic Study of the Child* (International Universities Press, Inc., 1962), Vol. XVII, pp. 42–81.

20. Jacobson, *The Self and the Object World,* p. 125.

21. Bernard Diamond, "Identification and the Sociopathic Personality," in *Archives of Criminal Psychodynamics,* Washington, D.C., Jan., 1961 (Special Psychopathy Issue).

22. Jacobson, *The Self and the Object World,* p. 94.

23. Sandler *et al.,* "The Ego Ideal and the Ideal Self," in *The Psychoanalytic Study of the Child,* Vol. XVIII, pp. 139–158.

24. *Ibid.*

25. *Ibid.*

26. Freud, *The Ego and the Id,* p. 44.

27. Bronfenbrenner, "Freudian Theories of Identification and Their Derivatives," in *Child Development,* Vol. 31 (1960), pp. 15–40.

28. Brown, *Social Psychology.*

29. *Ibid.,* p. 401.

30. Karl Menninger, *Man Against Himself* (Harcourt Brace and World, Inc., 1938).

31. Charles Odier, *Les Deux Sources consciente et inconsciente de la vie morale* (Neuchâtel: Éditions de la Baconnière, 1947), p. 222.

32. Freud, *Civilization and Its Discontents*, Ch. VII.

33. Freud, *The Ego and the Id*, p. 69.

34. Freud, *Civilization and Its Discontents*, Ch. VII.

35. *Ibid.*, p. 116.

36. *Ibid.*, p. 114.

37. Cf. Menninger, *Man Against Himself*, pp. 185 f., and Freud, *The Ego and the Id*, p. 76.

38. Jacobson, *The Self and the Object World*, p. 43.

39. Karen Horney, *The Neurotic Personality of Our Time* (W. W. Norton & Company, Inc., 1937).

40. *Ibid.*, p. 223.

41. Fromm, *Man for Himself*, p. 151.

42. Freud, Three Contributions to the Theory of Sex," in *Basic Writings* (Modern Library, 1938), p. 568.

43. Jacobson, *The Self and the Object World*, pp. 143 ff.

44. *Ibid.*, p. 146.

45. *Ibid.*, p. 147.

46. Piers and Singer, *Shame and Guilt*, p. 11.

47. Odier, *Les Deux Sources*, p. 221.

48. Wilfred C. Hulse, in *Report on Proceedings, International Congress on Mental Health* (London: H. K. Lewis & Co., Ltd., 1948), pp. 52–53.

49. Jacob A. Arlow and Charles Brenner, *Psychoanalytic Concepts and the Structural Theory* (International Universities Press, Inc., 1964), p. 81.

50. Jacobson, *The Self and the Object World*, p. 119.

51. *Ibid.*, p. 128.

52. See René Spitz, *No and Yes* (International Universities Press, Inc., 1957), pp. 9–11.

53. Freud, *Civilization and Its Discontents*.

54. András Angyal, *Foundations for a Science of Personality* (The Commonwealth Fund, 1941), p. 172.

55. Fromm, *Escape from Freedom*.

56. Fritz Redl and David Wineman, *The Aggressive Child* (The Free Press of Glencoe, 1957), p. 203.

57. Hugh Hartshorne and Mark Arthur May, *Studies in the Nature of Character* (The Macmillan Company), 1928–1930 (3 vols.).

58. Brown, *Social Psychology*, p. 414.

59. Joseph Finney, "What Is Sickness?" in the *Merrill Palmer Quarterly*, Vol. IX, No. 3 (July, 1953), pp. 205–228.

60. *Ibid.*, p. 211.

61. *Ibid.*

62. *Ibid.*, p. 214.

63. Arlow and Brenner, *Psychoanalytic Concepts*, p. 48.

64. Anna Freud, *The Ego and the Mechanisms of Defense.*

65. Arlow and Brenner, *Psychoanalytic Concepts*, p. 38.

66. Redl and Wineman, *The Aggressive Child*, p. 210.

67. Freud, *The Ego and the Id*, p. 75.

68. Mowrer, *The Crisis in Psychiatry and Religion*, p. 26.

69. Herman Nunberg, *Practice and Theory of Psychoanalysis* (International Universities Press, Inc., 1948), p. 193.

70. Odier, *Les Deux Sources*, p. 226.

71. Freud, *New Introductory Lectures on Psychoanalysis*, p. 92.

72. *Ibid.*, p. 92.

73. *Ibid.*, p. 96.

74. Jacobson, *The Self and the Object World*, p. 92.

75. Flugel, *Man, Morals and Society*, p. 58.

76. McKenzie, *Guilt: Its Meaning and Significance*, p. 48.

77. *Ibid.*, pp. 48–49.

78. Jean Piaget, *The Moral Judgment of the Child* (1st ed., 1932; Free Press, 1948), p. 118.

79. Brown, *Social Psychology*, p. 404.

80. *Ibid.*

81. *Ibid.*, p. 416.

82. *Ibid.*

83. Jacobson, *The Self and the Object World*, p. 125.

84. *Ibid.*, pp. 175–176.

CHAPTER V. Guilt in the Sociopathic Personality

1. Carl Frankenstein, *Psychopathy: A Comparative Analysis of Clinical Pictures* (Grune & Stratton, Inc., 1959).

2. *Ibid.*, p. 76.

3. McCord and McCord, *Psychopathy and Delinquency*, p. 43.

4. *Ibid.*, p. 14.

5. B. Karpman, "On the Need for Separating Psychopathy Into Two Distinct Clinical Types: Symptomatic and Idiopathic," *J. Crim. Psychopath.*, Vol. 3 (1941), pp. 112–137.

6. M. M. Cleckley, "Psychopathic States," in Arieti (ed.), *American Handbook of Psychiatry*, Vol. I, pp. 567–588.

7. Diamond, "Identification and the Sociopathic Personality," in *Archives of Criminal Psychodynamics*, Jan., 1961 (Special Psychopathy Issue).

8. Robert M. Lindner, *Stone Walls and Men* (Odyssey Press, Inc., 1946), p. 155.

9. Frankenstein, *Psychopathy*, pp. 6–7. (Italics not in original.)

10. Ausubel, *Ego Development and the Personality Disorders*, p. 57.

11. Jacobson, *The Self and the Object World*, p. 51.

12. *Ibid.*, pp. 51–52.

13. D. T. Lykken, "A Study of Anxiety in the Sociopathic Personality," in *Journal of Abnormal and Social Psychology*, Vol. 55 (1957), pp. 6–10.

14. D. C. Hodges, "Psychopathy: A Philosophical Approach," in *Archives of Criminal Psychodynamics*, Jan., 1961 (Special Psychopathy Issue).

15. C. J. Dalman, "Psychopathy and Psychopathic Behavior: A Psychoanalytic Approach," in *Archives of Criminal Psychodynamics*, Jan., 1961 (Special Psychopathy Issue), pp. 443–455.

16. J. Donnelly, "Aspects of the Psychodynamics of the Psychopath," in *Amer. J. Psychiatry*, Vol. 120, No. 12 (1964), pp. 1149–1154.

17. Redl and Wineman, *The Aggressive Child*, p. 201.

18. *Ibid.*, pp. 201–208.

19. Ephraim Rosen and Ian Gregory, *Abnormal Psychology* (W. B. Saunders Company, 1965), p. 361.

20. Albert Bandura and R. H. Walters, *Social Learning and Personality Development* (Holt, Rinehart and Winston, Inc., 1963), p. 45.

21. *Ibid.*, p. 98.

22. *Ibid.*, p. 103.

23. *Ibid.*

24. *Ibid.*, p. 124.

25. Lindner, *Stone Walls and Men*, p. 153.

26. J. R. Stabenau, J. Tupin, M. Werner, and W. Pollin, "A Comparative Study of Families of Schizophrenics, Delinquents and Normals," in *Psychiatry*, Vol. 28, No. 1 (Feb., 1965), pp. 45–59.

27. V. H. Sharp, S. Glasner, I. I. Lederman, and S. Wolfe, "Sociopaths and Schizophrenics—A Comparison of Family Interactions," in *Psychiatry*, Vol. 27, No. 2 (May, 1964), pp. 127–134.

28. Cleckley, "Psychopathic States," in Arieti (ed.), *American Handbook of Psychiatry*, Vol. I, p. 584.

29. Abraham H. Maslow, *Motivation and Personality* (Harper & Brothers, 1954), pp. 98–99. (Italics not in original.)

30. McCord and McCord, *Psychopathy and Delinquency*, pp. 145–176.

31. Cf. S. B. Maughs, "Current Concepts of Psychopathy," in *Archives of Criminal Psychodynamics*, Jan., 1961 (Special Psychopathy Issue), pp. 550–557.

32. McCord and McCord, *Psychopathy and Delinquency*, p. 144.

33. R. A. Craddick, "Wechsler-Bellevue I. Q. Scores of Psychopathic and Non-Psychopathic Prisoners," in *J. of Psychol. Studies*, Vol. 12, No. 4 (1961), pp. 167–172.

34. H. L. Kozol, "The Dynamics of Psychopathy," in *Archives of Criminal Psychodynamics*, Jan., 1961 (Special Psychopathy Issue), pp. 526–541.

35. I. Sipos, "The Influence of an Induced Frustration Situation on the Stability of Honest Behavior in Pupils," in *Ceskoslovenska Psychologie*, Vol. 8, No. 1 (1964), pp. 16–23. Also, M. Steininger *et al.*, "Cheating on College Examinations as a Function of Situationally Aroused Anxiety and Hostility," in *J. of Educ. Psychol.*, Vol. 55, No. 6 (1964), pp. 317–324.

36. R. D. Hare, "Psychopathy, Fear Arousal, and Anticipated Pain," in *Psychol. Reports*, Vol. 16, No. 2 (1965), pp. 499–502.

37. Bandura and Walters, *Social Learning and Personality Development*, p. 200.

38. J. Aronfreed, "The Effects of Experimental Socialization Paradigms Upon Two Moral Responses to Transgression," in *J. Abnorm. Soc. Psychol.*, Vol. 66, No. 5 (1963), pp. 437–448. (Italics not in original.)

39. Bandura and Walters, *Social Learning and Personality Development*, p. 243.

40. *Ibid.*, p. 213.

41. Cleckley, "Psychopathic States," in Arieti (ed.), *American Handbook of Psychiatry*, Vol. I, pp. 567–588.

42. George A. Kelly, *The Psychology of Personal Constructs* (W. W. Norton & Company, Inc., 1955), p. 502.

43. *Ibid.*, p. 504.

44. Viktor Frankl, *From Death-camp to Existentialism* (The Beacon Press, Inc., 1959).

45. M. H. Miller, "Time and the Character Disorder," in *The J. of Nervous and Mental Disease*, Vol. 138, Jan.–June, 1964, pp. 535–540.

46. Redl and Wineman, *The Aggressive Child*, p. 121.

47. Jurgen Ruesch, *Disturbed Communication* (W. W. Norton & Company, Inc., 1957), pp. 121–122.

48. Hans Jürgen Eysenck, *The Dynamics of Anxiety and Hysteria* (Frederick A. Praeger, Inc., Publishers, 1957).

49. Bandura and Walters, *Social Learning and Personality Development*.

50. W. Mischel and C. Gilligan, "Delay of Gratification, Motivation, for the Prohibited Gratification, and Responses to Temptation," in *J. Abnorm. Soc. Psychol.*, Vol. 69, No. 4 (1964), pp. 411–417.

51. *Ibid.*

52. *Ibid.*

53. Bandura and Walters, *Social Learning and Personality Development*.

54. Cf. Menninger, *Man Against Himself*.

55. *Time*, Nov. 26, 1965.

56. George W. Kisker, *The Disorganized Personality* (McGraw-Hill Book Company, Inc., 1964), pp. 230–231.

57. Frankenstein, *Psychopathy*, p. 187.

58. *Ibid.*, p. 188.

59. W. Bromberg, "The Treatability of the Psychopath," in *Amer. J. Psychiatry*, Vol. 110 (1954), pp. 604–608.

60. Lindner, *Stone Walls and Men*, p. 159. (Italics not in original.)

61. E. Bergler, "Psychopathic Personalities Are Unconsciously Propelled by a Defense Against a Specific Type of Psychic Masochism: Malignant Masochism," in *Archives of Criminal Psychodynamics*, Jan., 1961 (Special Psychopathy Issue).

62. Cleckley, "Psychopathic States," in Arieti (ed.), *American Handbook of Psychiatry*, Vol. I, Ch. 28.

63. Reported in Rosen and Gregory, *Abnormal Psychology*, p. 367.

64. Maughs, "Current Concepts of Psychopathy," in *Archives of Criminal Psychodynamics*, Jan., 1961 (Special Psychopathy Issue), p. 556.

65. V. Fox., "Psychopathy as Viewed by a Clinical Psychologist," in *Archives of Criminal Psychodynamics*, Jan., 1961 (Special Psychopathy Issue).

66. August Aichhorn, *Wayward Youth* (The Viking Press, Inc., 1935), p. 150.

67. *Ibid.*, pp. 159–161.

68. Redl and Wineman, *The Aggressive Child*, pp. 35–37.

69. *Ibid.*

70. *Ibid.*, p. 201.

71. *Ibid.*, p. 201.

72. *Ibid.*, p. 205.

73. *Ibid.*, p. 206.

74. *Ibid.*, p. 207.

75. McCord and McCord, *Psychopathy and Delinquency*, pp. 161–165.

76. Bandura and Walters, *Social Learning and Personality Development*, p. 205.

77. *Ibid.*, 212–213.

78. *Ibid.*, 245.

79. *Ibid.*, 250.

80. *Ibid.*, 240.

CHAPTER VI. NEUROTIC GUILT

1. Maurice Lorr, C. J. Klett, and D. M. McNair, *Syndromes of Psychosis* (Pergamon Press, 1964), p. 36.

2. Cf. D. Caffelt and A. B. Swaney, "Motivational Dynamics of Violent and Nonviolent Criminals Measured by Behavioral Tests." Paper presented to The Southwestern Psychological Association, 1965 Annual Meeting, Oklahoma City.

3. Milton Rokeach, *The Three Christs of Ypsilanti* (Alfred A. Knopf, Inc., 1964).

4. *Ibid.*, p. 134.

5. *Ibid.*, p. 327.

6. Boisen, *The Exploration of the Inner World.*

7. *Ibid.*, pp. 24–25. (Italics not in original.)

8. Cf. Joseph Wolpe *et al.*, *The Conditioning Therapies* (Holt, Rinehart and Winston, Inc., 1964); also Hans Jürgen Eysenck and Stanley Rachman, *The Causes and Cures of Neurosis* (Robert R. Knapp, Publisher, 1965).

9. Cf. C. G. Costello, "Behavior Therapy: Criticisms and Confusions," in *Behav. Res. Ther.*, Vol. 1 (1963), pp. 159–161.

10. Eysenck and Rachman, *The Causes and Cures of Neurosis*, p. 266.

11. Joseph Robert Cowen, in *Psychiatry*, Vol. 25, No. 2 (May, 1962), p. 187.

12. Freud, *Collected Papers*, Vol. IV, pp. 152–170.

13. Sandor Rado, "The Problem of Melancholia," in *International J. of Psycho-Analysis*, Vol. IX (1928), pp. 420–438.

14. Cf. Frederick C. Redlich and Daniel Freedman, *The Theory and Practice of Psychiatry* (Basic Books, Inc., Publishers, 1966), Ch. 15.

15. In Otto Fenichel, *The Psychoanalytic Theory of Neurosis* (W. W. Norton & Company, Inc., 1945), p. 412.

16. *Ibid.*, p. 405.

17. *Ibid.*, p. 412.

18. Emil A. Gutheil, "Reactive Depression," in Arieti (ed.), *American Handbook of Psychiatry*, Vol. I.

19. *Ibid.*

20. Freud, "Mourning and Melancholia," in *Collected Papers*, Vol. IV, p. 155.

21. Fenichel, *The Psychoanalytic Theory of Neurosis*, p. 391.

22. Rosen and Gregory, *Abnormal Psychology*, p. 249.

23. Fenichel, *The Psychoanalytic Theory of Neurosis*, p. 405.

24. Rosen and Gregory, *Abnormal Psychology*, p. 248.

25. Morton Deutsch and Robert M. Kraus, *Theories in Social Psychology* (Basic Books, Inc., Publishers, 1965), p. 132.

26. *Ibid.*, p. 132.

27. Sigmund Freud, *The Problem of Anxiety* (W. W. Norton & Company, Inc., 1936), pp. 53 f.

28. Sandor Rado, "Obsessive Behavior," in Arieti (ed.), *American Handbook of Psychiatry*, Vol. I, pp. 324 f.

29. Fenichel, *The Psychoanalytic Theory of Neurosis*, pp. 268 f.

30. Cited in Flugel, *Man, Morals and Society*, p. 158.

31. Cf. Sigmund Freud, "Notes Upon a Case of Obsessional Neurosis," in *Collected Papers* (London: Hogarth Press, Ltd., 1953), Vol. III, pp. 293–383.

32. Erik H. Erikson, *Identity and the Life Cycle* (Psychological Issues Monograph Series, International Universities Press), Vol. I, No. 1, 1959.

33. Rado, "Obsessive Behavior," in Arieti (ed.), *American Handbook of Psychiatry*.

34. *Ibid.*, p. 331.

35. Freud, *Civilization and Its Discontents*, p. 116.

36. Fenichel, *The Psychoanalytic Theory of Neurosis*, p. 292.

37. Freud, *The Problem of Anxiety*, pp. 53 f.

38. David Shapiro, "Aspects of Obsessive-Compulsive Style," in *Psychiatry*, Vol. 25, No. 1 (Feb., 1962), pp. 46–59.

39. *Ibid.*

40. Freud, *The Problem of Anxiety*, p. 57.

41. Rado, "Obsessive Behavior," in Arieti (ed.), *American Handbook of Psychiatry*, Vol. I, p. 339.

42. Kisker, *The Disorganized Personality*, p. 273.

43. Freud, *The Problem of Anxiety*, p. 56.

44. Freud, *The Future of an Illusion* (A Doubleday Anchor Book, 1957), p. 53.

45. Freud, *The Problem of Anxiety*, p. 45.

46. Ralph Metzner, "Some Experimental Analogues of Obsession," in *Behav. Res. Ther.*, Vol. 1 (1963), pp. 231–236.

47. *Ibid.*

48. Rado, "Obsessive Behavior," in Arieti (ed.), *American Handbook of Psychiatry*, Vol. I.

49. Fenichel, *The Psychoanalytic Theory of Neurosis*, p. 292.

50. Rado, "Obsessive Behavior," in Arieti (ed.), *American Handbook of Psychiatry*, Vol. I, pp. 328–329.

51. Fenichel, *The Psychoanalytic Theory of Neurosis*, p. 305.

52. Shapiro, *loc. cit.*

53. Fenichel, *The Psychoanalytic Theory of Neurosis*, p. 296.

54. Shapiro, *loc. cit.*

55. Fenichel, *The Psychoanalytic Theory of Neurosis*, p. 270.

56. *Ibid.*, p. 324.

57. Odier, *Les Deux Sources*.

58. *Ibid.*, pp. 211–239.

59. Cf. Albert Bandura, "Psychotherapy as a Learning Process," in *Psychology Bulletin*, Vol. 58, No. 2 (1961), pp. 143–159.

60. Cf. Metzner, "Some Experimental Analogues of Obsession," in *Behav. Res. Ther.*, Vol. 1 (1963), pp. 231–236.

61. B. F. Skinner, "'Superstition' in the Pigeon," in *J. Exp. Psychol.*, Vol. 38 (1948), pp. 168–172.

62. T. Ayllon, E. Haughton, and H. B. Hughes, "Interpretation of Symptoms: Fact or Fiction?" *Behav. Res. Ther.*, Vol. 3 (1965), pp. 1–7.

63. *Ibid.*

64. *Ibid.*

65. *Ibid.*

66. Eysenck and Rachman, *The Causes and Cures of Neurosis.*

67. Ralph Metzner, "Re-evaluation of Wolpe and Dollard/Miller," in *Behav. Res. Ther.*, Vol. 1 (1963), pp. 213–215.

68. *Ibid.*

69. O. Hobart Mowrer, "Freudianism, Behaviour Therapy and 'Self-disclosure,'" in *Behav. Res. Ther.*, Vol. 1 (1964), pp. 321–337.

70. Metzner, "Re-evaluation of Wolpe and Dollard/Miller," in *Behav. Res. Ther.*, Vol. 1 (1963), pp. 213–215 (note 58).

71. Eysenck and Rachman, *The Causes and Cures of Neurosis*, p. 138.

72. Mowrer, "Freudianism, Behaviour Therapy and 'Self-disclosure,'" in *Behav. Res. Ther.*, Vol. 1 (1964), pp. 321-337.

73. *Ibid.*

74. Mowrer, *The Crisis in Psychiatry and Religion.*

75. *Ibid.*, p. 74.

76. Mowrer, "Freudianism, Behaviour Therapy and 'Self-disclosure,'" in *Behav. Res. Ther.*, Vol. 1 (1964), pp. 321–337.

77. Freud, *An Outline of Psychoanalysis*, pp. 121–122.

78. *Ibid.*, p. 75.

79. Sigmund Freud, *A General Introduction to Psycho-Analysis* (Permabook, 1935), pp. 463, 441.

80. *Ibid.*, pp. 441–442.

81. Mowrer, *The Crisis in Psychiatry and Religion*, p. 118.

82. *Ibid.*, p. 20.

83. Hartmann, *Psychoanalysis and Moral Values*, pp. 15–16.

84. Mowrer, *The Crisis in Psychiatry and Religion*, p. 128.

85. Freud, *Civilization and Its Discontents*, p. 119.

86. Mowrer, *The Crisis in Psychiatry and Religion*, p. 161.

87. *Ibid.*, p. 162.

88. Mowrer, "Freudianism, Behaviour Therapy and 'Self-disclosure,'" in *Behav. Res. Ther.*, Vol. 1 (1964), pp. 321–337.

89. Mowrer, *The Crisis in Psychiatry and Religion*, p. 159.

CHAPTER VII. THE PSYCHOTHERAPY OF GUILT

1. Tillich, *Theology of Culture.*
2. Mowrer, *The Crisis in Psychiatry and Religion* (1961). Also, Mowrer, *The New Group Therapy* (D. Van Nostrand Company, Inc., 1964).
3. Charlotte Buhler, *Values in Psychotherapy* (The Free Press of Glencoe, 1962).
4. Donald Glad, *Operational Values in Psychotherapy* (Oxford University Press, Inc., 1959).
5. Werner Wolff, *Values in Personality Research* (Grune & Stratton, Inc., 1950).
6. Perry London, *The Modes and Morals of Psychotherapy* (Holt, Rinehart and Winston, Inc., 1964).
7. Glasser, *Reality Therapy.*
8. Drakeford, *Integrity Therapy.*
9. J. F. T. Bugental, "The Person Who Is the Psychotherapist," in *J. Consult. Psychol.,* Vol. 28, No. 3 (1964), pp. 272–277.
10. Goodwin Watson, "Moral Issues in Psychotherapy," in John R. Braun (ed.), *Clinical Psychology in Transition* (Howard Allen, Inc., Publisher, 1961), pp. 108–110.
11. Arnold P. Goldstein and Sanford J. Dean, *The Investigation of Psychotherapy: Commentaries and Readings* (John Wiley & Sons., Inc., 1966).
12. Robert Allan Harper, *Psychoanalysis and Psychotherapy: 36 Systems* (Prentice-Hall, Inc., 1959).
13. Carl A. Whitaker and Thomas P. Malone, *The Roots of Psychotherapy* (McGraw Hill Book Company, Inc., 1953).
14. Albert Ellis, *Reason and Emotion in Psychotherapy* (Lyle Stuart, Publisher, 1962).
15. John Rosen, *Direct Analysis* (Grune & Stratton, Inc., 1953).
16. Carl Rogers, *On Becoming a Person* (Houghton Mifflin Company, 1961).
17. August de Belmont Hollingshead and Frederick C. Redlich, *Social Class and Mental Illness* (John Wiley & Sons, Inc., 1958).
18. Arnold P. Goldstein, K. Heller, and L. B. Sechrest, *Psychotherapy and the Psychology of Behavior Change* (John Wiley & Sons, Inc., 1966).
19. J. D. Frank, *Persuasion and Healing* (Schocken Books, Inc., 1963).
20. L. Krasner, "Reinforcement, Verbal Behavior, and Psychotherapy," in *American Journal of Orthopsychiatry,* Vol. 33 (1963), p. 101.
21. Goldstein, Heller, and Sechrest, *Psychotherapy and the Psychology of Behavior Change.*

22. Charles B. Truax, "Reinforcement and Nonreinforcement in Rogerian Psychotherapy," in *J. Abnorm. Soc. Psychol.*, Vol. 71, No. 1 (1966), pp. 1–9.

23. Frank, *Persuasion and Healing*.

24. Fred E. Fiedler, "The Concept of an Ideal Therapeutic Relationship," in *J. Consult. Psychol.*, Vol. 14 (1950), pp. 239–245.

25. Glad, *Operational Values in Psychotherapy*, p. 46.

26. Eysenck and Rachman, *The Causes and Cures of Neurosis*. Cf. also Joseph Wolpe *et al.*, *The Conditioning Therapies*.

27. Mowrer, "Freudianism, Behaviour Therapy and 'Self-disclosure,'" *Behav. Res. Ther.*, Vol. 1 (1964), pp. 321–337.

28. Charles B. Truax and R. R. Carkhuff, *Toward Effective Counseling and Psychotherapy: Training and Practice* (Aldine Publishing Company, 1967), p. 21.

29. *Ibid.*, p. 141.

30. *Ibid.*, p. 150.

31. *Ibid.*, pp. 150–151.

32. H. Feifel and J. Eells, "Patients and Therapists Assess the Same Psychotherapy," in *J. Consult. Psychol.*, Vol. 27, No. 4 (Aug., 1963), pp 310–318.

33. Cf. A. P. Goldstein, *Therapist-Patient Expectancies in Psychotherapy* (The Macmillan Company, 1962), and Frank, *Persuasion and Healing*.

34. R. D. Cartwright and B. Lerner, "Empathy, Need to Change, and Improvement with Psychotherapy," in *J. Consult. Psychol.*, Vol. 27, No. 2 (1963), pp. 138–144.

35. Eysenck and Rachman, *The Causes and Cures of Neurosis*.

36. J. H. Cautela, "Desensitization and Insight," in *Behav. Res. Ther.*, Vol. 3 (1965), pp. 59–64.

37. G. Saslow, "A Case History of Attempted Behavior Manipulation in a Psychiatric Ward," in L. Krasner and L. P. Ullmann (eds.), *Research in Behavior Modification* (Holt, Rinehart and Winston, Inc., 1965), p. 288.

38. *Ibid.* (Italics not in original.)

39. Jay Haley, *Strategies of Psychotherapy* (Grune & Stratton, Inc., 1963).

40. Berne, *Transactional Analysis in Psychotherapy*.

41. Everett L. Shostrom, *Man, the Manipulator* (Abingdon Press, 1967), pp. 199 f.

42. Everett L. Shostrom and R. R. Knapp, "The Relationship of a Measure of Self-actualization (P.Q.I.) to a Measure of Pathology (M.M.P.I.) and to Therapeutic Growth," in *Amer. J. Psychother.*, Vol. XX, No. 1 (1965).

43. Philip Rieff, *The Triumph of the Therapeutic* (Harper & Row, Publishers, Inc., 1966), p. 87.

44. Tillich, *Theology of Culture*, pp. 118–120.

45. London, *The Modes and Morals of Psychotherapy*.

46. Quoted in Erikson, *Identity and the Life Cycle* (Psychological Issues Monograph Series), p. 49.

47. Shostrom and Knapp, *loc. cit.*

48. D. Rosenthal, "Changes in Some Moral Values Following Psychotherapy," in *J. Consult. Psychol.*, Vol. 19 (1955), pp. 431–436.

49. M. Rosenbaum, J. Friedlander, and S. M. Kaplan, "Evaluation of Results of Psychotherapy," in *Psychosom. Med.*, Vol. 18 (1956), pp. 113–132.

50. Glad, *Operational Values in Psychotherapy*, p. 5.

51. *Ibid.*, p. 231.

52. *Ibid.*, p. 236.

53. Krasner, "Reinforcement, Verbal Behavior, and Psychotherapy," in *American Journal of Orthopsychiatry*, Vol. 33 (1963), pp. 601–613.

54. J. R. Reid, "The Problem of Values in Psychoanalysis." Paper read at the annual meeting of the American Psychoanalytic Association, Los Angeles, May 4–7, 1953.

55. Carol Murphy, "Conscience and Psychotherapy," in *J. of Pastoral Care*, Vol. XVI, No. 2 (1962), pp. 81–84.

56. *Ibid.*

57. E. M. Pattison, "On the Failure to Forgive or to Be Forgiven," in *Amer. J. of Psychotherapy*, Vol. XIX, No. 1 (Jan., 1965), pp. 106–115.

58. Pfister, *Christianity and Fear*, p. 115.

59. Pattison, *loc. cit.*

60. Weisman, *The Existential Core of Psychoanalysis*, p. 195.

61. Cf. John Cumming and Elaine Cumming, "The Value Problem in Psychiatry," in *Psychother. Psychosom.*, Vol. 13 (1965), pp. 186–193.

62. Weisman, *The Existential Core of Psychoanalysis*, p. 181.

63. Cumming and Cumming, *loc. cit.*

64. Hartmann, *Psychoanalysis and Moral Values*, p. 62. (Italics not in original.)

65. *Ibid.*, p. 63.

66. Weisman, *The Existential Core of Psychoanalysis*, p. 184.

67. Reid, "The Problem of Values in Psychoanalysis."

68. Weisman, *The Existential Core of Psychoanalysis*, p. 181.

69. Rogers, *On Becoming a Person*.

70. Mowrer, *The Crisis in Psychiatry and Religion*.

71. Ellis, *Reason and Emotion in Psychotherapy*.

72. M. Brewster Smith, " 'Mental Health' Reconsidered: A Special Case of the Problem of Values in Psychology," in Nunokawa

(ed.), *Human Values and Abnormal Behavior*, p. 47. (Italics not in original.)

73. London, *The Modes and Morals of Psychotherapy*, pp. 163–173.

74. *Ibid.*

75. C. M. Lowe, "Value Orientations—An Ethical Dilemma," in Braun (ed.), *Clinical Psychology in Transition*, pp. 120–126.

76. Rosenthal, "Changes in Some Moral Values Following Psychotherapy," in *J. Consult. Psychol.*, Vol. 19, No. 6 (1955).

77. Timothy Leary, *Interpersonal Diagnosis of Personality* (The Ronald Press Company, 1957).

78. F. Perls *et al.*, *Gestalt Therapy* (Julian Press, Inc., 1951).

79. Shostrom, *Man, the Manipulator*.

80. Glad, *Operational Values in Psychotherapy*, p. 302.

81. Erich Fromm, *The Sane Society* (Rinehart & Company, Inc., 1955).

82. Cumming and Cumming, *loc. cit.*

83. Paul Tillich, *The Protestant Era* (The University of Chicago Press, 1948).

84. Buhler, *Values in Psychotherapy*, pp. 124–130.

85. Floyd W. Matson, *The Broken Image* (George Braziller, Inc., 1964).

86. Cf. also Werner Wolff, "Fact and Value in Psychotherapy," in *American J. of Psychotherapy*, Vol. 8 (1954), pp. 466–486.

87. Rieff, *The Triumph of the Therapeutic*.

88. Buhler, *Values in Psychotherapy*, pp. 27-28.

89. *Ibid.*, pp. 218–220.

90. Glad, *Operational Values in Psychotherapy*.

91. Shostrom, *Man, the Manipulator*, pp. 199 f.

92. Cf. Goldstein, Heller, and Sechrest, *Psychotherapy and the Psychology of Behavior Change*, p. 8.

93. Cf. *ibid.* for ways of encouraging self-esteem-producing changes via reinforcement of positive responses, pp. 237 ff.

94. Quoted from Harry Stack Sullivan, *The Psychiatric Interview*, in Glad, *Operational Values in Psychotherapy*, p. 117. (Italics not in original.)

95. *Ibid.*, p. 119.

96. Cf. Krasner and Ullmann (eds.), *Research in Behavior Modification*, pp. 285–304.

97. Hartmann, *Psychoanalysis and Moral Values* (International Universities Press, 1960).

98. *Ibid.*, pp. 29–30.

99. *Ibid.*

100. *Ibid.*, pp. 30–31.

101. *Ibid.*, pp. 64 ff.

102. R. B. Kurz, R. Cohen, and S. Starzynski, "Rorschach Correlates of Time Estimation," in *J. Consult. Psychol.*, Vol. 29, No. 4 (1965), pp. 379–382.

103. Fritz Redl and David Wineman, *Children Who Hate* (Free Press, 1951), p. 106. (Italics not in original.)

104. *Ibid.*, p. 109.

105. *Ibid.*, pp. 120–121.

106. *Ibid.*

107. *Ibid.*

108. *Ibid.*, p. 64.

109. Weisman, *The Existential Core of Psychoanalysis*, p. 195.

110. Redl and Wineman, *Children Who Hate*, p. 208.

111. Leopold Bellak and Leonard Small, *Emergency Psychotherapy and Brief Psychotherapy* (Grune & Stratton, Inc., 1965), p. 35.

112. *Ibid.*, pp. 56–57.

113. Sidney Tarachow, *An Introduction to Psychotherapy* (International Universities Press, Inc., 1963), p. 148.

114. Weisman, *The Existential Core of Psychoanalysis*, p. 182.

115. *Ibid.*, p. 229.

116. Cf. G. Chrzanowaki, "The Psychotherapeutic Management of Sociopathy." Address presented at the Fifth Emil A. Gutheil Memorial Conference for the Advancement of Psychotherapy, New York City, Oct. 25, 1964. Cf. also Glasser, *Reality Therapy*.

117. Berne, *Transactional Analysis in Psychotherapy*.

118. Cumming and Cumming, *loc. cit.*

119. Lewis J. Sherrill, *Guilt and Redemption* (John Knox Press, 1957).

120. David E. Roberts, *Psychotherapy and a Christian View of Man* (Charles Scribner's Sons, 1950).

121. Tournier, *Guilt and Grace*.

122. McKenzie, *Guilt: Its Meaning and Significance*.

123. David R. Belgum, *Guilt: Where Religion and Psychology Meet* (Prentice-Hall, Inc., 1963).

124. Drakeford, *Integrity Therapy*.

125. Pattison, *loc. cit.*

126. Fromm, *Man for Himself*.

CHAPTER VIII. GUILT AND THE RELIGION OF LOVE

1. Robert Lee (ed.), *Paul Tillich and Carl Rogers: A Dialogue* (at San Diego State College, March 7, 1965), p. 18.

2. Freud, *Civilization and Its Discontents*, p. 58.

3. Ira Progoff, *Jung's Psychology and Its Social Meaning* (Grove Press, 1953).

4. Tillich, *Systematic Theology*, Vol. I, p. 209.

5. Dietrich Bonhoeffer, *Letters from Prison* (The Macmillan Company, 1965), p. 195.

6. James E. Loder, *Religious Pathology and Christian Faith* (The Westminster Press, 1966), p. 142.

7. Teilhard de Chardin, *The Phenomenon of Man*, p. 291.

8. Freud, *The Future of an Illusion*.

9. Cf. Marc Oraison, *The Human Mystery of Sexuality* (Sheed & Ward, Inc., 1967), pp. 38–41.

10. Erich Fromm, *You Shall Be as Gods* (Holt, Rinehart and Winston, Inc., 1966), pp. 73–79.

11. *Ibid.*

12. Teilhard de Chardin, *The Phenomenon of Man*, p. 289.

13. *Ibid.*, p. 290.

14. *Ibid.*, p. 298.

15. Pfister, *Christianity and Fear*.

16. Reik, *Myth and Guilt*, pp. 422 ff.

17. Pfister, *Christianity and Fear*, p. 345.

18. *Ibid.*

19. *Ibid.*, p. 367.

20. *Ibid.*, p. 434.

21. *Ibid.*, p. 435.

22. Roy S. Lee, *Freud and Christianity*.

23. *Ibid.*, Ch. 8.

24. Mowrer, *The Crisis in Psychiatry and Religion*.

25. A. R. Eckardt, "Ventures of the Post-Freudian Conscience," in *Journal of Bible and Religion*, Vol. XXX, No. 4 (Oct., 1962).

26. Dietrich Bonhoeffer, *Ethics*, ed. by Eberhard Bethge (The Macmillan Company, 1955), p. 47.

27. Joseph R. Royce, *The Encapsulated Man* (D. Van Nostrand Company, Inc., 1964).

28. Tillich, *Systematic Theology*.

29. Bonhoeffer, *Ethics*, p. 46. (Italics not in original.)

30. Tillich, *Systematic Theology*, Vol. I, p. 240.

31. Weisman, *The Existential Core of Psychoanalysis*, p. 220.

32. *Ibid.* (Italics not in original.)

33. *Ibid.*

34. *Ibid.*, pp. 223–224.

35. Frederick Henry Heinemann, *Existentialism and the Modern Predicament* (Harper & Brothers, 1953), p. 39.

36. Joseph R. Royce, "Psychology, Existentialism, and Religion," in *The Journal of General Psychology*, Vol. 66 (1962), pp. 3–16.

37. Weisman, *The Existential Core of Psychoanalysis*, p. 234.

38. Elliott, in a paper presented to the Conference of Supervisors, 1960 Council for Clinical Training, held at Washington, D.C., Oct. 24–26, 1960.

39. Martin Buber, quoted in *ibid.*

40. Tillich, *Systematic Theology*, Vol. II, p. 77.

41. Paul Tillich, *The Courage to Be* (Yale University Press, 1952), p. 17.

42. I Corinthians 13:3.

43. Tillich, *Systematic Theology*, Vol. I, p. 13.

GEORGE ALLEN & UNWIN LTD
London: 40 Museum Street, W.C.1

Auckland: P.O. Box 36013, Northcote Central, N.4
Barbados: P.O. Box 222, Bridgetown
Beirut: Deeb Building, Jeanne d'Arc Street
Bombay: 15 Graham Road, Ballard Estate, Bombay 1
Buenos Aires: Escritorio 454-459, Florida 165
Calcutta: 17 Chittaranjan Avenue, Calcutta 13
Cape Town: 68 Shortmarket Street
Hong Kong: 105 Wing On Mansion, 26 Hancow Road, Kowloon
Ibadan: P.O. Box 62
Karachi: Karachi Chambers, McLeod Road
Madras: Mohan Mansions, 38c Mount Road, Madras 6
Mexico: Villalongin 32, Mexico 5, D.F.
Nairobi: P.O. Box 30583
New Delhi: 13-14 Asaf Ali Road, New Delhi 1
Ontario: 81 Curlew Drive, Don Mills
Philippines: P.O. Box 4322, Manila
Rio de Janeiro: Caixa Postal 2537-Zc-00
Singapore: 36c Prinsep Street, Singapore 7
Sydney, N.S.W.: Bradbury House, 55 York Street
Tokyo: P.O. Box 26, Kamata

EDWARD V. STEIN

THE STRANGER INSIDE YOU

Shakespeare advised, 'To thine own self be true', Socrates and the Delphian oracle called every man to the central challenge to knowledge with 'Know thyself'. Thus selfhood is man's classical and perennial concern. Dr. Stein wrote this book for the man who is seeking to know himself.

He sees this man as 'the mythical average person: one who has the usual preoccupation with sex, aggression, and guilt, an oblique exposure to psychoanalysis, a closet full of slightly faded certainties, some frayed values, a few psychic skeletons and a wobbly but hopeful perspective on the world in general – faith included'. Stripping psychology down to its 'essentials to live by', Dr Stein writes from his years of teaching psychology to seminary students who are seeking to integrate psychological insight with their pastoral tasks in the world where they will work. Seminars and many private hours of wrestling with the core concerns of searching people have convinced him that these are the subjects that many think about, worry over and want answers to.

The book moves from what is most unique and most general to one's self to reflections on the new knowledge of mind that Freud introduced into our world. The middle chapters deal with the cataclysmic changes most of us have been thrust into in this century of 'the psychological man'. The last chapter dares to suggest that in spite of the cyclonic winds blowing through our frenetic, manipulated, depersonalized and missile-taut world, there may be audible yet a still small voice to make sense of it all.

Simple, yet anything but superficial, *The Stranger Inside You* is faithful both to the needs of men in our modern hectic society and to the complexities of psychology.

GEORGE ALLEN & UNWIN LTD